THANK YOU FOR THE SHOES

ANNIVERSARY EDITION

THANK YOU *for the* SHOES

RAFFAELA MARIE RIZZO

THANK YOU FOR THE SHOES, Anniversary Edition
Copyright © December 2025
by Raffaela Marie Rizzo

First edition copyright © 2015

This is a work of literary nonfiction, based on the life stories of real people, actual locales, and historical events, brought to life by the author's creativity and imagination.

All rights reserved.

No part of this book may be used or reproduced in any manner whatsoever without the written permission of the author, except in the case of brief quotations embodied in critical articles and reviews. Contact: author@rmrizzo.com. By payment of the required fees, you have been granted the non-exclusive, non-transferable right to access and read the text of this book or e-book on-screen. No part of this text may be reproduced, transmitted, downloaded, decompiled, reverse-engineered, or stored in or introduced into any information storage and retrieval system, in any form or by any means, whether electronic or mechanical, now known or hereinafter invented, without the express written permission of the author or Giro di Mondo publishing services.

Published by Giro di Mondo Publishing
Fernandina Beach, Florida

Printed in the United States of America.

Cover and interior by Roseanna White Designs
Cover images from www.Shutterstock.com

SECOND EDITION:
    ISBNs: 979-8-9904398-0-1 (Hardcover)
                      979-8-9904398-1-8 (Paperback)
                      979-8-9904398-2-5 (Digital)

Library of Congress Control Number: 2025927303

*It has taken me decades to articulate this understanding
and to write this song of praise for my father and my mother.
I dedicate this Anniversary edition with much love to my granddaughter, Selena,
and grandson, Jackson— I hope you will learn from the history shared here. You
are our future; I pray you'll embrace it.*

*"Rejoice always, pray continually,
give thanks in all circumstances,
for this is God's will for you in Christ Jesus.*
1 THESSALONIANS 5:16-18 NIV

FOREWORD

In the ten years since the first edition of *Thank You for the Shoes*, I have made many subsequent trips to Italy and have continued to learn more about our family history there and in the United States of America (USA), as well as the conditions that prevailed in both countries during the period covered by this book. I was enriched by all those who wrote to share how the story moved them or helped them understand their grandfather or other elder relatives. This writer gratefully appreciates all the notes and comments. During this time, I learned of some errors, and while they were not substantive to the story, I still wanted to make them right.

Even in this modern world, we know that living in the USA, with an Italian last name or an ancestor with Italian roots often exposes us to a knowing bias that conjures up the word "Mafia."

The truth is that, for the few who fell to the seductive lure of the mob made famous by Mario Puzo's books and the cable TV series The Sopranos, millions of Italian immigrants embraced the new world with a fire in their bellies to do good for themselves and provide a future for their families. They arrived at our nation's shore to face unimaginable hardships. They persevered through honest, backbreaking work and with God ever-present as their guiding star.

While today, the word Italy conjures up visions of the magnificent art and architecture of the Renaissance or the ancient grandeur of Rome, the peninsula in the shape of a woman's high-heeled boot did not become a nation until the 1860s. It is a land of texture and color, shaped by its cultural history, hammered into a fine patina by numerous invasions, political divides, and regionalism. Curiously, the most significant wave of emigration to the USA started in 1870, after Italy became a unified country, and most especially from the Southern region, where many were dying of starvation.

As the clerks processed them through immigration, they labeled the new arrivals "Italian," but the individuals thought of themselves as Abruzzese, Calabrese, or Napolitani. They immediately became the fodder that helped build our country and, in doing so, became part of the fabric we call America. Among the millions who came was a thirteen-year-old, fatherless man-boy, baptized Michelangelo Rizzo, from the rural outskirts of a little mountain town called Platania in Calabria.

This story is about big hopes, enormous setbacks, and small triumphs. It is a story of love and legacy that I hope resonates with anyone who is a first- or second-generation immigrant from Europe or other parts of the world, and for the millions of people in the United States who have made tracing their roots a passion.

What follows are my thoughts and interpretations from conversations with my father and mother, as well as stories recounted to me by my older sisters, brothers, other relatives, friends, and *paisani* in Italy, Australia, and America. I have blended those numerous conversations and interviews with my research and investigation, experiences, observations, and imagination.

I offer this work in the spirit of love and remembrance.

~ Raffaela Marie Rizzo
November 2025, Amelia Island, Florida

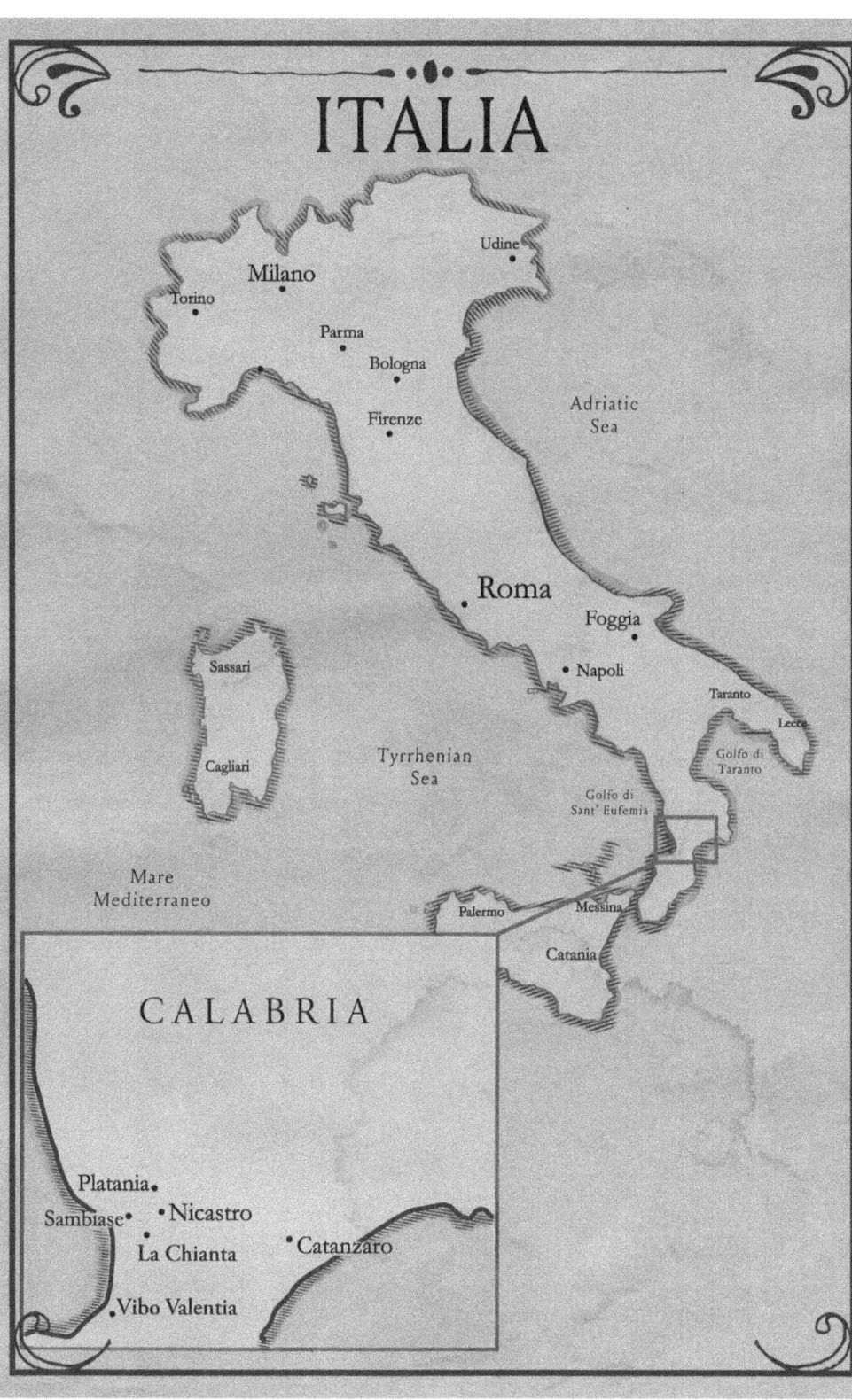

PART ONE

*Chine lassa a via vecchia e pia chilla nova sa chillu chi lassa
ma un sa chillu chi trova.*
~ old Platanese proverb

He who leaves the old road for the new knows
what he leaves but not what he finds.

PRELUDE

Southern Italy, October 1909

The moon was still visible, and the sun but a suggestion, clawing its way over the mountain crest as Michelangelo Rizzo trod slowly down the rock-strewn mountainside. He followed a path well-worn by the ancient Greeks who had settled in the southern Italian town called Platania centuries before. Heading toward Nicastro, the market city center in the valley below, the youngster was intimately familiar with the dirt and rubble road from Platania, having traveled it more than twice weekly in his short thirteen years. Michele (pronounced *meh-kele*), as his family affectionately called him, had etched the treacherous path in his mind so well that he could find his way down it in the dark.

As he made his way, he mentally noted the tremendous significance of this trek. He knew it would be the last time he descended the trail to the base of Monte Reventino. He did not intend to return, ever.

Once down the mountain, he would eventually head to the *Commune di Nicastro*, where he would catch a train later in the day to the port of Vibo Valente. A small vessel would take him to Naples, where he would board the *Duca D' Ostia* ocean vessel that would take him across the Atlantic Ocean to New York—America.

But first, he needed to detour to the outskirts of the *Commune di Sambiase*, an area in the valley known as *La Chianta*. Alternatively called *La Pianta*, depending on which dialect you spoke, it was where his *zio*, or uncle, Luigi Folino—his mother's brother—and his large family lived. Of all his many relatives on his mother's side, he especially wanted to see these cousins.

He loved all his Folino cousins but felt a special bond with Zio Luigi's children, Angelina and twin brothers Antonio and Michele. Their older sister, Petronella, had gone to America a few years ago and married there; he hoped to see her again when he was there. He had always felt more related to these four than all his other maternal cousins. He wasn't sure why, maybe because they were all close in age to him or because they all had radiant blue eyes and infectious smiles. He cherished their company and always felt at home with them.

His night had ended a few hours earlier when he bade his mother, Rosa, a last goodbye. It had been a gut-wrenching affair. Trekking along, he became lost in his thoughts and began reliving not just the scene from last night but also scenes from years past.

"*U shachu che nonti vido ciu, cum tu patre,*" his mother had wailed in the distinct Petronese *montagnaro*, Platania's mountain people's dialect. "I know I will never see you again," she keened. "You're just like your father. You were not yet four years old when we learned your father had died in America, " she sobbed. " From that time, I knew that when you were older, you would want to find some shred of him, something that would help you know him."

Michele's parents married in 1881, when Antonio Rizzo was thirty-one and Rosa Folino was twenty-four. Together, they had six children. Yet now, it was up to Michelangelo, the youngest and the only living male child of their marriage, to carry on the family name.

He was proud of his name. In fact, the main church in Platania was San Michele Arcangelo, the town's patron saint. Michael the Archangel, revered in Catholic tradition as the protector and defender of the Catholic Church, was part of the lore Michele heard often. He knew the saint was called an archangel because he was placed over all the angels as prince of the seraphim.

The itinerant priest who said mass at the tenth-century church in Piazza Vittorio Veneto, Platania's main square, said that San Michele Arcangelo was more than a defender against the devil; he was a special patron of the sick and mariners. Michele admired the church's statuary, which depicted the saint's emblems and powers—a banner, a sword, a dragon, and scales. He had called upon the angel often when he was little.

Now, as he descended the mountain, he realized it had been a long time since he had called on his namesake. So, he asked Saint Michael for protection and asked the saint to defend him against evil on his journey to America.

1

SEARCHING FOR A GRAVE

Platania, November 2, 1901

Each year, on November 2, all communities across the region of Calabria visit cemeteries to pay their respects to their lost loved ones. Michelangelo recalled his first Day of the Dead, or All Souls Day, just after he turned five. That day, the gray sky threatened rain, though the temperature at forty degrees Fahrenheit was no chillier than expected for this time of year. Michele's mother had prepared for the worst, wearing a black shawl to cover her head and shoulders, and her wool stockings. She had said aloud many times that the clothes she had bought with the money Antonio had sent from America were proving useful. As she muttered often, she did not know when, if ever, she could replace the wool stockings so vital in the mountain winters.

With Michelangelo in tow, as she approached the Nicastro cemetery, it appeared the whole valley was flocking to the site, bearing flowers and small tokens made from last spring's palms. It was an annual pilgrimage.

He remembered asking her, "Mama, where is my father buried? Why can't we bring flowers to his grave? Where did he go?"

"Stop. You are stabbing me in the heart," was his mother's response.

But he had pushed forward, his inquisitiveness unquelled.

"Are you doing this just to give me pain?" she had asked without expecting an answer.

"Mama, I don't understand. If Papa died, shouldn't he be here in the cemetery so that we can put flowers and light candles?"

She shushed him again as she strode to the grave of her parents. He wondered why it seemed everyone was staring at them. Everyone knew who she was—Antonio Rizzo's widow, Rosa, whose husband died before he could return from America. Several women who knew Rosa well stopped by to inquire about her situation and her children, making remarks about how fast Michelangelo, whom many also called Michele, as his mother did, seemed to have grown. They spoke as if Michele wasn't even there.

A few more paces, and another local woman stopped them. Spying Michele, who was trying to disappear behind his mother's dress, the nosy woman asked, "Who do you have here? Is that Antonio's last son?" Michele recalled his mother's lamenting responses to all the questions.

"I would have left Michele with Marianna, you know, my adopted daughter, but my son Carlo is so sick. It's difficult for her, and my Carlo struggles to breathe, so his disposition is not too pleasant. Poor thing, Marianna is grieving, too," Rosa continued.

"Michele is a good boy, but he asks a million questions. He's curious about everything. Between Marianna and me, we must keep our eyes on him every minute. Thanks to God, he is sturdy for such a small boy. He never complains about our long journey from our mountain abode to the valley and back up again."

As she walked, she encountered others; she shared with them that her parents were buried in Nicastro. It was well known that people from the valley of Nicastro felt superior to those of the mountains. To have a family member buried at the Nicastro cemetery was almost like saying you were wealthy. Otherwise, Rosa's local cemetery in Platania would be just a short walk.

After they left the cemetery and had almost scaled the mountain, as their modest home came into view, Michele announced, "Someday, I'm going to find my father's grave and bring flowers."

He looked up at his mother as a loud wail came from her mouth; her face had turned pale.

2

A SON NEEDING ANSWERS

"I see your father every time I look at you," Rosa often told Michele. He recalled how she would cling to him during those first few years after she was widowed.

Despite his continuous effort, he could not recall any memories of his father. Though Antonio Rizzo had died when Michele was three and a half years old, he had left for America when Michele was still a babe sucking milk at his mother's breast. There was no memory for the boy to conjure up of him.

Never having known his father or paternal grandparents, Michele did not even know any of his father's family; siblings, aunts, uncles, and cousins all died either before he was born or shortly afterward. Although Rizzo was a common name, Michele was the last living male in his lineage to carry it. This realization weighed on him, instilling a sense of responsibility to preserve his family's history and honor his father's legacy.

From a young age, Michele's thirst for knowledge about his father was insatiable. His relentless questioning of his mother and others was a testament to his unwavering desire to understand the man whose blood coursed through his veins. By age ten, Michele had pieced together the trials and tribulations that led his father to America. His only information about his father came from others, such as his mother's brother, Luigi, and his adopted older sister, Marianna. They well remembered Antonio, and Michele had asked them and others about his father almost since he first could speak.

When he questioned his mother, she provided only the bare facts. Whenever he pressed her for more details, she became defensive. This tone, coupled with her apparent guilt over having insisted Antonio take a second trip to America, often left Michele feeling frustrated and distant from his mother.

Their moments of togetherness had become rare in recent years, especially after Rosa remarried when Michele was nine. Around this time, he confided in his mother, expressing his belief that the answers to his questions lay in America, the place where his father had met his end.

3

CALABRIA, THE MELTING POT

Antonio Rizzo, son of Carlo Rizzo and Rosangela Gallo, was born on April 19, 1850, in Platania (often called Petrania in the local dialect), in the state of Catanzaro, in the region of Italy known as Calabria. Calabria, a melting pot of Mediterranean and non-Mediterranean cultures, is different from Rome, Florence, and Venice, which most tourists visit. Each state within Calabria (Cosenza, Catanzaro, and Reggio Calabria, plus a fourth state, Vibo Valente, which emerged in the 1990s) is as different as the countries of France, Spain, Italy, and Russia.

Dominated by the Apennine Calabro mountains, the Calabrian region is also surrounded by an 800-kilometer coastline formed by the Mediterranean, Ionian, and Adriatic seas. This coastline creates the bottom of the country's shape of a woman's high-heeled boot. Calabria stretches from toe to heel up through the instep. It ends just before the ankle of the boot, abutting the region of Campania. The state of Catanzaro, with its capital city of the same name, is the area from the instep to the arch of the boot. With a breathtaking coastal landscape, Calabria is much more mountainous than flatland, defined by its majestic pine and birch forests, lakes, and rivers.

Its natural beauty and historic sentinels are witness to the fragments of cultures and customs of the various visitors and conquerors, reflected in the faces, mannerisms, and dialects of the Calabrian people. Through the ages, Greeks, Iberians, Romans, Saracens, Byzantines, Normans, Jews, Aragonese,

Swabians, Spanish, Moors, Bourbons, and numerous others left their imprints behind in genes and influence.

Giuseppe Garibaldi, a renowned military leader and nationalist, commanded several campaigns in the mid-1800s that eventually led to the unification of all cities and kingdoms of Italy into a single nation in 1861, known as the *Risorgimento*. Although Garibaldi was acclaimed as a hero and the unification of Italy was desired and anticipated by most, for the Calabrese, it created misery and famine. After unification, highway robberies flourished in the region. The meager plots of land were heavily taxed to support the city dwellers. People from Southern Italy felt unrepresented in the newly formed government, which ignored their needs in favor of the North. And, while ordinary people in Southern Italy begged for change and political stability, Calabria received none, giving rise to brigandage. A lack of employment, high taxation, and lawlessness crushed the people of the South.

To be Calabrese could mean being a blend of the best of many cultures, or, as young Michele preferred to believe, it meant you were from a race of supreme survivors, people who adapted, grew, and conquered their circumstances, if not other people—a proud heritage. Sometimes, Michele felt that the blood that ran in his veins perhaps contained a fine blend of both.

When Michele's father, Antonio Rizzo, left Platania, he was part of an almost thirty-year migration to the New World to relieve the hunger, misery, and indignities of the time. During this period in Southern Italy, many children were born, but few survived past their teens. If they did, they often left to find a future in the Americas or in North Africa, where many Calabrese went to help build the Suez Canal in the 1860s.

In 1898, Antonio left for his second journey to America. Michele was twenty months old. His oldest sister, Angela, had reached an age when she would soon need a dowry. Antonio and Rosa were facing the realities of the times and circumstances. Their seven-year-old son, Carlo, suffered from congenital heart disease, and it was clear to his parents that he would not live into adulthood.

The Rizzos had also raised another child, Marianna, whose birth mother had died giving her life one day before their Angela was born. As Rosa was overflowing with milk, the couple's compassion prompted them to take in the motherless infant so Rosa could serve as her wet nurse. After baby Marianna's father remarried, his new wife showed little interest in the child, and Rosa and Antonio adopted the little girl, raising her as their own. Not uncommon in places of high infant mortality, a *figlia di latte*, or milk daughter, was a cherished member of many families.

Marianna was a humble girl devoid of even a trace of arrogance or guile. She had been a tremendous help to Rosa with Carlo, who suffered from an inability to walk due to reduced breathing capacity because of his heart disease. And when the new baby, Michele, was born, Marianna acted like a little mother to him.

Then, when both Angela and Marianna were fourteen years old, Antonio set off on his second trip to America in four short years.

On his first trip to America in 1894, Antonio soon realized that the stories of streets paved with gold were exaggerations promulgated by the owners of the coal mines and road builders to lure workers. Rosa's brother, Luigi, who had gone to America two years earlier, helped Antonio find work as soon as he arrived in Bridgeport, Connecticut, where Uncle Luigi had settled. The work as a day laborer building roads was backbreaking, but it earned Antonio decent money. Back at home, raising the desirable and prized silkworms to supply the cottage silk industries that peppered the mountains during that period, Rosa had helped supplement the family's earnings.

Antonio sent a steady stream of money home to his wife by living in a rooming house with other men who were doing similar work. Back home, the American dollars had afforded the Rizzo family more than just the ability to buy the food and supplies they needed. It had put them in a unique position compared with much of the Southern Italian peasant-class hillbillies.

Antonio missed his family. And, though there were Luigi and other fellow villagers from their area of Calabria, they all boarded at different houses because the immigrants had to lodge wherever there was an empty bed. Antonio was frugal to the point of being parsimonious because he wanted to save all he could.

As misfortune would deal him a short deck, his first trip to America was truncated. He arrived in America after a bank panic and financial depression that had evaporated many jobs. While he found some work right away, it wasn't steady enough. He was a day worker, unlike his brother-in-law, who had been there long enough to be put on the payroll as a regular. Thus, Antonio was assigned work on a sporadic basis.

Where he had planned to stay for two years, he returned to Italy after only a year and a half, despite the urging of many *paisani*, fellow Calabrians, who said, "Ride it out, America won't stay down for long."

Antonio went home, saying, "I don't need to be greedy. I've earned enough for my family to live in a bit more comfort."

After his return to Italy in December of 1895, he and Rosa used his savings to acquire a small plot of land to plant some vegetables and build a rustic stone house. Those who lived within the city, in the buildings near the square, would have described the Rizzo abode as little more than a hut. Nevertheless, the loose stone structure Antonio had built for his family was among the better ones in their area among rural mountain dwellers.

On their plot of land, not contiguous to their house, Antonio and his wife coaxed out a variety of vegetables, including potatoes, during the spring, summer, and fall seasons. Winters were harsh on the mountain, yielding almost nothing. During the producing months, they took the small harvest of whatever was in season to sell at the *Mercato,* the open-air marketplace in the valley.

The largest town in the area, Nicastro, had many well-heeled residents and professionals who would pay a few *Ducati* to help the Rizzos buy necessities they couldn't grow or make themselves. Though Calabria now used the *lira* established in 1861, Antonio and his family and friends all referenced the monetary unit of Venice—the *Ducati d'oro,* meaning the gold of the duke. The older currencies held sway in world trade, and many Southerners were skeptical of the unification and the new monetary currency.

With the birth of Michelangelo in September 1896 and the looming needs of a marriage-aged daughter, Rosa began to nag Antonio to return to the "well" known as America.

Rosa later told her son that his father lamented having to make a second voyage to America. Antonio had said that he remembered all too well the stench of the long trip in steerage class with no windows and people sick everywhere on that first trip across the Atlantic. Antonio expressed that he had pined for his family while away.

He realized that many men he saw on his first trip had no intention of ever returning to Italy. When Antonio came home, he vowed never to return to America without his wife and children.

4

BACK TO THE WELL CALLED AMERICA

Platania, 1898

By 1898, rather than improving, the economic and political situation in Southern Italy entered a downward spiral. Disturbing lawlessness prevailed, and famine was even more widespread. At the same time, there was growing talk in Nicastro that America was on the move again. A new president meant more work ahead, and the railroad bankruptcies of 1893–1894 were giving way to more building and construction. America needed good workers again.

Feeling the weight of his obligations toward his family and Rosa's persistent harping on the case for Angela's dowry since even before the baby Michele arrived, Antonio was softening. Moreover, now they needed to help Marianna, who had a boyfriend and was eager to marry.

But at forty-eight, Antonio said he didn't feel young enough to withstand the rigors of the strength-sapping voyage and the harsh conditions he had faced in America—bone-breaking work on roads and construction projects in the cold and heat, and squalid rooming houses, with as many as four men to one bed. He had always prized his own personal cleanliness, a trait he had imparted to his children. He knew that upon returning to America, there would be no luxury like personal space or cleanliness. Though they had little in Platania, Antonio felt they had a space of their own: sunshine, fresh air, and family nearby. However, he could not see a future here for his children.

Antonio had confided in Rosa that America was not the land of milk and honey that so many believed. Although Rosa knew her husband to be a truthful, honest man, she, like many townspeople, did not quite believe the stories of hard work, unscrupulous bosses, and challenging conditions. She felt that perhaps he had embellished a little to gain sympathy. How could it be that bad in America when many others had written letters about the riches there?

According to Antonio, those who had no intention of returning were the worst. They sent exaggerated accounts of easy riches. Indeed, many had amassed considerable fortunes, though often through dishonest means.

They spoke of wonders never seen in the *Mezzogiorno,* the traditional term for the southern regions of Italy, scorched by the midday sun. They spoke of the big houses that *i'mericani* owned. And they raved about how someday they would buy a big house, and then their families could come, too. They promised their wives would live like queens. In the meantime, they claimed to be saving every dime so that their families could reap the riches of America. Instead, Antonio observed that many didn't save a cent. After sending some of their earnings to their families each week, they drank away more than they sent back to Italy. And what they didn't drink away, they spent on evenings at the local brothels.

Antonio was ashamed of the behavior of those *paisani*. He also knew many who, like him, were homesick and dedicated to working, saving, and returning to their families. However, it seemed that those who were less than good, God-fearing sons of the *Mezzogiorno* had more money and received favored treatment from the bosses.

Rosa knew that her husband had no stomach for returning to America, but she often boasted that she had devised the ultimate lure. When Marianna was about to be married in the early spring of 1898, Rosa managed to sway Antonio. Marianna was promised to Augustino Caruso, a strong young mountain man. Eight years her senior, at twenty-two, Augustino was an industrious worker with a rough but kind demeanor. Antonio looked forward to the upcoming wedding.

While no one would have described her as beautiful, Marianna had even features, a pert little nose, and high cheekbones. She was scrawny and strong.

A sturdy worker with a big heart. While she would bring almost no dowry, the young man prized the woman who often worked alongside him to remove stones from the fields. He joked that she was more agile than a mountain goat. Marianna was a simple person, trustworthy and open. Thoughts flew from her head to her lips in an instant. Most of all, she had a loving and generous spirit.

Soon after her marriage, Marianna's husband would go with her adopted father, Antonio, on this second trip to America in 1898. Augustino and Antonio planned to stay for three years—from May 1898 to May 1901.

Rosa told Marianna, "When they return, they should have earned enough money to recoup what they paid for the passage, and they also can perhaps buy some additional land, where they can build a house for you and Augustino. In the meantime, they will send us money to keep us fed.

"Best of all," said Rosa, "I will be able to amass a proper dowry for Angela so she can marry well. We will present a good face to the community ... *La Bella Figura*. I know you understand what that means, Marianna." *La Bella Figura,* presenting a good face to the community, was central to Rosa's view of the world. "My family is from the valley of Nicastro." Rosa's own marriage and her move to the mountain with Antonio had seemed a step down in the eyes of others, but also in her own eyes. Yet her brother, Luigi, had often reminded her that Antonio had been worth it. He was loyal, faithful, trustworthy, and handsome.

Rosa told Antonio, with conviction, that their son-in-law would be doing a wonderful thing for himself and Marianna. Taking him to America on this voyage could help assure that their adopted daughter, who had been such a godsend to them, would have a stab at a much better life with the earnings her husband would send back.

5

A SURPRISING SECOND VOYAGE

Atlantic Ocean, 1898

Antonio Rizzo left Platania with his son-in-law, Augustino Caruso, to embark on the Britannia Ocean vessel from the port of Naples on May 17. Though long, the passage of twenty-one days to New York was not as horrible as Antonio remembered from his first trip across the Atlantic. Perhaps it was the better ship. Built in Glasgow, Scotland, the twenty-year-old three-masted ship with a single funnel was 350 feet long and thirty-eight feet wide. With compound engines and a single screw, it carried along its 654 passengers, almost all third-class, at a service speed of eleven knots. There were a handful of first-class passengers, but the small vessel scurried from Kalamata, Greece, to Messina, then to Naples, and finally to New York, profiting from the mass exodus to the Americas under the British flag for the Anchor Line.

Antonio had warned young Augustino of the rough seas and admonished him about not drinking wine, as it would increase his seasickness. Though bland, the food too seemed a little better to him than he recalled from his first voyage, though perhaps he was now familiar with what the English called food. He was just happy to get some.

The time passed more quickly than on his earlier voyage. Also, the seas appeared a little calmer this time of year. Though the quarters were crowded and filled with offensive odors, Antonio walked up on deck often to take in the fresh, salty air.

At night, he often played *scopa* and *briscola,* the card games endemic to Southern Italy, and sang songs with his fellow *paisani*. It was perhaps the time of year, or the companionship of his son-in-law, or that he had braced himself for the horror of his first trip. But despite the cramped quarters, the lack of privacy, and the heat below deck, Antonio thought this crossing tolerable. This time, the ship carried more families and fewer single men. And, where there were women, things were just a little cleaner.

This crowd of fellow steerage passengers seemed more jovial than on his first trip. He almost always heard someone singing, and sometimes people danced. Passengers sometimes became sick, but not to the degree of Antonio's first crossing. He had learned what to avoid, and his stomach fared much better. Regretting the difficulty he had caused Rosa over making this second trip, he focused not on the work he would have to do ahead but on the trip home and bringing money for a good dowry and a better life for his family and his adopted daughter. He began to fantasize about bringing Rosa and the children to America.

Though Augustino had been seasick for almost a week, Antonio's newfound optimism infected his son-in-law, and they both disembarked with smiles on their faces that spread from their first sighting of the Statue of Liberty and didn't even get defeated as they endured the dreaded Ellis Island processing. Soon, they were safe at 588 Pembroke Street, the home of a trusted *paisano,* Antonio Negri, a rented row house in Bridgeport, Connecticut. Negri, as friends called him, had been widowed with four children and then married a widow with two of her own. The family took in two boarders to make ends meet and somehow managed to accommodate ten people in the tiny space.

Antonio's letter to Negri, several months before their departure, had said he would need a bed for two. His response had been not to worry; we'll find you a place to board. When they arrived, Antonio learned that he and his son-in-law could stay with the Negri family. The wife would cook, wash, and clean for the whole brood.

"What's two more?" said Negri with a confidence unmatched in the face of his new wife of just one year. Negri had now been in America for five years.

When Antonio was there the first time, he and his brother-in-law, Luigi Folino, along with Negri, worked for the railroad as day laborers. Negri, though, had stayed and gotten a better position with steady work.

Angela Negri prepared a delicious meal for all of them, with the comforting aromas of Calabrian food. As they feasted on full plates of pasta and an oval-shaped meatball made from veal and pork, Negri bragged about his wife's cooking talents. They talked for several hours about the townspeople, their families back home, and the conditions in Platania and Calabria. Then Negri showed Antonio and Augustino the sleeping accommodations.

"*Dormiti qui*," he said. They would sleep in an area of the tiny house Negri called the *porcchia*. Antonio figured out that it wasn't Calabrese but an Italianization of the American word for *portico anteriore*, or front porch. Bone tired, the two men fell asleep in an instant, even though they shared a small sofa bed on the minuscule enclosed porch.

Despite the tight sleeping accommodations, they awakened rested to the blinding light of a sun-filled day with an azure sky, nary a cloud overhead, and zero humidity. The weather and beauty of the day invigorated Antonio.

Over coffee, Negri said he would be working a night shift so he could take Antonio and Augustino to find work that day; right after they finished their coffee and rolls, they set out.

Young Augustino couldn't contain himself. "*Sono in America*—I'm in America," he effused. The homes all sported colorful flowers and greenery in their tiny front yards. As they walked, Antonio explained to Augustino that spring here in Connecticut resembled Platania's. His earlier trip to Bridgeport had lasted long enough for him to experience the entire change of seasons.

Maybe the transatlantic voyage caused his exhaustion, but after the three-mile walk, Antonio felt winded when they arrived at a shack where a sinister-looking man smoking a cigar sat at a small table. The man barked what sounded like greetings, and Negri's English impressed Antonio as he listened to his friend express himself with such facility. Of course, he reminded himself that he could not judge Negri's English language skills, as he had none of his own.

After a long exchange in which Antonio and Augustino didn't understand a word, Negri announced, "We are all set; I struck a deal, and you start work tomorrow!"

Back at the house, Negri told them they would dig trenches for a new railroad line. There would be some blasting to clear the rock that was so prevalent in the area. Negri chuckled. "This Connecticut is full of hard rock. But nobody digs ditches better than we Calabrese do! And we know about rocks from our hometown, *Petrania,* which means rock-strewn. Well, at least that's what its over-name means," he joked, as he knew full well that the town's actual name, Platania, was named after a tree, the platen, which grows everywhere there, and not the rock-strewn nickname, though indeed the mountain and the town had no shortage of rocks and stones.

The next day, the two newcomers reported for work. Augustino came home at the end of the day with welts and blisters, a splitting headache, and his back screaming with pain. Though not unaccustomed to backbreaking work, the two men's muscles had been in disuse for a spell with getting ready for the trip, traveling to Naples, and the ocean voyage.

Antonio felt terrible for his son-in-law. Despite his own aching muscles and blistered hands, he helped get Augustino into the tin tub to soak in salt water. He told Augustino his muscles would adjust. "*Tu si, giovane. Tra pochi giorni ti sembra un giocco di ragazzi.* You are young," Antonio joked, "this will seem like child's play before long."

6

AN UNEXPECTED TURN OF EVENTS

Bridgeport, Connecticut, 1899

The days progressed with working, eating, sleeping, and letters to the family in Italy dictated to a *scrivano,* a letter writer who knew Calabrese. The spring weather gave way to the summer solstice, bringing hot, humid days. And the noonday heat was intense.

Augustino remarked to his father-in-law one morning, "I thought Americans were so smart, but unlike in Italy, where we work very early and get out of the sun and rest from one o'clock until four in the afternoon, before starting up again for a few hours, here they work right through with only a thirty-minute break. Don't they know that this intense sun is not healthy?"

While Antonio empathized with him, he said, "America is growing. They have no time for long rests. You make sure you drink lots of water during the breaks. That's all I can tell you. And do not suggest that Americans are not smart. They are smarter than our country, and even after unification, our government can't create jobs for us peasants willing to work. Remember how often you have gone to bed hungry before you dare criticize how they do things here."

Though he hadn't raised his voice, his tone had been excoriating, and the admonitions cowed Augustino. Antonio felt terrible about it and decided to keep his thoughts to himself going forward. Though they woke up each morning soaked in sweat and returned broken, burned, and exhausted, they both told Negri how grateful they were that he'd found work for them.

During the August heat wave, Antonio and Negri sat outside in the late evening after everyone had gone to bed. Negri smoked a shriveled, skinny cigar that the *i'mericani* called "guinea stinkers." Lulled by the air's heaviness and the cicadas' screaming pitch, Antonio explored new territory with his friend.

"What do you think it would take for me to bring my whole family here? I know Rosa would love to come to America."

Negri explained the process of getting his first wife and children here. He also described a hair-raising scene that happened to his second wife. When she arrived at Ellis Island, one of the children was sick. She had almost died of fright that they would turn the child back. They stayed in quarantine for a while. At last, the child's chest congestion cleared up, and they entered. "It's a good thing," he said, "because I'd be here with my motherless children going crazy."

Then, Antonio brought up his older son. "Based on what you've told me, it's clear to me that my Carlo would never get into the country with his heart condition. The examiners would spot his withered body and condition right away, and that's only if Carlo, against all odds, survived the ocean journey itself," said a dejected Antonio. He and his friend talked into the wee hours. Negri discussed when Antonio planned to repatriate to Italy.

"If you stay until you reach your goal of staying three years, you will return to Platania with a sizable sum of money," Negri predicted. "You could build a *palazzo* (an apartment building) in the center of town, perhaps. With the American money you will save, you and your wife and children could live like barons."

His jocularity evaporating, Negri said, "My poor first wife died so young. And my Angela's first husband the same. The arduous work and not enough decent food killed them; our homeland failed us. Now, we live in our adopted country and think of every way we can save a few pennies. Angela works night and day cooking, cleaning, and managing the children and the boarders. She also takes in sewing and ironing. It is no different here; the work is challenging. But I have hopes for my children. In time, they will live better than we are living.

"Tell me more about the situation back home. I was sure that Garibaldi would bring about significant changes for the better," pried Negri.

"Garibaldi was indeed magnificent, but in Italy, things are horrible. There are many bands of lazy rogues who roam the rural areas, wreaking mayhem and doing unspeakable things to women and children. There is general lawlessness. People are starving everywhere around us. If it weren't for the money sent from those fortunate to have family in America or make a trip or two ourselves, we would all be dead from hunger," Antonio added.

"My family is better off now, but not because of Garibaldi. But because of my first trip here, which is now long gone," he confided in his friend.

"I have no great desire to leave Petrania forever, but there is no future for the young people. Carlo is one matter, but Rosa and I are happy that at least the new baby, Michele, seems strong and healthy," Antonio said. "But I cannot shake the terrible foreboding that Petrania will not be able to sustain our baby Michele as he grows. At some point, he will do what so many have done. He'll grow up and leave us for other places. Unless we can all move here, we will spend our old age alone with no children around us."

"Cheer up," Negri joked. "Stay focused, Antonio, on the money you will bring back that can change your life and those of your children. *La moneta combia tutto.*" He raised his wine glass as he declared, "Money changes everything."

"What an interesting thought," mused Antonio, feeling a bit better. He vowed to tackle his labor with joy, although they had been blasting rock this past week, and he didn't fare well with each blast. Antonio felt as if his whole being was sucked out of him each time. Nevertheless, he made his friend's words, "money changes everything," a mantra. Along with his daily prayers, he felt he needed something to keep him going. An optimistic person by nature, these recent years had been a downer for Antonio. He didn't know why, but he felt an impending sense of doom. Whenever it overtook him, he worked to shake it off with a prayer to St. Antonio, his patron saint.

In his next letter to Rosa, he expressed his optimism that, with American money, the baby would grow up respected as a son of wealthy people. Their daughter, Angela, would marry a fine young man, and while nothing would change Carlo's condition, they could provide him with a more comfortable home and more care from the doctor.

7

TRAGEDY AT WORK

Bridgeport, Connecticut, 1900

Antonio and Negri didn't see much of each other over the next three months, because Negri had been working the night shift. They saw each other briefly in the mornings, and they tossed a joke or two and some pleasantries, but not much else.

One morning, Antonio and Augustino were basking in the solitude of the quiet, sipping coffee on the front stoop before heading to the blasting site. The household was still calm, as they often prepared the coffee themselves and left before six a.m., when Angela began waking the children and starting her day. With her husband working the night shift, returning around eight a.m., she had a short window to get the noisy chores done so he could rest after the children were off to school.

Then, out of nowhere, appeared two men. Antonio thought it odd that visitors would come when it was barely light out. He had a sudden flash of the marauders that often attacked the families in Southern Italy, snatching young girls and boys right before their mothers' eyes.

One of the men addressed the pair on the stoop in Calabrese. *"Tu se u fratti di Negri?"* he asked.

"No, I'm not his brother, I'm Negri's friend and boarder," Antonio answered. "Has something happened? Where is Negri?" He suddenly panicked.

"Mi dispiace," replied the stranger. "I'm sorry to have to bring bad news, but we must talk with his wife."

Before Antonio could go inside to knock on the door for Angela, she appeared dressed for the day with some mending in her hands. She stopped when she spotted the two men behind Antonio.

"What's happened?" she cried.

"Your husband collapsed at work."

"Where have they brought him? I must go to him."

"He's gone," said the other man in almost a whisper. "There was nothing to be done."

Stunned, Angela screamed. The children came running. In an instant, chaos replaced the stillness. Antonio had no words. He heard the men tell him that his friend Negri had not suffered. He felt at a loss as to what to do next. He and Augustino had to report to work, or the bosses would let them go.

He suddenly realized that he really knew nothing about his friend Negri's affairs and financial situation. He asked Angela if there was someone he could fetch for her. She sat limply in a chair, ashen, with all the children around her, their saucer-sized eyes incredulous.

As if out of nowhere, a neighbor woman appeared and seemed to take charge of Angela and the children. She begged Antonio to find out where Negri's body had been taken. The two men had already walked almost to the end of Pembroke, and Antonio ran after them. Shouting to Augustino to head to their work site and tell the boss that he would be along soon, Antonio went with the men to the undertaker to confirm the identity of the body.

After the painful identification, Antonio asked some questions about what would take place next, and he went ahead and arranged a small funeral for his friend, as his widow was in no condition to handle anything.

When he finally arrived at his worksite, Antonio was winded. Forcing himself forward, he went to talk to the railroad boss about Negri's family. He learned with relief that, unlike himself, Negri was not a day laborer, but a real employee. That meant this family was entitled to railroad insurance that would help cover funeral expenses.

The next evening at the visitation, Antonio was pleased that many of the *paisani* and some distant relatives had shown up. Dying was serious business among the *paisani*. Everyone respected the dead. Antonio had only met a few of them during his relatively short time in Bridgeport. Judging by the size of the crowd, Antonio surmised that his friend had known just about everyone in town.

At the funeral mass the following morning, the owner of Negri's house approached Antonio and asked if he wanted to rent the apartment. Antonio explained that he would not be staying in America permanently, to which the proprietor said, "I'm sorry then, I'm going to have to evict the widow and the children. Everyone will have to be gone by the end of the week. I have to rent the place."

After the funeral, Antonio and Augustino went to collect their belongings and asked what they could do for Angela and the children. Apparently, a distant relative was taking them in temporarily and the relative relayed that she would return to Calabria. There, her parents, though elderly, might be able to help her.

Disconsolate from the events of the past few days, Antonio and Augustino trudged to a rooming house on a nearby street that someone had told them about. The price was slightly higher, but certainly far less than if they had to rent an apartment.

Antonio couldn't fathom how Negri had paid for the house. Though he had boasted a few times about having saved a lot of money, when Antonio asked some of Negri's coworkers how Angela might access his savings, they didn't sound at all encouraging. They told Antonio that if Angela wanted to remain in America long enough to probate his estate, it could take perhaps a year or more, and even then, there might be nothing for her to inherit. She would have to let it go. She knew less about his money than his co-workers did, if indeed he had any at all.

Antonio found it all so bewildering. America, the land of milk and honey, was so fragile. He knew Angela was not looking to profit from her husband's premature death, but how would she manage? She told him she didn't even have the money to pay for passage to return to Calabria. Some of Negri's coworkers offered to take up a collection for her, but what would she and the children live on until then?

At once, Antonio wanted to get away from Bridgeport, Connecticut. The sooner the better. An inexplicable fear overtook him. The place must be cursed. The next day, he and Augustino returned to work, each wearing a black armband in honor of their dear friend. Antonio felt as depressed at the death of his friend as when he buried the last of his own relatives in Italy. He thought about how he had no parents, siblings, aunts, uncles, nieces, or nephews remaining on earth. His wife and children were an ocean away. Despite Augustino's companionship, Antonio suffered an enormous sense of abandonment; it was as if he were an orphan.

He scolded himself. "I'm a grown man with children. Orphans are children with no parents." Yet for all the pep talks he gave himself, he could not shake the feeling of a boat adrift without an anchor, helpless against the tide. He recognized that these feelings were an anomaly; he was usually an optimistic person.

Yet he didn't lose sight of why he was here in America. He summoned his reserves and resolved to see it through. However, Antonio no longer wanted to stretch the trip out into May of 1901 as he and Augustino originally planned. That night, they discussed what they could expect to earn and, though they now had higher expenses for room and board, they continued to live simply. Together, they determined that if they finished out the current year working in America, they would still have done well.

"If we work till then," said Antonio, "we will have earned good money. We can leave in November or December; it's only six months before we planned. We'll be home for the start of the new year!" He said that for Augustino's benefit, but he didn't feel the optimism that his words were imparting. "There is no work here in the dead of winter anyway," he continued, "it's all frozen. You well remember last January through March, when we were sweepers earning almost nothing."

For months, Augustino had moaned that if they waited until the spring to return, it would be three years since they had left. To the young man, it seemed an interminable amount of time to be away from his wife. He missed

Marianna so much. In fact, the young man spoke of nothing else. He often said he would get her pregnant the first night he returned.

"I know you miss her," said Antonio in a small, quiet voice, "as I miss my Rosa and the children. It seems like forever. But in the scheme of life, it's not much."

Yet he was more than happy to give in to curtailing the stay. The letters continued back and forth across the ocean to their wives lamenting their separation and how hard life was without them in America. As Antonio always included some money in each letter, Rosa felt the sacrifices were worth it.

As time passed, she wrote, "Our son Carlo grows weaker each day. On a happier note, Michele is now quite a little man, talking and helping us with small chores. At three years old," she reported, "he's smart enough that we can leave him to tend to his sick brother while Marianna and I go into town or to gather the silkworms. Michele fetches things for Carlo, who doesn't have the strength to walk across the room."

In America, the men left the railroad projects to work on a new dam for the Bridgeport Hydraulic Company near Beaver Brook, in the upper part of the area called Stratford. The bosses said this job would shut down at Christmas and not resume until late March. Armed with that knowledge, Antonio and his son-in-law set their return passage to Italy for December 24. While he would have liked to be home for Christmas, Antonio found the passage cost lower on that date; it would allow the two men to work till the last possible day.

Then, on December 17, a week before their planned departure, Antonio and Augustino were digging away at a frozen embankment while blasting was going on at another area of the construction. The blasting explosions had become routine, and no one really worried about them except Antonio. He hated them. His work group had just stopped for a water break. He stood with a ladle in hand and watched in horror as the crew where his son-in-law worked became fodder for the cave-in that occurred before his eyes.

Antonio saw the upper part of the frozen bank suddenly collapse, burying about thirty men below. Dumbstruck, he realized Augustino had just perished before him along with some of the men he knew.

In the chaos that followed, no one noticed Antonio as he gripped his chest and slumped to the ground. Seeing the disaster at the cave-in site, all the men he was with rushed there and started digging to extract the men. The area was quickly overrun with people and horses who brought three doctors from Bridgeport to the victims' aid.

When Antonio's co-workers finally spotted him on the ground, they assumed he had been overcome with grief. They carried him back to his rooming house, but never fetched a doctor until the second day, when they recognized that Antonio was barely moving.

When the doctor arrived, he announced after examining him, "This man has suffered a massive heart infarction."

The massive coronary had debilitated Antonio tremendously. In his weakened state, he asked his co-workers to contact his family. Unfortunately, even before a telegram could be dispatched, Antonio died.

8

CRUSHING SORROW AND FEAR

Platania, October 1900

The telegram delivery boy, universally perceived as an ill omen in Calabria where the main channel of communication was word of mouth, was dreaded by everyone. When Rosa saw the young man on the bicycle approach her door, she screamed. Then the boy read the telegram to her. She keened with rage and fury.

"Not only have I lost my devoted husband, but what am I to do with a little boy, a ten-year-old son with heart trouble who can't help work the fields, let alone take care of himself, and a daughter getting closer every day to the age of marriage," she wailed. "This is every Southern Italian mother's nightmare—no dowry with which to make a good match for my daughter."

In a singsong lamentation, she cried about her fears that Angela would be forever a burden to her family, not to mention the shame of an unwed daughter who was not in a convent.

And, of course, there was Marianna. Heartbroken. A widow at sixteen. "What are we to do?" Rosa screamed as she tore at her face. Her guilt at having practically forced her husband to go on this trip would follow her to her grave.

"It's my fault. I should never have insisted he go. I have sinned," she declared to the world.

Little Michele had developed a strong bond—a solid kinship—with his "milk sister," Marianna, from the day he was born. Though only a teenager, she had tended to Rosa during the birth. Even after marriage, having no children of her own yet, and later an absent husband, Marianna lavished the little boy with all her love and attention. His own mother, too, had paid considerable attention to the baby from the time he was born. His hazel eyes and full lips often led her to declare that he was her little cherub, the apple of her eye.

Though not quite four years old, he understood the seriousness of what he was hearing from his mother now—her anguished cries, then joined by Marianna's as the news reached her that her Augustino would not be returning. Over the next several months, Antonio's premature death rendered Rosa increasingly despondent. She paid little or no attention to her little son, *Michuzzu*, her pet name for Michele. Now, even more than working and tending children, she faced greater issues. Whatever money Antonio was saving had disappeared. No one knew what happened to either Augustino's or Antonio's stash of earnings.

Marianna had expressed her pain differently. She went around hugging Michele, doing chores by rote, weeping quietly. Her pain, she realized, was different than her mother's. Rosa screamed words at her that didn't register: "You are a young woman with no children. You'll soon marry another good man."

The distance, the lack of education, and the lack of knowledge about America made it impossible for Rosa to lay claim to anything. She went to the priest to see if he would write an official letter, but the priest, though accommodating, was not encouraging.

"Rosa," he said gently, "America is a wild place. If he didn't send it to you, then it's gone—no sense building up false hopes. Whatever there was is gone. It is God's will."

Dejected, she trod home, hugged her children, keened, ranted, and cried some more. Rosa knew that in a place where lawlessness reigned, a woman alone with two daughters, a baby, and a sickly son had much to be concerned about.

One afternoon after going to the *Mercato* in Nicastro, she detoured on her way back to Platania to pay a visit to her brother Luigi and his family, and to her aunts, uncles, and cousins in the compound at *La Chianta* in Sambiase. Her sister-in-law offered her something to eat. Tears slid down her face. She barely had anything to feed her children, she confided. Her relatives all advised her that finding and marrying some good widower was her only salvation. She protested that she could do it alone. No one could replace Antonio, she declared.

A few months later, when winter raged, she realized that she and the children were all getting weaker. Her family's words rang in her head, and it finally dawned on her that they were right. She needed to find someone who had lost his wife. She needed others to convince him that Rosa would be a suitable wife for him, for the sake of all of them. It would be a marriage of convenience. Unlike the love and burning attraction she had experienced with Antonio, this union would just help them stay alive.

Was there such a man who would have her? She wasn't young; the bloom had left the rose, she thought. She examined herself in the small hand mirror she had received as a wedding gift, which seemed eons ago. Her face lacked lines, though she was closer to forty than thirty. And her bosom was still ample. Yes, encumbered with children and problems; nevertheless, she went to call on a woman in the town known for bringing the *'mbasciata*. A matchmaker. She would help.

In the summer of 1904, as she approached her fourth year as a widow, Rosa married Domenico Scalizi, a widower with several older children. Michele was nearly eight years old.

A virtual little man, always helping his mother and serving his sickly brother, Michele had not been asked his opinion about his soon-to-be stepfather. Yet he had overheard his mother talking to his sisters and the town matchmaker, and it sounded like the match did not bring her joy. He had heard her say, "It's the best I can do; otherwise, we will all perish."

Six months into the marriage of convenience, Michele realized that the man his mother had married was providing a roof over their heads and food for their bellies. Still, he was also inflicting plenty of pain and suffering.

9

BECOMING A SURVIVOR

Platania, 1906

He had been living alone for almost a year now. Michele had left his mother and stepfather's home after he'd gotten into a fight with the man, trying to keep him from striking his mother again. The terrible scene had appalled him. But when his stepfather struck Michele as well, his mother did not defend him. She merely tried to hush him so as not to provoke further disputes. Michele could not stomach the abuse that his stepfather dished out regularly, not only to him but to his mother as well. This incident, along with others like it, strained their family bond, leading Michele to make a difficult decision.

Realizing that his mother had resigned herself to a situation that he wanted no part of, he left. At age ten, he moved back into the old Rizzo home they had abandoned when Rosa had married—the place his father had secured with the earnings from his first trip to America. A crude structure typical of the Mercuri area of Platania, where the peasants lived, fashioned from the plentiful loose stones, kept the elements at bay with clay, hay, and an eclectic collection of nature's throwaways shoved between the crevices. The living conditions were harsh, but Michele's determination to make the best of it, enduring the cold and the scarcity, was a testament to his strength and resilience.

In summer, the tangy mountain air, spiked with pines and crystal-fresh springs, kept the temperature much cooler than in the valley of Nicastro, where residents fled to the beaches to escape the intense heat of August. The mountain springs ensured year-round good drinking water for the Platanese, but for those in rural areas, it was a long walk to reach them. *At least we are better off than most of Nicastro, where lack of water is a way of life during summer,* Michele thought.

He had clean drinking water on the mountain. Still, water for bathing, cooking, and washing was difficult to secure during January, February, and March, when temperatures hovered around 0.7 degrees Celsius. Those who resided in the Platania town center had sturdier structures that kept out the wind and cold while retaining the warmth from *caminetti* and *scaldapiedi*—the fireplaces and foot-warmers owned by all the well-heeled townies.

However, there was little to fend off the bitter cold and ice in the more remote rural areas where Michele's family lived. While picturesque for three seasons of the year, Platania, in winter, cloaked itself in an aura of mourning, due to the scarcity of food and forage. Like most in his area, Michele's house turned into a meat locker, with the only chilled game being himself.

On a frosty Tuesday in February, Michele had gone on his usual expedition to gather *frasche,* forest branches, sticks, and kindling for a fire. He would also look for small game birds or dig up some roots that he might sell or help contribute to the simple meal his sister Marianna would cook. His feet, bare most of the year, were wrapped in old rags, which did little to stave off the numbness.

He had set out at first light since the winter days were short. This morning, he had awakened with a stiff neck. His arms and neck hurt. He had not undressed because it was so cold, but his body felt itchy, and he noticed a rash on his abdomen. He felt generally unwell and sluggish. Yet he pushed on.

He was working his way to Marianna's house, arriving there close to noon so that he could help her. Marianna had married again, well before his mother had, within two years of losing her first husband. Michele had been Marianna's comfort when she was first widowed, and he had her undivided attention. She had smothered Michele with hugs and kisses, but her unbridled display of affection lessened when she married Francesco Fruscino. A sturdy peasant, he was a good man, simple, amiable, and hardworking. Two years older than Marianna, he had a handsome face, but best of all, he had a good heart and adored his wife.

While Marianna no longer lavished Michele with hugs and kisses, he knew she loved him very much. Most mornings, she and Francesco worked their small parcel of land on the hillside or walked approximately five kilometers into Nicastro to sell their meager produce—almost nonexistent this time of year. During the warm months, Michele often joined Marianna in going to the *Mercato*, thus leaving Francesco behind to work the fields. The pair would make the return trek at the height of the mid-afternoon sun after the market closed at one o'clock. Somehow, the thought of the cooler temperatures in Platania made the uphill trek home more tolerable.

Now, in the dead of winter, Marianna and Francesco greatly appreciated the bundle of branches and small food bits Michele brought. Michele helped make the fire for cooking on most winter days while Francesco tended the goat. The three would eat their shared meals together, a simple yet comforting respite from the harsh realities of their lives, a warm oasis in the cold winter.

Like many peasants in the Mercuri area, Marianna and Francesco's home consisted of one sparsely furnished room. Marianna noticed her young brother seemed ill, and as she stretched Michele out on the bed, she was shocked to find that his body appeared to be burning up with a fever. When Francesco arrived less than five minutes later, Michele was delirious and talking nonsense.

Francesco did not need to be told. He knew how many had succumbed to the awful sickness of the previous year—cholera, they had called it; several of his family members had not survived it. He didn't need to be told what to do. Turning on his heel, he ran to the doctor's house in the town center, thirty minutes away. When he returned with the doctor, Michele's body was not only burning, but his brain was too.

The small, neatly dressed man immediately went to Michele's side. He started feeling his neck, under his armpits, and abdomen, all while pressing Marianna for information. He then administered a series of treatments, each one a desperate attempt to save Michele's life.

"*Da quando e` cosi?* How long has he been like this?" His grave look and probing questions told Marianna and Francesco that time was of the essence.

"Before he became delirious, he said he had awakened ill when it was still dark out and that he had been sick to his stomach, and his head and neck hurt terribly." Too shy to look at the doctor because of her extreme consciousness of the class difference, Marianna went on, "Michele said he felt itchy with a rash. We saw him yesterday, and he looked and seemed fine. Doctor, please help him to be all right," she implored.

The doctor had no trouble understanding her mountain dialect with the words clipped at both ends.

"We do not know if we have gotten it early enough, but we may have since he appeared well yesterday," he told her. "It's good that he made his way here because the Lord only knows when someone would have found him."

Marianna felt embarrassed by the doctor's presence in her modest home. She knew he tended to the town's fine families as well as to the rural population. Still, those who lived in the countryside mostly saw the doctor when they went into town to his office. She offered him coffee but at once realized that what she had—made from boiled dandelions—was probably not what the doctor drank.

To her relief, the doctor said, "Thank you so much for your graciousness, but I had just had my coffee when Francesco arrived."

In short order, he announced in what Marianna thought was the most learned voice she had ever heard besides Monsignor at San Michele Arcangelo on Sundays, "Meningitis meningococcal." The doctor spoke in the mountain dialect, refined by his years away at medical school in Catanzaro and now used only to put the rural people at ease. "*C'e pocco che possiamo fare*," he said with a grave look, shaking his head. "There is little we can do."

He reached into a leather medical bag with his neat, uncalloused hands. Emerging with an eight-inch hypodermic needle in his right hand, he plunged the needle into a clear vial filled with fluid. Knowing what was coming, Marianna turned her head to avoid watching as the doctor jabbed the needle into Michele's thigh, and then he pressed slowly on the plunger until all the contents vanished. Michele flinched and moaned.

The doctor told Marianna the shot would help him only if they had gotten it in time. He explained the meningitis disease came from Africa but could occur anywhere, and, like the cholera of the year before, it was now sweeping through the area in epidemic proportions. He said the next forty-eight hours would be critical.

"Stay with him, place wet compresses on his forehead, and try to get him to accept small sips of clear broth," he urged. The doctor showed her how to wet rags to cool Michele's body, but he offered little hope that Michele would survive.

Determined that he would not die, Marianna kept vigil throughout the night, continually wetting the rags and bathing Michele's body. When it grew colder, she kept the chilling breezes off him by wrapping him in a woolen blanket. In his delirium, he raved about things that did not make sense. Trembling with fear, she sent her husband to alert Rosa. While she waited, she rocked back and forth, citing a litany of requests to the Lord to save her brother.

Hearing the news, Rosa started gathering some of her precious stock of medicinal herbs. She fell to her knees and began keening a litany of pleadings to God when her husband forbade her from going to her son. Rosa knew he would strike or leave her if she disobeyed him. She had often been on the receiving end of his quick hands, which had caused her son to leave their home. Every day, she regretted the marriage. Filled with self-loathing, she squirreled the herbs into Francesco's pockets and told him that she would pray to God to spare her son.

She cried, "Dear God, not him, too, like his father and brothers." Her heart bled for her youngest son, who she felt had never known a happy moment. She cried for herself, her dead husband, her dead children, and the one who was now at death's door. How could all this tragedy be heaped upon her? What had she done to deserve this pain? Her rosary in her hands, she prayed it aloud.

More than forty-five hours after the fever's onset, God answered Rosa's and Marianna's prayers. The next morning, Marianna saw a slight stir. When she checked, she found Michele's body cooler to the touch, though his lips were crusted and dried. She placed a moist rag to his mouth and shouted for her husband to come and sit with him while she went for fresh water at the public fountain, at least a ten-minute walk each way. After wrapping a handkerchief into a cruller shape and placing it on the crown of her head, she set a jug upon it and went to fetch the water.

She yelled to her adopted mother as she passed her dwelling. Since Domenico had already left the house, Rosa scurried to Marianna's place to get a peek at her son. Once there, she moved slowly toward him, touched his forehead, then fled quickly lest her husband return and suspect she had been to see him. Michele's eyes opened at her touch, and he thought it a dream when she said, "I prayed to God, and he answered me that you would get well."

Back at her house, Marianna made a fire to prepare a hot broth for Michele. She added some grasses and herbs to the water, and she got him to take microscopic sips within an hour. She spent each day coaxing a little broth into him and praying for full recovery. Slowly regaining some strength, Michele realized that not only was he wobbly on his feet, but his eyesight had somehow been impaired. Elated to be alive, he did not complain, yet he struggled to see things clearly at any distance more than a few feet away.

Later that week, the doctor looked in on him. When Michele mentioned his vision, the doctor told him it was often a result of the fever—that, and a weakened heart. But he felt sure that Michele would be all right because he had been a strong and healthy boy before the attack of the debilitating disease.

As the weeks passed and life returned to normal, Michele moved back to his own house as temperatures grew warmer and the days grew longer. A month later, he found himself at Marianna's door. Looking in, he felt his heart swell with love for this simple woman, his adopted sister. Others thought she was slow or behind in her mental development, but she had a huge heart. She was full of love for everyone, especially for him, often referring to him as *tesoro mio*, my treasure. That morning, he realized that without her loving attention, he would have died. He would be forever grateful for that and for her many kindnesses.

10

THE DREAM GROWS CLEARER

Calabria, spring 1907

As the mountain began its annual ritual of cloaking itself in flowers of every hue and umpteen shades of green, Michele realized that, although his bout with meningitis had impaired his eyesight, he had grown even more sharply focused on his dream.

Early in 1907, Nicastro was abuzz with the usual men who wore their best jackets, talked politics, and expressed their views on leaders, their decisions, and their impact on everyone. Every market day since he was very little, Michele had listened to even the tiniest morsel of news concerning not only the local items but also those beyond Italy. He especially paid attention to anything with a connection to the United States of America, mainly referred to as 'merica by the locals. Recently, he heard it discussed that America continued to grow bigger. The current president, Theodore Roosevelt, a robust and courageous man, was bent on expanding the nation.

One morning, Michele overheard a man he often saw in the square holding forth. This man, always well-dressed, spoke educated Italian. Each day, he sat on the same bench in *Piazza D'Arme* reading the daily newspaper. He invariably was joined by a group of similar-looking men within thirty minutes after he arrived. The other men referred to him as Professor Julio.

"I read in the paper that America has just gotten larger. Why, they are going to add another state called Oklahoma, before the end of the year," the man declared.

Michele inched closer to hear the conversation better without appearing to be eavesdropping.

"They do great things in America," effused one of Professor Julio's cohorts. "A few years ago, two brothers flew like birds in something they built called an *aeroplano*."

Through these bits and pieces, Michele learned that America was seeking strong workers because it wanted roads and trains to drive across the vast continent. In the opinions of these local men of politics in Nicastro, it would not be long before the United States annexed the entire continent. Then they would need more Calabrese to build roads, lay train tracks, and dig ditches. They gave a hearty laugh at this discussion because they said no one could dig ditches better than the *montagnaro Calabrese*—the Calabrian hillbilly.

They spoke of how rich everyone was in America. They all had shoes and several changes of clothes. Suits and outfits you would never see here, with extra clothes—some for Sunday and others for every day. "They throw away more food than anyone here has to eat for a week!" This notion caught Michele's attention. His belly ever unsated, he struggled to understand that kind of wealth.

Michele absorbed these crumbs of information. Later, he would find someone to chat with at the *Mercato* and ask questions he did not dare ask the *politica*. The rules about getting into the country interested him most. He gathered every morsel from knowledgeable people, understanding that some travelers faced the possibility of being turned away upon arrival after paying for their passage and enduring a long journey. This knowledge would help him prepare effectively for his own journey. This particular morning, he wrapped up the sale of his small basket of produce he had brought down from the mountain, and he slipped away before the stores and offices closed at one o'clock for the afternoon.

It was ten minutes to one when he walked into the travel agency, three blocks off the market square. Hearing the door, the man at the desk stood to greet him without looking up. Once at the counter, he took one look at the boy and thought to himself, "Steerage." As he glanced at the clock, he knew it would be but a few minutes before closing time, for nothing interfered with the four-hour midday meal and rest break of the office worker, a cultural norm deeply ingrained in Italian society. However, business was business.

"*Che cosa vuoi?* What do you want?" the agent asked curtly.

Michele answered modestly, *"Buon giorno. Per favore mi dice quanto costa un biglietto di seconda classa per America?* Good day. Would you please tell me what the ticket to travel second class to America costs?"

The agent was taken aback. He had never had a peasant, especially one from the mountains, come to inquire about a fare above steerage class. Michele, through his relentless inquiries, had learned that traveling at least second class reduced the risk of being turned back by the customs agents in America. Despite his fears about his eyesight and health, he was determined to avoid steerage, even if it was cheaper but riskier.

The man told him the ticket price and assumed that would be the end of the conversation. Instead, Michele thanked him at once and then asked a barrage of additional questions.

"How much ahead of the ship's sailing do I need to buy the ticket? Where does it depart from? How do I get to Naples? Is there a time of year when the ticket costs less? What documents do I need?" Lastly, Michele broached the immigration questions with the agent.

The agency worker, initially stunned by Michele's request, made a mental decision that this boy had something different in him. He chose to help him. The agent's abrupt manner dissipated, and he answered Michele's questions patiently, a glimmer of kindness in his eyes.

"Ocean liner fare is generally less expensive from November through May, then it goes up dramatically," he said. "You will need to take a train to Vibo Valente; there, you can board a small vessel to Naples. There, you go through a presentation of your documents and then board your ship to America."

The agent also explained, "To be admitted, you must have some money with you. Not too much, but you need to carry at least the equivalent of twenty-five American dollars. You will have to declare that money upon your arrival. Those who are without money or too poor are often turned back. You will need the address of a relative or friend, someone you claim you will be visiting; it's essential. If you don't have it, you can't go in."

Michele was eager to learn everything the agent had to say, hanging on every word as if his life depended on it.

The agent continued, "With the steerage fare, after you arrive in New York harbor, you will be transferred to another smaller ship and transported to a processing center called Ellis Island. Everyone going through Ellis Island undergoes a health examination. If you are found infirm, ill, or they think you are crazy, they will send you back."

"Does everyone have to undergo a health examination?" Michele asked.

"No. It is mandatory for those traveling in steerage class. Higher classes of fare only go to Ellis Island if, when they ask some general questions, you are a suspected criminal, act crazy, seem sick, or don't have someone in America who is expecting you."

Michele took the brochure and for a few moments stared at it intently as if it would tell him something he did not know. Expressing his gratitude, he said to the agent, "I will be back."

He left the office in May of 1907 more adamant than ever that he would make this happen before long.

Throughout the next couple of years, he looked for every possible way to earn a little more money. While other young men his age had already started finding their way to the cantinas to buy wine, he never did. He had no use for waste or creature comforts. All that could wait until he went to America. Deep in his gut, he knew as surely as there was a God that it was his destiny.

Then, in May of 1909, his mother suffered another terrible blow. Though not unexpected, his brother Carlo died in his sleep, his heart finally giving way.

At the wake, his mother said to Michele, "Carlo is finally at peace with the Lord."

Walking home afterward, he pondered that in Heaven, Carlo would be united with their father and other siblings.

When Michele arrived in America, he would find his father's grave and pay his father honor by placing flowers at his gravesite. He felt compelled to make a solid connection with the man he imagined his father to have been. Every one of his relatives who had known his father had said Michele looked, sounded, and acted like him. He often felt no connection to his father, yet at the same time, he felt that he was his father incarnate. It was a strange feeling.

Somehow, Michele knew with certainty that he would find what he was seeking in America. He lived for nothing else.

As God planned it and time would teach him, Michele was both right and wrong.

11

THE QUEST BEGINS

Platania, October 1909

When the rooster crowed, Michele awoke from jumbled dreams and poured water from the terra cotta jug into a small basin. The icy water served his washing needs and cleared his grogginess. He pulled on his pants and shirt and grabbed a small bundle containing one change of pants, shirt, and underwear. Before starting down the mountain, he had one essential thing to do.

As he walked, he could hardly believe the time had come. He had paid for the passage. He had the documents he needed. He was mentally ready to leave everything and everyone he knew behind him. Yet he knew he would miss Marianna very much, as well as his Folino cousins, the children of Uncle Luigi. He would say goodbye to that family once he descended the mountain before heading to the train station in Nicastro.

Though still dark, Marianna had been waiting for him.

"*A Michuzzu.* There you are," she greeted him in her distinctive mountain dialect.

Tall and scrawny, almost his height, she did not have an ounce of fat on her. A virtual mountain goat, he had thought hundreds of times as he'd watched her trek easily up and down the mountain carrying produce and other goods bought or sold at the *Mercato* in Nicastro. In his mind's eye, he always pictured her with the *vozzo*, an earthen jug containing water, on her head. He stared at the hardness of her calloused hands that had so tenderly cared for him.

She grabbed his shoulders and made him look right into her face as she continued in a tone that sounded like she was chastising him. Still, instead, it was her way of expressing deep affection. *"Stai attento, non farti amici con quelli che sono nella vita malvagia. Quando diventerai ricco, torna a trovarmi,"* she had ordered. Be careful; don't make friends with those who live an evil life. When you get rich, come back to visit me.

A huge smile replaced her frown as she hugged him, and then her eyes lit up, welling with liquid love that poured from them in giant drops.

He smiled. He had been Marianna's baby for his entire life, more so than his own natural mother's. He thought of how destiny had brought him and Marianna together; she needed a mother and father, and he needed the same.

Marianna's husband also hovered around Michele. In his limited Petronese dialect, Francesco said he would miss him, mainly when they worked together. He begged that Michele never forget them, especially his sister.

Michele was elated that his sister had found love to replace the husband she had lost. He knew that together, Marianna and Francesco would someday have children and have a wonderful family. Though she loved Francesco, she still occasionally spoke of her first love to Michele. She would often say, "I pray God has embraced him in his bosom."

Michele broke from his thoughts and said, *"È tempo che mi ne vado.* It's time for me to go."

They hugged again without words. As they separated, Michele watched as Marianna bent down, untied her shoes, and took them off. The work boots were a present from Francesco when they got married. Almost no one in the rural area had shoes. It was clear to Michele that the two had discussed what happened next.

She said, *"Michuzzu, non voglio che arrivi ala America squazzo come tutti l'altri montagnari. Va culle scarpe mia e ti fai un riccune subbito."* She seemed to think that if he didn't arrive barefoot, as so many other mountain people did, he would get rich quickly in America.

Stunned, Michele stared at the boots. He had been barefoot all his life.

In winter, like many of the Petronese peasants, he had wrapped his feet with whatever he could find—bark, large fig leaves, and rags bound with raffia. For the remainder of the year, they developed hardtack soles from the stones and brambles as they went barefoot.

Gathering his emotions, Michele insisted he couldn't possibly accept this gift.

"This is too much. You've already done so much for me. You packed some bread, *supressate*, and cheeses that I know you were saving for the Christmas dinner in December," he protested, pointing to the bundle wrapped in a *tovagliolo*—a cloth dish towel tied securely in a knot. He knew the food would sustain him through his arduous journey until he reached Naples, where he would board his ship to America. The agent had told him that his passage included meals for the transatlantic crossing.

Marianna ignored his protests and insisted that he put on the shoes. Reluctantly, he consented. He realized he had not given much thought to luxuries like shoes, but he would need them because he wasn't traveling in steerage class. Without shoes, he would stand out in second class.

Suddenly, an overwhelming sense of gratitude seized him. His adopted sister, whom all regarded as simple, had been more thoughtful and a much better judge of what was needed than he had.

With threatening tears, he laced up the leather boots, finding them even a bit too big. As he stood, Marianna said, "You will grow into them." She and Francesco beamed at him. Over his protests, they shooed him along.

He tried to say a proper goodbye, but his voice failed him. He choked up and hoped that Marianna could see the love and gratitude in his eyes. He hugged Francesco.

Then he took the shoes off and said, "I don't want them to get dirty before the trip." He would only wear them once it was time to board the ship. He also wanted to feel every rock and sharp bramble down the mountain for one last time.

With his shoes tied together and slung over his shoulder, the tears that had stayed misty until he left Marianna turned into a waterfall as he descended to the valley. Sooner than he expected, he caught a glimpse of Nicastro's lights.

12

A STRANGER IN UNKNOWN TERRITORY

The Port of New York, November 1909

"*Sie solo raggazzo?* Are you alone?" asked a smartly dressed middle-aged man. When Michele answered yes, the man quickly responded in a low voice, saying, "Stick with me; I'll take you under my wing."

Michele recognized the dialect as Sicilian. Through his foggy brain, he remembered his cousins' admonitions about strangers; lessons they learned from their father's multiple forays to America. Instead of following the Sicilian, Michele turned and moved into the crowd to lose the man.

His legs seemed made of rubber. The dizziness and nausea he had experienced for many days on board the ship had left him totally depleted. He had not been able to eat for most of the trip; when he did, he soon lost most of it. He didn't know if it was just seasickness or something else. He felt extremely weak and was fearful that if he looked sick, he would not be admitted, despite his second-class passage.

People around him were speaking rapidly. Most of it he did not understand. Now and again, he would pick up a word or two and recognize it as Calabrese. He was shoved into a line; he saw that those around him were much better dressed, carrying real leather valises, unlike his cloth bag.

As confusing as the activities swirling around him were, his research soon paid off. Disembarkation was organized by class, then by cabin number. He listened for his number, and then he and the men who had shared his cabin filed along. It was so close, yet America seemed an eternity away.

He could see two official-looking men in uniform asking questions and reviewing papers as each passenger came before them. Fear filled him as he waited his turn. He tried, however, to appear confident and assured. His stomach was in knots, and despite the cold air, he felt sweat gathering on his back. This morning, he had put on the only clean shirt he had, saved for the disembarkation. His inquiries had led him to believe that even though he was not traveling in steerage and automatically subject to Ellis Island, he still needed to look strong, healthy, and sane.

The agent in Nicastro had warned, "They will move you to the Ellis Island line in a heartbeat if you look lame, disoriented, have oozy eyes, or show any impairment whatsoever."

He watched intently and noticed that a family with a babe in arms was sent to the other line. The little girl appeared to have red, weepy eyes. He held his breath and prayed as his turn came up. Indeed, God would not allow him to be turned back after all he had been through. When asked, he answered the questions as forcefully as possible to the agent, who spoke Italian and English. The Italian was difficult to understand, and it differed drastically from Calabrese.

His voice faltered slightly at the start; he stated his name. Yes, he answered forcefully that he had someone waiting for him in South Norwalk, Connecticut, a cousin. Yes. He had money in his pocket. The official showed no reaction to his answers,

Michele concluded that he must have answered satisfactorily and looked okay because the agent pointed him toward the gangway to disembark. He finally breathed a sigh of relief. He felt tears welling up. He did not undergo the "examination." It had cost him dearly. Almost all his savings, along with the proceeds from selling his father's land and house, were gone, and after the expensive ticket, he was left with only a few dollars to start a new life in America.

In what seemed an instant, he found himself dumped into the great New York City.

The strength he had mustered to get himself through the disembarkation process left him, and a choking sense of doom replaced it, fueled by the days of continual seasickness and resulting dehydration. Perhaps he had dreamed the whole thing, and he was now dead and in hell.

What struck him about America was the noise and confusion. His brief time in Naples, a stop after leaving Vibo Valente, had also seemed noisy and confusing. Still, this place teemed with even stranger people and vehicles pulled by many horses. The stench of horse droppings everywhere, along with other unknown smells, brought the nausea back. Surely, this was not America. People hurried on their way to somewhere. Others looked at him strangely. Strange-sounding languages surrounded him. Everything was a whirlwind. He felt himself falling.

At the last moment, he saw a stone wall. He sank against it with a thud. As he slumped over, he said to himself, "I am here, America. Now what?"

The *padroni* were well known at New York's port. The *padrone*, or boss, was supposed to function as an employment agent, travel agent, and sponsor. These men were free to swindle the ignorant immigrants, and they often did. Originally, the *padrone* would go to Italy to recruit unemployed peasants, paying for their passage and providing jobs in the U.S.—often overcharging for these services and failing to provide suitable living quarters. Most took a fee from the employers while charging the immigrants for finding them jobs. They mostly overcharged for transportation to job sites and levied exorbitant interest rates on loans.

Michele had been warned. He had explicitly avoided signing on with a *padrone* before leaving Italy. However, some had approached him in Calabria and then again at the port of Naples. Even if one didn't sign on before arrival, once in America, the peasant immigrant was easy prey. Michele knew that to get a job, you needed an intermediary. Still, he knew he needed to be very careful. These men were a necessary evil, especially since he and his fellow immigrants did not know the language. Despite horror stories about the men, Michele had heard that some *padroni* were honest and genuinely trying to help their own compatriots. He learned that these men were satisfied with the employer's fee payment, and perhaps you only needed to offer a small token of gratitude once you settled into a job. Despite its shortcomings, this *padrone* system brought short-term relief to the bewildered immigrants.

Now, Michele could barely remember his name or where he was from. The bewildering cacophony swirled around him. Coupled with weakened equilibrium from the voyage, dehydration, and disorientation, he found himself speechless when several men approached him and asked him questions.

He thought that one of them spoke what sounded like Neapolitan, another sounded Sicilian, and one spoke Abruzzese. How could he discern whom he should trust? So, when they asked him questions, he did not respond.

Instead, he watched as many people left the Lower Manhattan Battery toward what they had told him was a thirty-block walk uptown to Mulberry Street. What he had heard discussed on the ship that first night was that a large group would be walking with their belongings to a place known as *Piccolo Italia* or Little Italy. The distance would have been nothing for him usually. He had walked up the mountain longer distances than they described. But now, he felt so unsteady that it seemed as far as walking back to Calabria. He recalled all the overheard conversations and admonitions. He decided he wanted no part of New York's *Piccolo Italia*.

He didn't know if it was the right decision, but he felt that to succeed, he needed to be in America, not in some smaller version of what he had left behind. Unbeknownst to Michele, the slums of London that Charles Dickens wrote about in novels like *Oliver Twist* held about 175,000 people per square mile—yet the Lower East Side of New York City at the beginning of the twentieth century had almost 300,000 people per square mile. One tenement might house 1,200 or more immigrants, ten to a room if they were all male workers or all of one family. Without knowing these statistics, the reputation of the squalid living conditions in "little Italy" had crossed the ocean and reached Michele loud and clear; even his hard life in Platania seemed better than that.

Like most Southern Italians, Michele was self-sufficient. Most Italians chose not to seek help from institutions. In 1909, there were more than 2,000 mutual aid societies in New York City. Still, typically, most Italian immigrants shied away from them. Michele had grown up understanding that you could not trust the government or its so-called aid. Like his *paisani* friends and relatives, he distrusted most organizations. Most importantly, like most Calabrese, he preferred work over charity, no matter how menial the job.

As he sat slumped against the stone wall, he felt a blackness enveloping him, and he thought it would be easy to let himself slip away to another world. *If you want me, God, I'm ready,* he thought. He leaned against the wall and closed his eyes.

He was nearly gone when a man who clearly looked the part of the *padrone* he had been told about shook him and offered him a cup of water. As he sipped, the man came into focus. He spoke Italian that Michele only partly understood. He wanted to pull out his cousin's address to ask for directions on how to get there, but he needed strength. Michele understood that the man said he had work for him, a place to sleep, and something to eat.

Despite all his concerns, he slowly accepted the man's outstretched hand to help him stand up, saying in Calabrese, "I need to go to Bridgeport."

The *padrone* said he would put him and the three other young men with him on a train. Michele had understood that he needed to get on a train to find his cousin. The man asked about the money he had on him. Having strapped the cash and the paper with the address to his body in a sash, he was reluctant to expose it, so he said nothing. The man took it that he was penniless, and Michele thought he understood the man saying that he could pay when he got to his destination.

The walk with the man and the others seemed interminable; in reality, it was only about ten minutes. Sifting through the noise and bustling streets, they found themselves at a junction of tracks and a long line of box-type cars with open sides. The *padrone* jumped in one, then extended his hand to pull up one of the other men; that young man pulled, and another, who had not yet boarded, pushed Michele into the car. Michele flopped to the floor and didn't move for hours. He was aware that, at some point, many more men joined them in the boxcar.

As the world went in and out of focus, Michele noticed another man associated with the *padrone* doled out some water from a tin and something to eat, something he had never seen before. It looked like a sausage wrapped in soft, spongy bread. Michele nibbled at the corners and then clutched it tightly. He had no idea how much time had passed; suddenly, he realized the train car was moving and felt a wave of the all-too-familiar seasickness flood over him. Still, he clutched the uneaten portion of the sausage, his instincts from Platania, where food was scarce, kicking in. Nausea passed, and he fell asleep.

Hours later, they arrived at a station where someone shouted, "Philadelphia." Could he be back in *Filodelfia,* the Calabrian mountain town by that name? Then he broke from his reverie and turned to the source of a voice yelling that they needed to get off. He and the forty or so other men who had occupied the car, without seats or benches of any kind, poured out in the early evening twilight and walked off the tracks into the street.

On the sidewalk, the *padrone* stood looking official with a stack of papers clipped to a board and a pencil with barely a point. He asked each for their names, when and where they were born, the birthplaces of their parents, and whether they could read or write. After each responded, he was asked to sign his name on a sheet of paper.

When it was Michele's turn to sign the completed paper, he hesitated. The man gave him a hard look and, in a cold dialect that Michele barely understood, said, "If you don't sign, you cannot work; if you don't work, you don't eat." Grasping the unstated meaning, Michele put his X where he was told, knowing full well that the paper had more to it than what he had provided in answer to the questions. Michele would eventually learn that the document said that he was three years older than he had told the man. It promised that he would reimburse the *padrone* for the transportation, food, accommodations, and other assistance the man provided in his first earnings.

As all the men finished signing, a large horse-drawn wagon pulled up, and Michele and several other men were told to pile in. Michele asked the *padrone's* assistant, who had handed out the water and sausage, if they were going to Bridgeport. The reply, "*Certo, Andiamo a Norristown, e Vicino Bridgeport*—certainly, it's close to it," lulled Michele into thinking it wouldn't be long before he saw familiar faces.

One of the men in the wagon said to another, *"Andiamo alle minieri*—let's go to the mines!*"* Michele knew what that meant. He just needed to learn how he got to this point or why he would work in the mines. He had heard so many terrible things about the work in the coal mines—the accidents, explosions, and the appalling air you had to breathe. But somehow, it seemed he was headed there now.

After a bumpy hour, he and the others filed into what looked like a campsite. Tents and makeshift shacks with dirty-faced children outside and the smell of cooking wafting in the air. A man dressed in a coverall came to meet them, saying, "*Benvenuti, povere diavole.* Welcome, you poor devils."

Michele was assigned to one of the shanties with eight other men. He flopped onto the cot they pointed to. When he woke, despite the cold, he was soaked in sweat and full of terror. He looked around and, in the dark, he realized it had been just a horrible dream. However, as he took stock of his surroundings, he realized he had awoken into a dream just as terrible. Where was he?

"Where is this?" he asked one of the others.

A young man, obviously from Naples, responded, *"L'inferno!"*

Michele lay awake for a long time. As others arose, he asked where he could relieve himself. A man pointed to an outbuilding. Unlike Platania, everything here was made of wood. As he came out, the same man pointed to a shanty and said, "*Mangia.*" He knew that there would be food there.

Two women were ladling out a hot chocolate coffee-type drink. They chatted back and forth in a Sicilian dialect. He took the hot drink and moved along to another woman who ladled out something and said, "*Polenta 'mericana*—cooked cornmeal."

Looking straight at her, he responded, "*Grazie,*" noticing her blue eyes. *They are just like my mother's,* he thought.

He looked around at the rough-hewn tables and benches and decided to stand near the egress. Worried that he would not keep the food down, he ate cautiously, ready to run outside if he felt sick again. A quarter of a teaspoonful at a time, he ate the porridge, which, compared with *polenta* at home, was tasteless, and he drank the beverage, replenishing himself immensely. When he finished, he felt a little better. Then, someone yelled his name and motioned for him to follow.

In another one-room structure, a man not much older than Michele, sporting a barely-there mustache and wearing a white, buttoned shirt that looked like he had slept in it, appeared to be in charge. He called a few men forward, surname first. He spoke to each from behind a table where he sat with papers stacked in three piles. When Michele's name was called, he stepped forward and stood uneasily as the man stared at him, clucking his tongue as if he had done something wrong.

After a long pause, Michele asked, "Is there something wrong?"

Finally, the man spoke in a tone that exuded empathy. "You are too young to work in the mines, though you look old enough; they are cracking down now. Unions are making all kinds of trouble, so we will send you to work for the steel mill instead. We must find you a place to live, so you'll probably be here for a day or two. Don't worry, we're gonna look out for you, kid."

Again, Michele inquired about Bridgeport, but he had his address in hand this time. The man looked at him as if he were crazy. "You do know you are in the wrong state, right?" Michele's heart sank. "This address is in Bridgeport, Connecticut. We are in the state of Pennsylvania, and we have a town called Bridgeport nearby, but you won't find your people there. The Bridgeport you want is closer to where you disembarked in New York."

Then the man lowered his voice as if he were taking Michele into his confidence. In his Neapolitan dialect, he said, "You would be better off not to mention or show this address to the *padrone*. If you do, you might get hurt. You need to work where he sends you for a while, pay off your debt to him, and then down the road, you can go and find your family if that's what you want."

Michele didn't say another word. He knew now that he would have to repay what the *padrone* had invested in him even though the place where he worked would most likely pay the man a finder's fee.

Michele swallowed hard. "How far is this steel mill I will work at? When will I go, and who will take me?"

"Well, the *padrone* knows a lot of people, so he feels certain he can get you there in a few days. Here, we process people. Find out what they can do, and we will send workers where needed."

13

OFF TO THE MINES

South Pittston, Pennsylvania, early 1910

Michele had spent almost a year at the Lukens Steel Company in Coatesville before moving on to the coal mine area in South Pittston, Pennsylvania. His first job was cleaning latrines at the steel mill; he also swept and moved debris from the various work areas. It was dangerous to crawl under equipment and disgusting to clean the toilets. Still, Michele was too young to work elsewhere, so he was grateful.

When he turned fourteen, Michele moved on as soon as the hiring agent could arrange other work because, at the steel mill, he was paid next to nothing once he was done paying his expenses. The agent had said the mines were where you would make your money.

Michele's eagerness to go to the mines turned sour quickly. At the camp, each morning before dawn, he left to walk down the dark streets leading to the mines. Outside, he would meet other young boys headed to the collier, a machine that sorted the coal. He remembered eating some hard bread with his coffee and taking the tin pail with his lunch prepared by the woman who ran the shanty where he lived with a dozen others. Wearing a cap and coat over his threadbare clothes, he approached, with fear, the tall, gloomy structure where the coal was broken and sorted.

From the first moment he arrived, he hated the job. Inside the breaker, he found a large, noisy room with high walls and a flight of narrow steps that climbed past the blackened wooden beams and grimy windows. Long iron chutes ran from the top to the floor. He and many others sat on pine boards placed astride the chutes.

Michele had learned that some things that came out of the mine were not coal. It was a mixture of coal, rock, slate, and junk, all called "clum." Like the other "breaker boys," his job was to pick out the clum as the coal flowed down through the chutes.

As each full coal car emerged from the mine, a long steel cable pulled it to the top of the breaker. There, a man threw a lever, the crate on wheels tipped, and the coal rushed out into a shaking machine, which pushed the coal toward the chutes.

As the coal streamed down the chutes, it spewed clouds of coal dust, steam, and smoke, which settled over him and the other breaker boys like a blanket, and their faces and clothing turned black. They wore handkerchiefs across their mouths to keep from inhaling it. The overseer taught Michele to use his feet to stop the flow of coal. He removed the clum from the chutes and lifted his feet so the coal could continue to the next boy. All around him was the monstrous, deafening machinery that crushed and separated tons of coal into various sizes.

When the work was at its peak, he would toil until six or six-thirty in the evening. His back ached from sitting in a hunched position all day. The bosses' rule of not wearing gloves, under the pretext of being unable to distinguish between coal and clum, took a toll on his hands. The first week, his fingers swelled from the sulfur on the coal, and the sharp edges of the coal shredded his hands.

The town outside Pittston, where Michele and the other workers lived, was even smaller than Platania, but a nearby river was crucial to the mine's operation. At work throughout the day, he was always on the alert because many of the young men were often hurt; some were maimed or killed. It took a good half-hour each night after work to wash the soot from his face and hands. Still, even after a thorough scrubbing, it clung in the creases of his neck, ears, and nostrils.

When one of the *capos*—leaders—complimented him, saying, "You do the work of three men; keep it up, and you will soon be old enough to go deep into the mine. That's where you earn the real money," the words had scared Michele, even more than when he had encountered the threatening *mafiosi* near the mine.

That had been in his first week at the breaker, earning seventy cents daily. As he was leaving the area where he had collected his money, a group of thuggish-looking chaps approached him and said, "You need to give us half your money so we can protect you; there are lots of bad people here who will hurt you."

The pay envelope had elated Michele. The boss explained the deductions, and after transportation reimbursement, tools, food, and lodging, it was a paltry amount for his work, but there would be a little left over after expenses. It had been brutal work, but he now had some money for his labor, and there wasn't anyone going to take it away from him.

Michele had stood as tall as he could, looking into the eyes of what appeared to be the group's leader, and said with fierce determination, "Get away from me! I will give you nothing. I know your kind, and you won't get anything from me."

He was surprised by the shocked look on their faces. He figured most people didn't stand up for themselves and, like sheep, forked over the protection money. He had been through too much to give up his wages without a fight. To his puzzlement, they walked off and never bothered him again, a moment of triumph in his struggle.

Before the breakers, his first job had been as a janitor at the steel mill, and after his fourteenth birthday, the bosses brought him over to the mines, though he had learned that you had to be sixteen to work in the mines. Michele felt sure there had to be more and better opportunities for him somewhere in this vast land. Close to a year after his arrival, he concluded that he wasn't getting the best of America yet—although he didn't know where that best was. That night, after being complimented by the *capo* at the mines, Michele said aloud to himself, "I didn't leave everyone I knew and sunny Platania for this."

14

OPPORTUNITY KNOCKS IN OHIO

Cleveland, Ohio, 1911

Now that he was in Ohio, his days were long, but Michele didn't mind. With a steady diet that included chicken or meat at least once a week, he could keep up with older and bigger men. Michele noticed he was growing—his work pants, which had been too large at first, now fit. The work here was backbreaking, but this road-building project in Cleveland had been a godsend.

He reflected on how he had come to Ohio, recalling that fateful evening in the pub in Pittston, Pennsylvania. While he had no interest in alcohol, he went to the pub most evenings to catch up on the news and learn about the local happenings. It also offered camaraderie away from the watchful eyes of the *capos* or bosses.

He was gaining a clear picture that the breakers worked on a sporadic schedule and only real coal miners made any money. He was too young to work deep in the mines, and even if he wasn't, he recognized that coal mines were dead ends. In his heart, he was sure he did not want to live and die underground.

Then, an agent for the road-building project in Cleveland, Ohio, had come to recruit men at an area near the pub in Pittston. Michele knew these arrangements had to be kept confidential. You couldn't let the bosses know until you were about to leave. There were too many stories, whether true or not, of those who tried to leave meeting bad accidents.

As he spoke with the agent, his eagerness to go caused the agent some worry. The agent knew that the mine bosses wanted to avoid others poaching their workforce. The agent wondered if this strong-looking young man might be a plant for the people at the mines. But after questioning him for about ten minutes, the agent realized that the young man had no family or obligations, did not appear to be involved with the Mafiosi, and seemed like a good worker. So, the agent felt confident he was not in danger of retaliation.

Then he asked what Michele thought an odd question. "Do you plan to go back to Italy?" Michele's answer was, "No. I have no one there to see."

"Good. Then we can use you. You look strong and sturdy, and I don't want you to work for a few months and then run back to the old country like so many do. We have a lot of work. I could keep you busy for a few years."

Michele was thrilled at the chance to leave the mine's oppressive atmosphere behind. The unfamiliar yet intriguing name of the destination, "Cleveland, Ohio," sparked his curiosity and filled him with a sense of adventure.

With the agent paying the fare, Michele made the train trip from Pittston to Scranton and then on to Cleveland. He had traveled with three others destined for the same job.

By this time, Michele understood a good bit of the language. He had gone to some of the English classes offered nearby. But most of the writing instructions didn't make sense to him without knowing how to read or write in Italian. However, he had a good ear and picked up the speaking part pretty quickly. He learned to write his name and recognize letters. He found that most people responded well when he tried to speak "Americano." Often, they would laugh and coax him to say it correctly. He chuckled with them, and he'd try again. He enjoyed the challenge because he was desperate to become American.

That first winter in Cleveland had been the coldest he had ever experienced in his life. The winds coming off Lake Erie were as cutting as the sharpest knife. He had been freezing in Platania, but as he thought back to those days, he realized he had never been without shelter from early morning until evening, in subfreezing temperatures and bitter winds.

He knew the road construction work was dangerous. Marianna's first husband had died at a similar site in another state. It was that disaster that had precipitated his father's heart attack and death. Michele knew he was vulnerable to a similar fate.

After about two years in Cleveland, Michele began to feel drawn by the thin, wrinkled paper with the address of some of his family living in America. The shred of paper that had started as fragile as a butterfly's wing was now in danger of disappearing into dust. He was adamant that he would go to Connecticut at some point. He longed to see and feel some contact with family, but he also knew his relatives lived somewhere close to his father's grave in Bridgeport. So he decided to find his cousin by using the address on the flimsy piece of paper.

That night, he slept, dreaming about what to do when he got to the cemetery. In his dream, he placed a wreath of flowers on the grave and said prayers for his father's soul. He saw himself talking with him and telling him how glad he was to find him.

The Cleveland road work was steady, and he felt he was getting ahead. He needed to work here for a bit longer to afford a train ticket to Connecticut and still have some money left.

Before coming to Cleveland, his wages had almost equaled his living costs. Yet he was better off than others in the camps who owed the company money at the week's end. He had been careful, never wasting money on smoking, drinking, or women. When he had an extra few cents, he would find someone who could write in Calabrese and pay the going rate to have them craft a letter, sending his greetings to Marianna and her husband.

He recalled his gratitude and pride when he had put a whole American dollar in the first letter to her, saying, *"Questo e per le scarpe."* This is for the shoes.

By now, it had become a transatlantic joke between them because, after the first letter, she had begged him to stop sending money.

"The shoes were a gift," she insisted in a letter written for her by someone else. Nevertheless, Michele kept sending the money whenever he could. He wanted her to know he would never forget.

Michele now lived in a rooming house with several men who were much older than he. The German woman who ran the establishment at 2124 Woodland Avenue cooked meals that, though bland, filled him up well. Once a week, she washed his and his housemates' few belongings and returned them folded in a neat pile. Every Saturday night, she allowed the men a tub full of hot water for a bath in their shared bathroom.

As he reveled in the water heated on the wood-burning kitchen stove, he was pleased that he was just the second one to use the bath water this evening. It was not as cloudy as on most other Saturday nights. The warmth of the water flooded his mind with visions of Platania, where the water from the public fountain fed by the mountain springs was frigid in the winter months. Michele often questioned his own fastidiousness. He wondered where he had gotten this curse to wash and clean himself so frequently. Perhaps his father had been like that. His mother had kept the house clean but was less than fastidious with her personal care.

He could withstand all the swill and dirt while working, but he detested being dirty when he sat to eat. It didn't matter if it was a simple piece of stale bread, the dandelion coffee they made, or a holiday *Soppressata* (a Calabrian homemade cured salami). No matter the fare, he felt his hands needed to be immaculate and his face clean. He had washed his mouth out with water and combed his hair every morning since he could remember.

After his Saturday bath, he walked three miles to the train station instead of going to bed. He asked the night agent at the desk what it cost to buy a ticket for Connecticut. As he returned to the rooming house, he calculated how long it would be before he could go.

Once he climbed the stairs to the room with multiple cots, he undressed down to his underwear and slipped under the single cover. He made the sign of the cross and said his silent prayers as he had done every night for as long as he could remember. He asked God for forgiveness for any wrong he might have committed and for his continual stubbornness. He thanked God for the job and for his strength to do the work. And he thanked God for the food and for the woman who cooked and let him live where he was. He asked God to protect his mother, sisters, aunts, uncles, and cousins.

In closing, he begged God to help him find his way to his Papa's grave. Then he said to himself, "Just a few more months." As he drifted off to sleep, he was already there.

15

CONNECTICUT, HERE I COME

New York and Connecticut, 1912

Michele watched each town along the train route. He noticed the subtle changes in the scenery as the view transitioned from city to farm country and then back to the city. Some towns were as filthy as Pittston and Scranton had been with the black soot of coal dust draped on them. Others were lush green, planted with some crops. He wondered what they grew there. America was indeed a vast place, he reflected.

When he heard the conductor say, "New York, Grand Central," he knew he would need to change trains there. All at once, it was dark. He hadn't expected the train to pull in underground. Once stopped, he found himself amid a cacophony of people, sounds, and smells. He realized this was the same New York City where he had disembarked from the ship that brought him across the ocean just a few short years ago. He would never forget that momentous yet frightening day. But now, he was not sick. He felt strong and excited. He followed the crowds up some concrete stairs into what appeared to be a huge waiting room. Across the cavernous hall, he spied a row of metal-barred windows where he assumed he would find the ticket agents.

From somewhere in the station, he heard strains of the words and music of Enrico Caruso's song, *"Addio."* He heard the song for the first time about a month ago at the rooming house where he lived. The owner had something called a gramophone. He had asked plenty of questions regarding the song with the words and title that meant goodbye. It had a beautiful melody, yet it evoked some nostalgia he had promised himself he would not feel. It made him think of his mother, sisters, and cousins, as well as the life he had left behind in Italy, and he realized he missed his people.

From the first time he heard of Enrico Caruso, he was smitten. He reveled in this man's magnificent voice and the beautiful, poetic songs, which seemed to garner worldwide adoration. He had learned that Caruso had been a poor Neapolitan just a short while ago, and now he was world-renowned.

This feat amazed Michele, marking the moment when he first became aware that all things were possible in America. Look at him now. He was riding a train on his own. No unscrupulous agent bought a ticket for him at usury rates, and there was no trickery about a great job and fantastic living conditions that turned out to be the direct opposite. He was doing this himself through the sweat of his work and determination.

As he took his place at the end of a long queue in front of the ticket window, he became mesmerized by all the sights and sounds enveloping him and went off into a reverie. After what seemed an interminable wait, he reached the window and somehow made himself understood by the agent by showing him the address on his worn piece of paper. The agent said Michele had just missed the train leaving for South Norwalk. He would have to wait for the next train in an hour—at 8:26 p.m. Michele would arrive at his destination close to ten o'clock.

He paid close attention to try to understand what the man was saying. "You'll have to take the train to New Haven, but get off well before that in South Norwalk."

When Michele said, "Scusa me; whatta you say?" a woman several places back in the line repeated the man's statement to him in a Neapolitan dialect. Michele thanked her and asked the agent, "How many stoppa to get off?"

The man said to listen for five stops. His stop would be the one right after the town called Darien. The woman from the line, again assuming the role of translator, said to Michele in Italian, "*Cinque fermate. La tua e quella doppo Darien.*"

Mike memorized the word "Darien" and repeated it to himself: "*Cinque fermate."* He paid the twenty-five-cent fare and tucked the change and ticket into his jacket pocket. As he turned to go, he thanked the woman who had helped him.

He was awestruck by the station. An enormous clock in the great hall's center revealed that he had enough time to get something to eat. Carrying his cloth bag in one hand and his cap in the other, he walked toward the source of the aromas that made his stomach growl. Stalls with food from every nationality beckoned him. Feeling it was too expensive, he passed them and stepped out onto the streets of New York City. He wanted to see if anything had changed since his arrival in late 1909. But he had not been to this part of New York on his brief visit the day of his arrival in the country.

Now, he exited the terminal on 42nd Street. Looking around, he thought the people seemed more well-heeled than he remembered from that first day. There were dozens of food and merchant vendors, as well as shops with clothing displayed in their windows. Not grasping the vast difference in location from where he had disembarked at the port, he concluded that New York had prospered in the past two and a half years.

He thought, *Money in my pocket. I've got two pairs of underwear, three shirts, and pants in my bag, a wool cap, and a sturdy pair of work shoes on my feet.*

His sister's precious gift of the boots, which had started too large, he had worn to death, casting them away only two months ago. By that time, the soles had worn through, and his feet were cramped in the toes, so much so that a nail on his left foot had become embedded and then infected. The kind woman at the rooming house had taught him how to clean, bathe, and wrap it each morning and night. She had told him he needed to see a doctor. He told himself if it didn't get better, he would part with the money he was saving for his departure, but not now. As it began to heal, he stopped thinking about seeing a doctor and saved his money.

He had cut a hole in his sister's shoes to relieve the pressure on his toe, but in the second week of his toe-relief effort, the foreman had noticed and said he could not work with his toe exposed. With that, he decided to use some of the precious money he had saved to purchase new footwear. They were not the best shoes by any means, but as he parted with the two dollars they cost, he vowed that someday he would buy himself the best men's shoes available.

As he walked a little farther, he heard a peanut vendor singing an Italian ditty, and he bought a small paper sack of hot roasted peanuts. Walking to the corner of Vanderbilt Avenue, he found a hot dog stand and bought one of his American discoveries. He had learned to love the salty sausage-looking meat with a yellow, spicy cream called mustard. The hot dog had become one of his favorites.

Lost in his thoughts, he realized it had grown dark. He scurried to find the clock in the center of the great hall and saw that the small hand was on the eight and the large hand at the one. The ticket agent had said the train tracks were a flight down the stairs. He reviewed in his head what he needed to do. Get on the train going toward New Haven, Connecticut, and listen for the stop that was South Norwalk; it would come right after the station called Darien, he repeated to himself.

Asking several people where the New Haven train was, he found the correct one just moments before the conductor yelled, "Last call; all aboard." They closed the doors behind him as he sprinted aboard, the doors almost catching his bag.

He sat beside a man in a business suit, reading a newspaper. When he finished, the man asked if he wanted to look at the paper. Michele thanked him and glanced at the pages as if he could read. As he flipped through the newspaper, he was fascinated by the arrangement of the letters, columns, and pictures. He wished he could read. He wondered what it would take to learn to do so. He was doing well now, writing his name. He had practiced and practiced at the schools they had at the steel mill and at the breakers.

He returned the paper to the man, saying, "Thank you lots." Then, he sat with his bag on his knees, imagining the joy of seeing his cousin Petronella when he surprised her with his arrival. He wondered if his mother's sisters, his aunts Giovanna and Maria, and his cousins would be there. It wasn't long before he heard the conductor announce, "Stamford station." He had more room after most people disembarked, including the man beside him. He noticed the man had left the paper behind, but for some reason, Michele picked it up and tucked it under his arm.

Then, in no time at all, he heard "Darien." Two people got off the train, and it moved on. Within minutes, he heard "South Norwalk!" This was it. He stood by the doors as the train rolled to a stop. As the doors opened, he stepped onto a deserted platform. No one else got off with him that he could see. Michele searched for someone at the windows of the small station, but everything was shut tight. It was so different from New York City that this place seemed eerie.

He was unsure of what to do. He had the paper with the address, but there was no one to ask or show it to.

He thought he would find somewhere nearby to stay, but nothing appeared open. He saw lights in the distance, but where would he go without knowing? He spied a long wooden bench on the platform and sat. He recognized it would be a long time until someone opened the ticket sales window in the morning. He was glad he had eaten something.

Thoughts tumbled through his mind. Would he stay here, where there was family, or would he move on? He did not know yet where he would call home in this vast country of America. He needed to see more of it to be sure. After a long while of musing, he stretched out on the bench, tucking his bag under his head for a pillow and spreading the newspapers like a blanket over his chest and shoulders. Michele became aware that he was homeless again. For a moment, he worried about robbers. He prayed to God for protection and forgiveness and drifted into a fitful sleep.

16

A STRANGE WELCOME

South Norwalk, Connecticut, 1912

Michele awoke to a cheerful sun and trembling cold. The fall air was damp. He felt chilled to the bone. As he opened his eyes and sat up, he saw signs of life around him. Two men in coveralls pushed a big, flat, green wooden cart with oversized wheels and red spokes. They moved toward what appeared to be a baggage room and began loading trunks and crates from it onto the cart.

Michele gathered his things and found the station's public bathroom, where he freshened himself up. Feeling confident, he threw his shoulders back, stood as tall as possible, and walked up to the ticket window. Looking the man straight in the eyes, he said, "Good morning."

Without greeting, the man asked, "Ticket to Grand Central?"

Instead of answering his question, Michele handed the agent the slip of paper. "You knowa where? Maybe I can getta taxi?"

The man studied the thin, worn-out scrap and then looked up at him, wondering if he was joking. It looked as if the kid had slept outdoors. Taking pity on him, the agent pointed toward the left and said, "Burbank Street is right out back. Since you are already on the eastbound side of the station, go down those steps. Then, you walk just a short way down this street, and it's right there. If you get to Wood Street, you've gone too far. Number 22 should be the corner house."

Michele missed the meaning of some of the agent's words, but he understood the phrase "short way" and gathered from the man's pointing that it was nearby. Shocked to think he could have walked there last night had he known, he sloughed it off, saying, "Thanks," and rushed in the direction the man had pointed.

At the bottom of the station steps, Michele couldn't remember if the man said to turn right or left. He thought he had pointed to the right, but as he was walking from the station area, he spotted a man pushing a luggage handler loaded with trucks and other bags, and thought it couldn't hurt to check.

"Good morning," he said. The black face looked wary at first, then broke into a huge smile. Michele asked, "You knowa where Burbank Street is?"

Recognizing the accent, the pleasant man pointed Michele in the general direction, making sure that he knew to turn left onto the first street he came to. The man pointed and said, "That house is right on the corner."

Smiling while thanking the man for his kindness, Michele started to walk away. But the man wasn't done with him. He smiled as he warned, "Watch out for Mr. Fred; he's tough."

Michele knew the word "tough" but didn't understand what the man meant. His heart raced as he approached the house with the number 22 posted near the door. He perused the three-story wooden structure and thought it impressive. All the cousins in Italy said that Petronella's husband, Fortunato, had done well in America.

The house sat behind a chain-link fence. The gate was locked. As he was trying to figure out how to get past the vicious dog barking by the front door, a woman he recognized came out. Looking at him, she asked in a gruff tone, "What ya wanta?"

"Petronella, *non me conosci*? Don't you recognize me?" Michele asked.

When she had departed for America, he was a little boy. Then, a light went off in her head. The voice could belong to only one person.

She scurried to put a key into the padlock and throw open the gate. Then she hugged and squeezed Michele until he couldn't breathe. When he was able to pull away, he noticed she had a scar down the left side of her neck, reaching her collarbone. She was four years older than he, yet she looked much older, thin, and worn.

Michele inquired if she was all right, and she shushed him, saying, "It's nothing. Have you eaten?" He noticed the tears in the corners of her eyes.

Climbing the stairs to the third floor, she cried and laughed at the same time. She urged Michele to sit as soon as they arrived on the third floor. "I'll fix you coffee. I have some good bread that I baked yesterday and some cheese so sharp it will make your mouth pucker," Petronella said in her native dialect, peppered with some American words.

Sitting, drinking coffee, eating homemade bread, and smelling the sharpness of the cheese jolted Michele into realizing how long it had been since he had had a proper meal. While he sipped and munched, a million questions and comments flew in rapid succession from Petronella's lips.

"Where have you been all this time? My sister Angelina, from Italy, wrote more than two years ago saying you were coming. I had given up hope." He was about to tell her when she cut in, saying, "Eat now; tell me later."

The warmth of Petronella's smile and the embracing environment of her kitchen made him feel at home. The kitchen was a sanctuary, with its immaculate floor, lace curtains at the windows streaming with sunshine, and the comforting aroma of cheese and bread.

They had just finished their coffee and his quick story about what he had been up to since arriving in America when she jumped up as if bitten by something.

"I have work to do," she said. "We have turned the first two floors of the house into a rooming house. I cook and clean for a dozen men who are boarders."

Then, something seemed to dawn on her. "Michele, stay here!" she exclaimed. "There is a lot of work nearby, and I have an empty bed downstairs in my boarding house." He asked how far Bridgeport was from South Norwalk. "It's not far by train," she told him.

"Do you know our aunt, Zia Giuanna, lives near us here with her husband, Zio Michelangelo Gallo? They have a little boy, Natale, whom they call Christopher in English. He's close to four years old. And Zio Pasquale

Nicolazzo brought our Zia Maria here with the two children after he earned some money. Then they had a third child, Pasqualina. It is so sad, though; Zia Maria died last year, leaving a two-year-old without a mother."

Michele wondered when she would stop talking. But without taking a breath, she continued.

"Zio Pasquale is such a nice man. His oldest girl, Innocenza, looks after the two younger ones, Michelangelo and the baby, Pasqualina. The Nicolazzo and Gallo families both live just a few streets away. We will visit them tomorrow. Today is my washing day."

At last, Michele got to ask her how much she charged for the room and what he could expect to make in wages in the area. She did a quick mental calculation and told him the numbers.

He favored staying with her, but Michele thought he would wait to answer until he met his cousin-in-law. "I will think about it," he said.

The night arrival at the train station and sleeping outside on the bench had made the area seem bleak and desolate. But now, the place reminded him of Platania in this spectacular morning sunshine. It was not as pretty as Platania, with its majestic pine trees and incredible mountain vistas. Still, all the houses he had passed while walking from the station had little gardens in the front yards. On the downside of the growing season, they still appeared bountiful. He longed for a patch of dirt where he could once again grow his favorite vegetables.

Wanting to make himself useful, he finished eating and followed Petronella to help her care for the men and the rooms. They spent the entire day chatting and working. She shared all she had heard from the letters she'd received from her sister and twin brothers in Calabria. She updated him on the events in Platania and the *Chianta*. He was saddened to hear of some deaths and elated that new babies had come into his distant family.

"Have you heard anything about my sister Marianna?" His voice was tentative, fearing what she might tell him. But his cousin had good news.

"She and Francesco had a little girl less than three months ago. She visited my sister, Angelina, to ask whether they had heard from you. My sister said in her letter that the little girl was adorable. They named her Maria."

Though Petronella noticed he had not inquired about his mother, she said nothing. But she did keep remarking on how handsome Michele was and whether he had a sweetheart.

"No sweetheart," he told her. "No time for girls; I have just been working and saving." She gave him a look and laughed, saying she didn't believe him.

They worked away at the chores. It was well past noon, and Petronella hadn't even discussed lunch. But after they finished the last bed, they sat for a few minutes to have a tomato-and-cucumber salad. Then she made some fresh coffee. The delightful aroma made him feel like he had been at Petronella's forever.

"It will be a while until supper time, but I will need to start cooking soon," she said, adding with a smile, "When the wolves arrive, they are famished."

As they sat with their steaming coffee, Michele told her he had decided to stay. Though he cautioned, he didn't know how long.

She jumped up and kissed him many times as if he had just arrived. "Wonderful! Get your bag, and I'll show you where to put it and show you your bed. Also, I must collect the money for the room and board up front. My husband always insists on it. I know you are my family, but I can't break the rules, or my husband will be furious."

Michele dug into the inside pocket of his jacket and, with reluctance, pulled out his eleven dollars.

He said, "I paid just eight dollars a week in Ohio."

"Fortunato won't let me charge lower rates even for my cousin," she said.

As they cleaned vegetables and scrubbed potatoes, the time flew. The day was almost gone. Petronella alerted Michele that her husband would be arriving soon. Michele was reflecting on what a wonderful day it had been when Fortunato arrived.

As Petronella introduced Michele to her husband, Michele noted that Fortunato was from Mileto. This ancient Calabrian town was once the Norman capital, located a little farther south than Platania. A dark, short, brutish-looking man, his tone was less than welcoming.

He expressed not the least pleasantry, instead getting right to business.

"I'm glad you have arrived, Michele, because we have an empty bed in our rooming house."

Michele pondered his words and manner. The man had never expressed joy that his wife now had more family nearby. Petronella informed Michele that the locals called Fortunato "Fred," and they had even changed his last name from Prestia to Presty.

Fred pulled out a chair and sat at the kitchen table, and immediately, his wife started placing food and wine in front of him. He tore into the food without prayer and without inviting Michele to sit with him, let alone join him in the meal, a rudeness that would never have happened in Calabria. The man did not even look up at his wife. Michele had noticed that he hadn't greeted her when he first arrived. Instead, he started barking orders at her—"get me this and fetch me that." Yes, this was the Mr. Fred that the kind black man at the station had warned him about.

Petronella seemed cowed by him. She tended to him like a servant instead of a wife. Michele wondered again about the long scar on her neck. She had not offered him any explanation. Without a word, he went down the three flights of stairs to the first floor to introduce himself to the other boarders and to eat the evening meal with his roommates.

The following morning, before Michele left to scope out the town, Petronella had a bit of good news for him.

"Michele, tonight I will take you to visit our relatives."

17

AT LAST, AMONG FAMILY

South Norwalk, 1912-1916

That evening, they walked the short distance to the Gallo home, at number four, Laura Street. When the door opened, a dizzying array of his mother's extended family welcomed him.

"What are you doing here?" Zio Michelangelo Gallo joked. Zia Giuanna's husband was a kind and generous person, unlike his wife, who was a tough cookie with a stern look that never softened.

Also, there was Zio Pasquale Nicolazzo, whom Michele hugged and offered his condolences. His wife, Maria, who had been Michele's mother's youngest sister, had passed away six years after joining her husband in America. Zia Maria had been the gentlest of the three sisters, and his mother and Zia Giuanna, more matter-of-fact, toughened by difficult lives. Not that Maria's life had been much easier, but her husband had sent her good money while he was in America, and his family had helped her with the children when she remained alone in Platania.

The Gallo and Nicolazzo families had settled among a neighborhood of people from Ungeria, or Hungary, as they said it in America. There was a church, St. Ladislaus, for Hungarian Catholics, just a short walk from where the Nicolazzo and Gallo families lived as tenants.

"We are among the few Italians in the neighborhood," Zio Michelangelo told Michele.

"I've lived on almost all the streets right around here before Burbank Street," said Petronella.

"In fact," joked Zio Michelangelo, "it won't be long before these streets, as well as Ely Avenue, will be taken over by Italians." Petronella's laughter at the joke made her eyes crinkle up, turning into slits with the azure blue just a sliver.

Michele basked in the scene around him. He loved seeing Petronella, the uncles, aunt, and cousins. Until then, he had not realized how good it would feel to be back among family. He had intended to visit for a while and then move on, but now he was beginning to think about staying in Norwalk.

Zia Giuanna made coffee and, in her raspy barking voice, asked him to sit and share all that he had experienced since leaving Calabria.

When asked about his life so far, Michele shared a sparse list of facts, omitting all the details and giving no clues about his heartache and loneliness. He did not feel it was anything he needed to share.

Zio Pasquale said, "Michele, there's a family of Hungarians here named Ritzo! They write their names differently from Italians. They are good people who mind their own business. They work hard." He paused, then shifted his conversation to the topic of his wife's premature death.

"We waited so long to be together. Now that we were all together in America, she's gone," his voice choked up.

"I'm trying to move my family to Bridgeport; I think we can do better there," he said.

Michele's ears perked up. "Bridgeport," he said. "I want to go there. Can we go tomorrow?"

Zio Pasquale said, "It's too far to walk. It is more than forty miles. We can get there by train, but Bridgeport is a big city, and things are very spread out. I think I've found work there, and if that job comes through, I will move the whole family there. Then you can see Bridgeport."

Michele remembered the two older Nicolazzo children from Italy, his cousins Innocenza and Michelangelo, though they had left for America with their mother when he was nine. Innocenza had been eleven years old; the boy, also nicknamed Michele and now called Mickey, was six. The little girl, Pasqualina, now called Lilly, had been born in America.

Now sixteen, Innocenza announced that she would marry in the spring. Beaming, Michele said, "If I'm invited, this will be my first American wedding."

His cousin Mickey was approaching thirteen and was a small, wiry youngster. Good-looking and cocksure, the boy boasted, "I can take you to Bridgeport, cousin."

Michele spent late into the evening among his relatives, talking about jobs and where he might go to seek work. Zio Michelangelo offered to take him around to find a job in the morning. The consensus was that he should be able to find a job right away. They all saw him as strong, and the bosses would snap him up right away, they joked.

The following three days, he spent the mornings helping Petronella with chores and then going out with his uncle to find work, calling on various companies his uncle knew were seeking employees.

On the third day, Michele had become a bit discouraged. The Harris & Gan Company on Water Street said they had hired two men and did not need help now, but they said, "Check back with us next month." The Ferris Coal Company on Washington Street said they needed help starting in two weeks.

As if he had read his thoughts, his uncle said, "Don't worry, Michele, there's going to be someone needing you now. We need to call on a couple more companies. I feel certain of it. Did you see how that Ferris Coal man insisted we return in two weeks? He saw your strength, but the timing wasn't right for them."

As if on cue, the next place they went was a coal, brick, lime, and cement supplier in the same general area as the earlier stops. The man at Bishop and Lynnes looked at Michele and said, "Can you start today?"

All the companies paid about the same wages for laborer work. Michele liked this company because he could start right away, and they had a second location in the next town, Norwalk. Michele liked having options.

The work was hard, but nothing compared with what he had experienced before. He shoveled lime and coal, stacked and loaded bricks as they filled orders or made room for inventory delivered nearly every day.

The foreman and his workmates changed Michele's name to "Mike." He didn't mind. He was happy to have a steady job and be near relatives.

Mike, as he now thought of himself, also made friends with some co-workers and found the whole atmosphere much more convivial than where he had been before. At the end of the work week, he went out for a beer with a couple of the men and smoked his first cigar.

However, by his third week at Petronella's boardinghouse, he got more of the taste of the evil man his cousin had married. Fred remained unpleasant after that first evening and did not warm up. Petronella went with Mike almost every evening to visit the relatives at Laura, Podmore, and Cliff Streets, but her husband never joined them.

Mike was in his room on a Friday evening; he and the other boarders had stretched out on their cots after dinner and were talking. They heard footsteps bounding down the stairs.

Fred walked into the room and said, "Something smells bad here." Then, he said, "Mike, it's your feet! I don't want anybody here with bad-smelling feet."

Mike was horrified. His feet did not smell. In fact, he was the only one whose feet did not smell. He wanted to say, "It's your own feet you smell." Though he was offended, he didn't say a word in response.

After making his grand pronouncement, Fred turned and went back upstairs.

Mike brooded all night. By morning, he decided this was Fred's way of saying, "Get going." It was clear that Fred had been upset that he had helped Petronella with her chores. On more than one occasion, Fred commented that Mike liked to do women's work. Mike felt that Petronella did not notice that her husband was a tyrant. He recalled how he had not stood still when his stepfather struck his mother. He knew he would be unable to restrain himself if he saw Fred hit his cousin, which Fred appeared ready to do at least on two occasions.

Tomorrow, I will look for a room elsewhere, he thought. Though he enjoyed his cousin's pleasant manner and delightful personality, he did not want to spend any more time than needed in the presence of her tyrannical husband.

On Saturday, he walked to the Central Hotel at the corner of Monroe and Chestnut Streets and negotiated a room and board for twelve dollars a week; they had wanted fourteen. The place was clean and comfortable. The owner told him the Italian social club, where men played cards on Sunday afternoon, was nearby. As a bonus, the room gave Mike more privacy than the boardinghouse his cousin ran. The hotel owner, Mr. DiSesa, was a decent fellow, ran a bar and a band, and was full of good stories.

Petronella was upset when Mike told her he was leaving. He comforted her by saying, "You'll always be my cousin and have my respect. I won't forget what you did for me, taking me in. Blood is blood."

"You're going right now?" Petronella asked. Then, she kissed his hands and got teary, but in her heart, she realized it was for the better. Fred obviously did not want anyone related to her in the house to see his comings and goings. Petronella knew he slept with the prostitutes who frequented the bar that he ran.

The scar she had on her neck was from a knife wound early in their marriage, when she had complained that she had seen him go into a back room of the bar with one of them. The scene had turned ugly in a flash. The words came out of her mouth, and he seethed, "Don't you ever question my authority or anything I do. I will kill you if you dare to say a single word about what I do."

At the time, she didn't yet know his capacity for violence. When she tried to explain, he picked up a kitchen knife and slashed her neck, warning her that his words were not empty threats. The neck healed with an ugly scar, and she had learned to keep her mouth shut. Within six months, she had contracted a venereal disease from her husband's continual promiscuity. The infection wreaked havoc, and she had to undergo a hysterectomy. As a result, she would never bear children, something she wanted more than anything. What could she do? She felt trapped. A woman without a man was as good as dead. Such was the case with many women; she resigned herself to it. She prayed for her husband's black soul, and she prayed for a child that might come to her through some miracle.

Mike had arrived at her lowest point; he had been great company and brought joy to her life. But his presence was not worth upsetting Fred. He was her husband, and she needed to obey him. As sad as she was, she determined it was good that Michele was leaving. She shuddered as she thought about what might happen if her cousin intervened when Fred was in one of his dark moods. She could tell that Michele was not like many of the black folks around the neighborhood, who Fred intimidated with his threats. Petronella did not want her husband and cousin to tangle. She knew in her heart that it could be disastrous.

18

AN AMERICAN-ITALIAN WEDDING

South Norwalk, 1912

As Mike walked up the hill, he passed the Hungarian Catholic church and went to Cliff Street, where Bouton Street intersected, to visit the Gallo family—Zia Giuanna, Zio Michelangelo, and their son, Natale, now called Chris. This Sunday dinner, he would also find his Zio Pasquale and the Nicolazzo cousins, who had moved to Bouton Street. It was all within just a stone's throw. Still, the families had moved into actual apartments instead of a one-room, shared-bathroom situation. At dinner, the family's topic was the upcoming wedding.

Zio Pasquale's daughter Innocenza, whom everyone now called Jennie, was getting married. It would be Mike's first American-Italian wedding. His aunt Giuanna served as the bride's mother, so Jennie would have all the information she needed to help her prepare for marriage.

Zio Pasquale was ecstatic. He liked his son-in-law-to-be and was thrilled that his children seemed to be faring well despite lacking a mother.

However, he worried a lot about his son, Mickey, who seemed more than a bit wild. He was learning to work hard like his father, but, as Zio Pasquale confided to Mike, it appeared to him that it was all about wheeling and dealing for young Mickey. He didn't like his son's friends. He urged Mike to take the boy under his wing, even though Mike was just four years older.

For his part, Mike didn't have the heart to tell his uncle that he was right not to trust the people his son called "pals." They were not of the good life. Mike felt nothing good could come from his cousin Mickey's association with that crowd. But he thought he had to try because it was a request from Zio Pasquale. After dinner, Mike invited Mickey to play cards with him at the Italian social club. The tension between them was palpable, a silent battle of wills.

After an hour of conviviality, Mike broached the subject of Mickey's dubious friends. No sooner were the words out of his mouth than Mickey retorted with conviction Mike had not seen before in his cousin, "Mike, I know everything I need to know about my friends."

Using the pejorative term for Italians, he said, "The *guineas* think if they work hard and save their pennies, they are getting somewhere. I won't be like my father, who works every day like a dog. For what? So he can pay rent to someone else, so only four of us share a place to sleep instead of eight? That is not for me. I remember how often my mother, sisters, and I went to bed hungry in Petrania. It's not enough to fill my belly; I want to be somebody!"

Mike tried to interject, but his cousin had more to say. With heated passion, he spat out, "People are gonna respect me!" His naked ambition charged the air like a lightning bolt.

The conversation ended with young Mickey storming down the stairs and out of the clubhouse. For a moment, Mike remained seated, trying to digest his cousin's passionate outburst. Then he decided he should go after him. When he got to the outside porch, he watched Mickey take off with some of his wise-guy buddies.

Then Mickey looked back, seeing his cousin, and yelled over his shoulder, "Cousin, don't tell my Papa that I didn't stay with you all afternoon." Mike couldn't help but feel concerned for his cousin's future, realizing that Mickey's ambitions might lead him down a dangerous path.

PART TWO

Aqua passata non macina mulinu.
—old Platanese proverb

Water that's passed won't turn the millstone.

1

CHARTING A DIFFERENT PATH

Norwalk, Connecticut, 1916

Mike was impressed by the thriving businesses and companies that dotted Norwalk. Despite being a fraction of the size of New York City, Norwalk was a melting pot of cultures, a place he had grown to love in the few years he had lived there. His work with people of every nationality, religion, and race deepened his admiration for the city.

His greatest challenge was finding common ground with those who identified as "Italian." Many were involved in what he considered "the bad life"—engaging in illegal activities such as running numbers, women, and liquor. Mike chose a different path and instead bonded with men of Irish heritage like his friends Magner and Leonard. He found them honest and loyal; he often sought their counsel. He took their shared belief in "the future of Norwalk" to heart.

Just a few years ago, the towns of Norwalk and South Norwalk merged into one city called Norwalk, with designations for East Norwalk, South Norwalk, Norwalk, and Rowayton also included. Working and living in South Norwalk, Mike gave serious thought to moving to the northern part of the city, away from the Italian community.

The Gallo family and cousin Petronella remained in the same general area where they had always lived. Early in 1916, to Mike's disappointment, Zio Pasquale had moved his family to Strafford, just outside Bridgeport's big city.

He loved the man and was fond of his daughters, Jennie and Lilly. Mike felt that his uncle was under the mistaken impression that if he took his son, Mickey, away from his circle of questionable friends, he would help him start fresh.

Mike worked hard and saved his money. He told the truth. He never spoke ill of anyone; without trying, he found that people responded well to him. He often recalled the words his cousin Mickey had spewed. The boy was right: Your friends are important, and if you want to be respected, you must do what it takes to earn respect. Where they differed was the method of achieving that goal.

It was a cold Sunday morning. Mike had boarded the train to Bridgeport from the South Norwalk train station, and the landscape from the train car's windows showed the promise of spring. Today, he was making another attempt to find his father's grave. The last time he had tried to find it, he had been ill-prepared. It had been within the first two weeks of his arrival at his cousin Petronella's place.

On that trip, once in Bridgeport, he had made several inquiries about the cemetery and learned there were three cemeteries where they could have taken his father. He also knew about the devastating news that the church had had a fire in 1906, which had consumed the records for all the Catholic cemeteries in the Diocese of Bridgeport to that time. This news left Mike crestfallen. There was no documentation he could ask them to check. How could it be that all traces of his father had dissipated?

He'd insisted someone show him where the cemeteries were located. He had gone to one cemetery there, called St. James, walked the grounds, and looked at almost every headstone and footstone with his uncle, who could read the inscriptions.

His dream of laying a wreath on his father's grave was shattered. Instead, he placed the wreath he had brought with him that day on the large statue at the entrance, bowed his head, and said a prayer for his father as well as for all those buried here, a solemn act of respect for those whose families might not know where they were. He and his uncle returned to South Norwalk that night without speaking. He couldn't believe there was no recourse to finding the grave. He was unwilling to give up his quest. The physical and emotional strain was taking its toll, but he remained determined.

Over the past four years, Mike had learned a lot in bits and pieces, each piece giving him new hope. He'd learned that St. James had stopped taking new burials well before his dad died in 1900, so that's why he wasn't there. This information was a small victory in his search, but it also meant he had to start over.

Although the other two cemeteries in that area had no records due to the same fire, he thought he could visit family members who could read and have them walk each cemetery with him. He would find a marker with his father's name on it. The blanket of snow during the months following his arrival in South Norwalk made checking other cemeteries impossible. Then, work demands, the distance, and his transportation limitations prevented him from returning to Bridgeport sooner.

It was almost two years before he could explore the second lead, St. Michael's Cemetery in Stratford. Still an active cemetery, it had taken burials from before his father's death and since then. On that occasion, Mike's heart, filled with hope and beating with anticipation, was disappointed once more to come up with nothing.

Then, he learned of the St. Augustine Cemetery, the most probable one to have taken his father for burial, someone at the Bridgeport Diocese office told him, because it was closest to where most of the immigrant workers lived. The area had many immigrant boardinghouses. Located on the east side of Bridgeport, it was the first Roman Catholic cemetery in Fairfield County.

Consistent with the ethnic makeup of greater Bridgeport in the mid-to-late 1800s, most of the burials were of Irish heritage—however, there were also a good number of Polish, Czech, Italian, Russian, Hispanic, and other ethnicities' graves. No one knew precisely how many individuals lay there. During Mike's inquiries, the diocesan office staff mentioned the range of 1,000 to 2,000 graves. Because of its location, it had been vandalized countless times.

Today, he was meeting Zio Pasquale, and together, they would walk around the graves in St. Augustine's Cemetery. They had chosen early spring because the snow had stopped, and there was not yet too much undergrowth.

As he prepared to meet his uncle, Mike was filled with hope, though it was tempered with a healthy dose of realism. He knew the odds were against him, but was unwilling to give up.

While searching for the grave several times, Mike started to realize he might never find it. He resigned himself to learning the general area where his father may have been buried. Later, after he had met his future bride, Raffaela, and planned to marry, he would place a wreath at the entrance to the last cemetery in memory of his father. He had decided he would honor his father by naming their first child, Antonio, after him; the thought had brought Mike great comfort.

2

DISCOVERING A TREASURE

Norwalk, 1917-1918

Working as a laborer on the tracks for the Connecticut Railway Company, Mike had found an apartment at 19 River Street in Norwalk, just off Wall Street, to bring his new bride, Maria Raffaela Russo, whom he called Raffaela. He had rented the place in the fall of 1917, right after they decided they would get married. Despite the preparations, it wasn't until the couple obtained their marriage license just before Christmas that the impending marriage seemed real to Mike.

The three rooms were dark and tight, but the apartment afforded Mike and Raffaela some marital privacy, even though Salvatore, Raffaela's brother, had come to live with them.

As she went about sewing, cleaning, and preparing meals, Raffaela felt overwhelming gratitude that God had sent her this gift. She had thought she would never marry. Now, she often reddened with embarrassment at the open adoration of this young man, Mike, who was almost nine years her junior. She felt that the unexpected way he had entered her life was a gift from God.

As a girl, she had lost her mother and then tended the three males in her family in Mileto, a small town in Calabria, twenty-five miles southwest of where Mike hailed from. After three earthquakes between 1905 and 1908, her father and her older brother, Giovanni, had emigrated to America, promising to send for her and her younger brother as soon as possible. Raffaela became the mother of Salvatore, just six years younger than her.

Antonio Russo knew the time would come for his daughter to get married. He had often told her she was a beautiful girl. He had been adamant with his sister, Concetta, to keep a watchful eye on his growing girl while he was gone. After a few years, Raffaela and Salvatore joined their father and older brother in America.

Raffaela felt herself change after coming to America. She had blossomed into a full-bodied woman. Her father and older brother wanted her to be happy. They encouraged her to attend regular gatherings where most of their *paisani* lived in South Norwalk. On the other hand, Salvatore, sour and demanding as a youngster, only grew more so with time. As a teenager, he followed in his father's and brother's footsteps—first as an apprentice and later a full-fledged cobbler. He later split from his older brother's business and opened his own shop.

Raffaela worried about him night and day. After their father died in 1913, Salvatore seemed to develop an exaggerated possessiveness for her. Then, Giovanni asked Antonietta Zambarelli to marry him.

Instead of being elated for his brother, Salvatore declared, "Everyone is leaving me!" He begged his sister never to leave him. By the time he was seventeen, he had developed a reputation as a rogue—taking up smoking, drinking, and gambling—and quite a reputation with the young women, with fathers wary if he noticed their daughters. Raffaela was distressed by the fact that he seemed devoid of commitment.

On the other hand, Giovanni felt his sister needed a life of her own. At twenty-eight, she was considered an old maid in their social circle. Their *paisani* considered a woman hopeless if she had reached the age of twenty without at least an engagement. It wasn't as if there hadn't been suitors, but the ever-devoted Raffaela had turned them down when the offers came because her "baby" brother needed her.

It seemed after she turned twenty-two, there were no longer any marriage-makers sending the *'mbasciata*—the message delivered by a go-between communicating an interest in a match. No one seemed to cast an eye in her direction any longer. Men who had been interested when she was younger were long married with children, not that any of them had intrigued her. Despite her thick, wavy hair, tiny waist, and ample bosom, she seemed to fade into that category of the unseen.

Her limited outings encompassed church, the market, and home. However, once Giovanni married, Raffaela's sister-in-law Antonietta, became an avid matchmaker on her behalf. But Raffaela seemed disinterested. Her sister-in-law urged her to attend the numerous gatherings her family held with Miletesi, people from the same town or province they came from. These gatherings rarely included outsiders. However, it did happen now and then.

In late April, the Connecticut sun began to warm a little from a long, arduous winter, and the tulips responded, casting pretty splotches of red, yellow, and purple on an otherwise dead canvas. Giovanni Russo took the occasion of the start of preparations for the feast of the Holy Mother, slated for May 8, as an opportunity to invite a non-*paisano* to a game of *bocce* at the St. Ann Club on Ely Avenue. The gathering after *bocce* always involved food, work, and planning for the upcoming festival in honor of the Holy Mother, the daughter of their patron saint, Anna.

Raffaela hadn't wanted to go, but Antonietta had said they needed help with the food and writing the petitions to the Holy Mother Mary. Antonietta appealed to Raffaela's beautiful penmanship.

"I beg you to come. You are the only one who has the script worthy enough to craft the petition letters that we will pin on the statue of Madonna," she implored. The club paraded the statue of the Holy Mother, with all the intercessions pinned to it, as part of its annual ritual.

The intercessions started coming into the club around the beginning of March, so they were already piling up. The locals organized this event each year in the traditions of their town in Italy. Most of the immigrants in the area could not read or write. Yet Raffaela had gone to the third grade back in Mileto, and she had learned her lessons well—the teacher had complimented her on how well she had mastered them, enough to teach others better than those who had attended school far longer. Her teacher had also felt that Raffaela's penmanship, her "hand," as she called it, was exquisite. A gift from God that she should share for good purposes, she had often told the girl.

Contrary to her homebody nature, Raffaela accepted the plea to attend the social gathering at the St. Ann Club on that semi-warm day in late April. With great reluctance, she went with a dish of eggplant parmigiana, her contribution to the buffet, and her fountain pen, which she treasured like gold.

There she sat with a handful of women dictating their petitions and what they had been told by others, Raffaela translating them onto the small scraps of paper torn by hand from a much larger sheet.

After the *bocce* rounds wrapped up, the men washed their hands and filed past the table laid out for a feast. One by one, they filled their dishes and sat at the makeshift table and long wooden benches fashioned from planks and stacked cement blocks.

Mike Rizzo had spotted Raffaela seated with pen in hand from the *bocce* court. He was intrigued by the scene. He didn't know many men in his group who could write, let alone a woman.

He noticed her beauty. He had been very respectful and asked someone who she was. They said she was the *zitella* Russo; Mike was stunned. He was almost twenty, and she looked his age. How could she be a *zitella*, an old maid?

He was gripped by a mixture of awe at her intelligence and beauty and a permeating sadness. He couldn't believe they referred to her in such a pejorative manner. At the same time, he felt elated that she wasn't married.

Driven by some unknown force, he walked over toward the women. As he approached, he heard her voice when she spoke to another woman, "I'll go in and check on putting out more parmigiana."

At the sound of her lovely voice, he was smitten. Though she never reappeared from inside, he sat there, hoping that he would get to talk with her.

Though disappointed, after the planning and his promise to help on the day of the feast, hope sprang eternal as the men invited him to come back the following week for another round of *bocce*, food, and festival planning.

She wasn't there on his subsequent visit, though he enjoyed the camaraderie and the food. On his third outing among the *Milatese,* he went to speak to Giovanni, Raffaela's brother. Mike worried about her because he had not seen her again after his first visit and hoped she was not ill. Her brother explained that she didn't often attend these gatherings, but the women had tapped into her good nature regarding the petition letters.

Mike tried not to betray his intentions lest Giovanni rebuffed him. However, Giovanni recognized the signs, and because he loved his sister so much and had grown fond of the young Platanese man, he asked Mike to join them for dinner at their home the following Sunday.

Looking back, Raffaela reflected on the strained gathering that had been her match-making meal. She had come to realize that her prospects for marriage were slim. She had devoted herself to her younger brother's needs and selfish demands and had become an old maid.

And yet, here she was now, a married woman. Stirring within her were conflicting emotions of regret, resignation, and a glimmer of hope for the new life that fluttered within her. She had found the courage to embark on a new chapter of her life.

Despite the cold, the wedding had been a warm and enchanting affair in St. Mary's Church on West Avenue on January 7, 1918. The church was filled with love and joy as Giovanni walked Raffaela down the aisle amid the lace and ruffles of the gown she had made herself. An experienced seamstress, she took great care with the most important dress she had ever worn. Her husband looked so handsome, and the warmth of the occasion filled the church.

Mike had insisted they have a wedding portrait taken. An extravagance they couldn't afford, but he had been adamant. The photographer told them they could pay a little at a time for the portrait, and once they finished paying, they could take it home. After fourteen months of marriage, the colorized full-length portrait decorated the wall of their tiny place. She basked in the thought of it all as she gazed at it often throughout the day, these past two months since they had made their last payment. Her dedication to their marriage was apparent in her care of their home. She stole frequent glances at their portrait as she worked throughout the day.

Since Raffaela's marriage, her brother Salvatore had become almost unbearable. He frequently expressed his feelings to his sister. "This boy-man has fooled you. He isn't smart or handsome," he had said just this morning. "You have made a terrible mistake." It wasn't the first time he had said it. She expected it wouldn't be the last. Salvatore often argued that Mike was taking her heart, time, and life.

Despite his vehement objections to the marriage, he seemed to hold the mistaken notion that even though she was married, she would remain his surrogate mother, devoted only to him. His constant disapproval and demands added an emotional strain to her new life.

Raffaela reminisced over her first year of marriage, a year of wonder and discovery for her and Mike. They learned how much they had in common, and their shared experiences deepened their connection. They now knew what it was to adore someone more than yourself. At first, she felt embarrassed that Mike was much younger. Yet he had proved to be a serious and committed husband. There seemed to be none of the failings she had heard so often from other women. He appeared oblivious to other women except as people. She was the apple of his eye, and his eye remained focused on her.

She had been pleased that Mike had agreed to have Salvatore come live with them. She had told Mike she couldn't marry unless he did. However, the two didn't get along well. Often, she felt torn. It was true that Salvatore treated her as his doormat, as Mike had said to him whenever they exchanged harsh words. Raffaela was in a bad spot. She loved Mike but felt guilty and obligated toward her brother. Sometimes, when Mike was out, Salvatore said such horrible things that she thought to herself, *Perhaps I should not have gotten married.*

She had become pregnant for the first time only two months after the wedding, but her body had aborted the baby almost as soon as she realized she was pregnant. The midwife had comforted and upset her in one sentence: "Don't worry; it is very common to lose the first one." Then the woman had crushed her hopes by adding, "Often, 'older' women never can carry a baby full term."

But happily, a few months later, Raffaela found herself expecting again.

3

THE JOYS OF PARENTHOOD

Norwalk, 1919-1920

As summer approached, the baby grew inside her, kicking, turning, and alive, and Raffaela was busy sewing and knitting the baby's layette. Today, she was beaming full of love as she sewed the gown her child would wear at baptism. She used the fabric from the train of her wedding dress, and her joy danced around her like pixie dust. She reflected that the larger her belly grew, the more her brother became. In the same moment, she smiled, thinking, *As my belly has grown, it seems Mike beams from morning until he falls asleep at night.*

"Rosa, that's what we will name her," Raffaela declared when their infant arrived in July. Before Mike could say anything about it, his wife had decided that tradition would prevail, and his mother's name would be passed along. Their first child, a beautiful girl with a head full of dark hair, cried with life. He had not given any thought to a girl's name. He had been sure it would be a boy, and he would name him Antonio.

But that wasn't to be, at least not yet. Mike had ambivalent feelings about his mother. But his feelings for this exquisite creation, his daughter, were crystal clear. An overwhelming sense of love and protectiveness for the mother and child born at home washed over him. He didn't want to leave them for even a minute. His brother-in-law Salvatore was the one who went to the town hall to register the baby's birth.

Now close to a year old, Rosa had become Rosie or Rosina to them and had begun to take her first steps. She was their joy. Not long after Rosie's birth, Raffaela had become pregnant again. The new baby would be born in September, just two months after Rosie's first birthday in July. Mike's cup was full.

Their second child, a girl, was born on September 9, 1920. With Raffaela again dictating the naming traditions of their heritage, they named her Angelina after Mike's oldest sister, who now lived in Argentina. The child became Lena to everyone as soon as she was born. Unlike her sister in personality and temperament, she, too, was a beautiful baby with gorgeous hair, a ready smile, and a dimple on her cheek.

The family had now outgrown the apartment on River Street.

"We need to move," Mike said to Raffaela. "We have a little money saved. I don't know if it's enough yet to buy a place, but I need to start looking for a place to rent. If something good comes along, and we can afford to buy, that would be best."

With her ever-present needle in hand, she nodded her agreement.

They needed more room and a place they could own, but he didn't know if he could afford both. He spent the day talking to people he knew in the shops, inquiring about property for sale and potential apartments. He had learned early on that if he could find something through word of mouth, it was often more affordable or negotiable than properties reported in a newspaper or listed with agents. Everything he looked at was way out of his reach. He had some savings now, but they were meager when he factored in the need to pay the loan, eat, and provide for a family of four on his labor wages. He knew he would save enough money in a few years, but they needed space now.

Mike decided to talk with his friend Jim Magner at the funeral home before returning to River Street.

Jim said, "You know, Mike, you are doing the right thing, looking for a property to purchase. I heard there was a house for sale on Henry Street. It backs up to the Center School property. It's a big house you could convert into a multi-family dwelling."

When Mike went to look, it was indeed enormous. He calculated that if he could come up with the down payment, he could rent out part of it, cover his mortgage, and have a place for his wife and children. He liked the street; the house had an ample yard to grow his vegetables. Excited, Mike took his wife, kids, and brothers-in-law to see the place. Everyone remarked on how much work it would need to make it livable, but Mike was no stranger to hard work. Raffaela became excited about the prospects. Her brother Giovanni had just bought a home nearby on Cross Street.

There was just one problem. When Mike went to the bank for a mortgage note, he didn't have enough of a down payment.

He talked with Giovanni, whose compassionate response, though of no help, opened another path. "Look, I would do anything for you and my sister, but as you know, a few months ago, I bought this place for my family. I don't have the money now. I know my brother, Salvatore, has money. He is a rogue, but he's making good money, and he has been living with you and my sister, paying no rent and spending no money on food. I think he would lend it to Raffaela if she asked him."

Mike faced a dilemma. He didn't want to be beholden to his ne'er-do-well brother-in-law. The only disagreement Raffaela and Mike had between them was about her brother. Feeling torn about whether to ask him for a loan, Mike swallowed hard and did it for Raffaela and his daughters, despite the emotional turmoil it caused him.

The very next evening, he approached Salvatore when he wandered in smelling of liquor at about eleven-thirty.

At first, Salvatore responded in a sweet falsetto voice, "Of course, you want my money. First, you took my sister; now you say that the money is for her and the children. Sure. Sure. I can lend you the money." The docile attitude tinged with sarcasm left Mike a little frightened.

Then Salvatore began banging doors and slamming things down. The children started crying. Raffaela left the bedroom in her nightgown and spoke to her brother in a barely audible voice but with an unmistakable firmness.

"You say you love me. Yet you try to destroy anything that makes me happy. These children are all you may have someday when you are old, and I am gone. They are the love of my life. As much as I love you, I love them more. My husband works every day to do the best he can for all of us. You live under his roof and eat his food, you ungrateful oaf. When will you wake up? You are biting the hand that's feeding you. We need the money. We will pay you back. If you don't lend it to us, pack your bags now and get out."

She turned and returned to the bedroom, shutting the door in his face, leaving him to grapple with the weight of her words.

Shocked, he knocked at the door and begged her forgiveness.

Humbled, he turned to Mike and said, "How much do you need? When you buy the house, I will give it to you at the bank. I will not live with you when you move. It's time I go out on my own."

After that night, Salvatore's change of heart and decision to help, despite his initial reluctance, were a step towards repairing the strained relationship with his sister and brother-in-law.

4

HOUSE FILLED WITH A GROWING FAMILY

Norwalk, winter 1924

"It's very cold," said Raffaela softly to Mike as he arrived from his night watchman's job at eight-thirty a.m. "We have almost finished the wood to burn."

They huddled close in the small apartment on Godfrey Street while two of their three daughters played on the kitchen floor, the warmest place in the house. Raffaela and the children already had a simple breakfast of latte and biscuits. It was Wednesday, and they would have meat on Saturday when he went to the butcher and bought some ground chuck.

Raffaela had some food waiting for him as he came in, so he rushed to wash his face in the enamel basin she had heated on the cast-iron wood-burning stove. That wood stove had kept them snug the past four years since they bought the house. With no central heating, the house was nothing more than a large wooden box with a flat roof.

Mike had worked several jobs at a time to buy the place. It cost almost $2,300, but when the opportunity came before they had enough to put the down payment on it, Salvatore had lived up to his word and loaned them the $400 they needed to make up the difference. They were shocked at the bank when Salvatore requested that his loan be treated as an official lien on the property in case they didn't pay him back. More than a little offended, they swallowed hard and said nothing in front of the bank officials. They had offered to write up an official note of the loan and payment, separate from the bank loan. But Salvatore kept saying, "No, no need—I'll meet you at the bank and give you the money then." They walked out of the bank owing two mortgages.

Despite owing money to her little brother and paying every six months on the note from the seller, they had done well. They paid Salvatore back, and he removed his lien on the house. Moreover, Mike had done enormous work to turn it into a four-family dwelling and make each apartment livable. He improved the plumbing and added kitchens to the three units that didn't have them. Mike and his family lived in one of the two upstairs apartments. He now collected rent on the other three apartments. This income helped provide the cash to pay the two mortgages.

They had rented the first-floor apartment to a family from New York with children. And a childless couple rented the small two-room apartment also on the first floor In the second upstairs apartment, backing up to theirs, lived a childless couple from Calabria.

The Rizzos' second-floor apartment was the larger of the two. More spacious and pleasant than the dark and airless rented apartment on River Street, the Godfrey Street apartment seemed quite large when the Rizzos moved in, but now it just about contained them and their three, soon-to-be four children. Despite the house's lack of aesthetic beauty and the never-ending need for repairs, Mike often basked in the noble feeling of home ownership. He hoped there would come a day when he could take the entire upstairs for his family.

The three little girls were growing up with beauty and charm. The third one, Concetta, named after Raffaela's aunt, had been born two years after Lena. They all had gorgeous smiles. Now, Raffaela was pregnant with their fourth child. Mike loved his little girls but hoped this one would be a boy. He wanted so much to have a namesake for his father.

He had never been able to locate his father's grave. With all the records destroyed by fire, no matter what he had done, he couldn't find it after searching in the three possible cemeteries. When he and Zio Pasquale had walked through the abandoned St. Augustine Cemetery, the stone markers had been knocked over; it was impossible to discern anything. According to the caretaker at the church where they had gone to see if there was any other recourse, some of the graves had been marked with wooden crosses. Those that survived the fire had been ravaged by the snow- and ice-laden winters.

That day, he had stared for a long time at the small number of crosses that still stood. He felt at a loss to assume that any of them marked his father's burial site. At first, he was heartbroken as if his father had just died. As time passed, he began to feel better after deciding to honor his father by naming his first-born son after him.

The cold weather in late 1923 didn't let up until April 1924. It was May, and they had had almost a month of beautiful weather; it wouldn't be long before the unbearable heat would descend upon them.

That morning, as she was fixing coffee, Raffaela doubled over in pain, and Mike realized she was in labor, though she was not due for a couple of weeks yet. He ran down the stairs two at a time and knocked on the house next door, imploring Mrs. Tavella to contact the midwife, who appeared about thirty minutes later.

He wanted to hold Raffaela's hand through her pain and delivery, but once the midwife arrived, she scolded and banished him from the bedroom, saying this was women's work. Instead, he focused on taking care of the three girls, bringing them outside to help. His thoughts wandered. He had been at work when Concetta was born and was so happy to be there with Raffaela for this birth.

He heard Raffaela's screams from the street and through the open windows. Then, all went quiet. He held his breath. Then someone shouted from the window, "Daughter number four."

He bounded up the stairs, elated to see Raffaela, tired and drained as she was. Her first words to him were, "I'm so sorry I didn't deliver you a son."

He said to her in a choked voice, "It's okay, we'll name her Antonietta after my father, Antonio. He will be smiling in heaven."

5

AN UNWANTED DETOUR

Norwalk, July 1924

Godfrey Street ran perpendicular to Main Avenue. Its positioning was excellent for the bus line and a reasonable walk into the north part of the city's business and retail area. Most important to Mike, it was on the opposite side of town from what was known as the center of the Italian population, South Norwalk. The road where his house sat had originally been named Henry Street, which the city had to change after the consolidation of Norwalk and South Norwalk revealed that there were two streets with the same name.

When he had purchased the house, it backed up to land owned by the town where the Center Elementary School stood—the school the girls would attend. However, most of the property was an empty, wooded area with rolling small hills that extended to the parallel street to School Street. Now, right behind his house, the town was constructing a new school on the empty part of the parcel. The new building would house the middle-grade students. He was pleased that his children would not have to walk far in the nasty winters until high school. The area was covered in trees, and the clearing before construction was now underway.

It was a comfortable morning at seventy-two degrees, nearing the end of July of 1924, when Mike noticed that the workers behind his house were taking the felled trees and cutting them up with an enormous chain-run buzz saw. The next day, he had gone to talk to the workers. Thinking ahead to the cold winter sure to arrive later in the year, he asked if, at night after they quit work, he could use their equipment to cut up a few of the trees himself to use in his wood-burning stove for heat.

The head worker told him, "Yeah, come in the evening after we finish or the day; we don't have a problem with that. You just can't be here while we work. You'd be doing us a favor because we need to get rid of everything before the construction can start."

A few evenings later, after he had worked a long day at his job, at about six-thirty he went over to the school construction site; the area was visible from their apartment window.

"You are so tired; go tomorrow," implored Raffaela as he headed to the site.

"I'm fine. I'm just gonna work for a few hours, and then I'll come and eat my dinner," Mike replied. "You worry too much."

She went to the window to watch him leave their house. From the window, she shouted, "Be careful," as was her custom.

The headline in the local paper the next day read, "Arm horribly mangled by buzz saw is amputated at Norwalk Hospital."

As Mike was using the chainsaw, he had bent over to move one of the cut logs away. He lost his footing. As he slipped, the chain caught his shirt sleeve.

Raffaela, watching him from the window, saw him go down. She ran, yelling for the neighbors. Mr. Bredice, a local man with a brand-new car, drove around, along with the next-door neighbor, picked up Mike and took him to Norwalk Hospital. However, the car didn't have enough power to make it up the steep hill to the hospital at the top of Stevens Street. From there, the hospital personnel carried him the rest of the way. He lost a tremendous amount of blood and was hanging on by a thread by the time a physician attended to him.

The doctors realized that to save his life, they would need to amputate the mangled limb. The cut came just above his elbow.

For several days afterward, he was delirious and unaware of his surroundings. He slowly came around and opened his eyes to see the worried faces of his beautiful wife and her brother Giovanni. Mike had no recollection of the events that put him in the hospital. He saw their concerned, tired faces and realized he was forever left-handed.

He made a protracted recovery, but after an extended stay, they let him go home. He watched with guilt as his beloved Raffaela, with three small children and a baby in tow, waited on him hand and foot because of his incapacitation. Raffaela hugged him and cried, too. Before long, the oldest girl, Rosie, came over and hugged and cried with them. He spent the next couple of months wallowing in self-pity.

Friends and family came to visit, expressing their sympathy for him. Their pity, though well-intentioned, was depressing. His self-flagellation about what he had done was relentless. Three months after the accident, his friend Jim Magner came by and gave him the scolding he needed.

Unlike all his prior visitors, Jim's demeanor and words were stern and unsympathetic. When his friend entered the bedroom where Mike had holed himself up, Jim's usual compassionate manner was absent.

"Get off your ass, Mike," he bellowed. "You are a strong man, young, and a hard and industrious worker. There is no reason for you to stay inside nursing your wounds. Get out there. Take care of your family and stop feeling sorry and blaming yourself for what happened. That will not put any food on the table!"

It was a hard blow. Stunned, Mike sat, not saying a word.

After about three minutes of ranting, his buddy paused and said, "I don't care if you ever talk with me again, but I just had to tell you."

To Jim's surprise, Mike said after a long silence, "Thank you. You are a very good friend."

The next morning, he told Raffaela to leave him alone when she asked if he was ready to have her help him dress. Instead, Mike told her to care for the children and that he would rest a little longer. With the door closed, he got up and tried to put on his clothes for the first time without help.

He struggled but kept at it. Right-handed all his life, he realized his left arm was almost useless. Then he'd scold it, "You bugger!" He'd chastise its clumsiness. But he did not give up. When he came out of the bedroom, Raffaela was surprised to see him somewhat dressed.

"Why didn't you call me so I could help you?" she asked.

"I need to do this myself. You work so hard with the children; you don't need me to be another one of your babies," he said, his voice catching to stop the tears.

Within a week, he mastered washing himself and putting on his clothes.

In rapid succession, he moved to help his wife with the household chores as he had in the past. By the end of October, he could hang the washed clothes on the line with one hand. He even managed to tie his shoes. He held his infant daughter and played with the girls.

Each night, he made his sign of the cross with his left hand. He prayed morning and night, imploring the Almighty, "Dear God, help me do what I can and make the most of what you give me."

6

A CRUSHING LOSS

Norwalk, February 1927

What an angelic child, he thought as he looked at his daughter Concetta sleeping. At the other end of the crib was the baby, Antonietta. She would be three this coming May. Antonietta had a smile that could seduce the hardest curmudgeon. He walked over to the other small bed where the two oldest girls slept, Rosie and Lena, both gorgeous youngsters. If asked, he couldn't have said which was the prettiest. At seven and a half years old, Rosie seemed the most adult, though not quite fourteen months older than Lena; she was an enormous help to her mother with the younger children.

It had been a freezing winter, and they were still in its grip. Mike had been doing laborer work all day at Young's nursery in the farm area north of Norwalk called Westport. He and two other men had covered the plants, wrapped the shrubbery, and stoked the heaters to ensure the greenhouse protected the plants from the cold. The days were short, and the cold seemed to whip through the windows. He wished he had as much material at home as they did at the nursery to keep the elements at bay.

His left hand touched the girls' heads one at a time. Then he sat down to eat his very late dinner that Raffaela had kept warm. She had seemed quiet and tired these last few days. He didn't know what was wrong; she said she was fine when he asked. He wondered if she was pregnant. He had asked, but she said she didn't think so. As they whispered between themselves so as not to wake the children, he ate his dinner in his usual slow manner. He didn't turn on the radio as usual, deciding that the morning would be soon enough to hear of the events around town and the world and listen to music.

It had been almost three years since his stubbornness had cost him his right arm. He had fought to get back on his feet, and once he did, he made great strides in getting back to work. Despite initially being viewed as damaged goods, his reputation as a hard worker spread fast. Supervisors often picked him in the first round of the labor lineup for day-laborers,

Now, he had found some more steady employment at the nursery. He and his two co-workers handled everything from digging and potting seedlings to repairing and reinforcing the structure to keep the cold out. In the spring, they would remove the glass and wood and expose the many plants to the sunshine and warmth. Now, in the middle of February, that seemed a long way away.

Gardening, landscaping, tending the land, and the plants were in his blood. He had learned how to coax vegetables from a stubborn soil in Platania. Every year since he had bought the house, his backyard was lush with vegetables. After he lost his arm, he found he could still wield a shovel and plant the fresh vegetables his family needed. The business of landscaping and tending plants was a good place for him to work.

While waiting for him to come home from work, Raffaela had cut out a dress for Rosie. Her seamstress talents ensured the children always looked well-dressed, a testament to her resourcefulness in their meager circumstances. She was always looking for price-reduced fabric at the dry goods store, ready to pounce when she found a good deal. She'd fashion a pattern, cut and sew each little dress, going through the lineup of daughters one at a time. Now, she was back at the oldest, the other three each having gotten a new dress over the past six months.

Admiring the small cut-out form of the dress, she said, "Rosie will love this little blue fabric."

"Let's get some sleep," Mike said to her. "You look exhausted; you work too hard."

They readied for bed, and he waited for her to join him as she went in to take one last look at the girls. The full moon flooded the room with light through the windows. He kissed her forehead when she came to bed, and both closed their eyes. They cuddled close to keep warm.

She suddenly complained of a terrible headache and turned her head up to him. In the moonlight, he saw her contorted face and recognized that something was wrong. Within moments, she made a convulsive sound.

He screamed, "Raffaela, Raffaela, talk to me," but no other sound came.

He pulled on the lamp chain and reached out for his pants, intending to run next door for help getting her to the hospital. But before he could even get to them, her eyes rolled back into her head.

His body hugging her, he began screaming like a wounded animal. The screams woke the tenants from the apartment below. They roused and banged on the door.

The commotion awoke little Rosie, who began to cry. But she let the couple in when he shouted to her to open the door despite her tears.

They found him with his wife in his arms, screaming, "Don't leave me. Don't leave me."

Three days later

"She looks so pretty, like she's sleeping," Lena whispered to Rosie. The girls sat quietly as friends and neighbors viewed the open casket where the beautiful mother of four lay. The girls couldn't understand why their Mama would not talk to them. The neighbors had told them she had gone to heaven to be with God.

The casket sat in the church among a vast array of flower arrangements brought by friends and relatives. Connie leaned over to her father and asked with an innocence only a four-year-old could express, "Why did she have to go?"

A vise gripped his heart; he felt he couldn't breathe. He tried to say something comforting to his daughter, but his voice choked, and the faucet of tears he had been working so hard to control opened up full blast. The pain of losing his wife was unbearable, and he felt he was drowning in a sea of grief.

The death certificate said she had died of a cerebral hemorrhage.

"This aneurysm had been like a ticking time bomb in her brain for many years before now," the doctor told him.

Mike sat in a daze throughout the visitation and funeral mass. He was inconsolable. He had had angry words with Salvatore, who accused him of killing his sister. Salvatore's words had cut to his heart. Perhaps it was his fault. She was a bit older than most women when she started bearing children. *Could that have been the cause?* He wondered.

7

CARE FOR THE CHILDREN

A week after the funeral, Mike was no better. He had slipped into an abysmal depression. His friend Jim stopped by the house to check on him and was appalled at how he looked. Mike nodded to acknowledge Jim's presence, but no words came.

Filled with compassion, Jim spoke in a gentle tone to his friend, hoping to get him to register the world around him. "Mike, you've got to get yourself out of this; you've got these four children. Only you can help them."

Mike heard the words as if through a dense fog, struggling to focus on them. His sense of loss was so vast that he'd sunk into a deep well and couldn't find anything to grip on to pull himself up. After Jim left, Antonietta, his youngest, who had been in the care of a neighbor for the first few days after the funeral, crawled onto his lap and hugged him. Looking at her dirty face, Mike felt ashamed. How long had it been since he'd noticed his children?

In a flash, he realized his girls were the incarnation of his beautiful wife. This thought jolted him out of despair, and he knew he had to step up and take care of his children.

His thoughts ran together, overwhelming him. He sat for a long while sorting things out in his head; all the while, the children, who had seemed afraid to approach him, came close and hung on him. Their touch brought him back to reality. He knew he had to work. How would he take care of them? In a daze, he got up, washed their faces, and helped them change into clean clothes.

Then, as if struggling through molasses, he began to work out arrangements where the two youngest girls would be cared for by a nearby woman who could come to the apartment to watch them, at least for a short while. The two older ones were in school during the day, and he'd worked it out so his brother-in-law's wife could watch them after school. Balancing work and childcare was a constant struggle, but he was determined to make it work for his daughters.

Two days of that routine—going to work and returning to find the youngsters dirty and hungry—were enough to demonstrate that this plan wouldn't work. With his one hand, he tried to clean them up and make them some food as best he could. Then, on the third day, the woman left before the appointed time, leaving the two smallest children alone.

When he arrived, they were screaming in terror. He pulled them onto his lap and cried with them. Calming himself, he thought there had to be a way he could get them through the next few years. By then, Rosie would be old enough to help with her younger sisters.

The next day, he didn't go to work, figuring he would need to make other arrangements for his daughters. However, someone had already reported to children's services that four little girls were in peril. The knock on the door sounded like another death knell.

"Mr. Rizzo, it has been brought to our attention that there are four neglected children here."

He was stunned. However, he knew how it must have looked to the case worker. The house was not clean. The girls weren't dressed properly; their faces weren't spotless. He felt a stab of total despair and then brushed it away. *I have to be strong for my daughters*, he thought.

He listened respectfully as the woman said. "Unless you bring in a nanny or get married, we must bring the girls to the Children's Home on Westport Avenue. There, they will be treated well, given proper meals, appropriately bathed and dressed, and sent to school."

Then she said in a low voice, "I must be honest with you; bringing them to the children's home makes them eligible for adoption. You will be declared an unfit parent, and they will become wards of the state. They are lovely girls; someone will adopt the two younger ones right away."

He could not speak for several minutes. Then, in a whisper, he asked, "Will they be kept together?"

"I'm sorry, there are no guarantees. I will be honest with you, it's not likely. I can't think of anyone in a position to adopt all four," the social worker said as if she were talking about something no more important than taking out the trash. He was silent for so long that the social worker grew impatient and prompted, "Have you been listening to me, Mr. Rizzo?"

He struggled to keep the tears from his eyes and to get his voice under control. "I will come to talk with you on Monday. I will be here with them over the next three days, and I know I can get my sister-in-law to help me with them for a few days."

"We can do all the paperwork then, Mr. Rizzo," she said as a parting shot. He shut the door, sat in a chair, and cried. The pain was unbearable. He'd lost Raffaela; now he would lose her daughters.

The girls, who had gone into hiding when the woman was there, came out, hugged and kissed him.

Rosie had understood everything. "Why do they want to take us away, Papa?"

He wallowed in his misery that entire afternoon and evening. The next morning, he bundled them all up and walked them to his brother-in-law's house on Cross Street. Hearing what had transpired, Giovanni, who was now known as John, empathized with the predicament.

After some discussion, John's wife, Antonietta, had a suggestion. "Mike, there is a widow we know who would make a good mother to the girls and a good wife to you. She has two children of her own."

"I can't," he said. "I can't take that chance."

"What chance?" Antonietta asked, mystified that he would not jump at the idea.

"What if someone mistreats them? How can I do that to them? They are innocent children. My girls should not be punished for their mother's death. It's my fault; I will make this right. I don't know how, but I will make it right."

"Antonietta," John said, "please make some lunch for my nieces," as he beckoned Mike out to the front porch. The sun was bright, but the temperature was twenty-six degrees.

Once out of earshot of his wife and the girls, John said, "Mike, what are you gonna do? You can't stay like this. They are too small yet."

"I know there are women who take in children as boarders. I just don't know how to find them," Mike sobbed. "You know so many people through the shoe repair shop; someone you know must have a lead on a name. I beg you to help me find someone."

Before returning inside, John said, "I will do what I can."

After they had stayed a while and had a good meal, Mike took his tiny band home. Once there, he heated water, bathed them, put on their nightclothes, and put them, two each, in a bed. Rosie slept with Antonietta, and Connie slept with Lena. He hugged them for a long time. It was cold, and they giggled as he snuggled them.

He looked in on the girls a while later, then turned on the low radio to hear music. Sitting in the quiet with the soft broadcast, he heard the chugging train, the music, and the words to a popular song: *"I see a new horizon, my life has only begun, beyond the blue horizon, lies a rising sun."*

As if something had jolted him with a wire, he said aloud, "I will never give them up for adoption! I don't want anyone to split them up, and the only way I know no one will mistreat them is for me to raise them. Dear God," he cried, "please help my girls, even if I'm a wretched, worthless sinner. Please help me find a way!"

On Sunday morning, the woman from downstairs, Mrs. Perri, knocked on the door. "Do you need help getting the girls ready for the day?" she asked, smiling broadly. Catherine Perri had heard Mike's cries from downstairs the night before. She felt a deep empathy for those beautiful children. Childless herself, she hoped that he would offer one of them to her for adoption.

He opened the door and accepted her gracious offer with a nod. After the girls were all dressed and fed, she announced, "My husband and I are going to the noon mass at St. Mary's Cathedral. Mike, you and Raffaela always went to mass—now is not the time to stop. You and the girls need God's grace and peace."

He agreed. Mrs. Perri helped them put their coats on, and off they went. He had first felt angry with God for taking Raffaela. Then, Mike had self-flagellated in his belief that he had killed her. Now, two months after she was gone, he was mired in a quiet resignation filled with sadness and easy tears. During mass, Mike thought, *Dear Lord, I have to get hold of myself. I don't want to upset my girls more than they already are.*

Leaving mass, he ran into Mr. Bredice, the man who had saved his life when he drove him to the hospital after the chain-saw accident. Mr. Bredice was as polite as ever. He chatted with the girls first, then looked up at Mike and said, "How are you faring, Mr. Rizzo? It must be so hard with the young girls and you with one arm."

The empathy on his face made Mike confide in him, though it was uncharacteristic of Mike. He felt this man was kind, knowledgeable, and trustworthy. As he shared his desire to keep his daughters, Mr. Bredice nodded.

"There has to be someone," Mike said, "who could take care of them until the baby is a little older and Rosie is old enough to help me look after them and tend them when I'm at work."

Then, as if the heavens had heard him, Mr. Bredice had a brainstorm. "Mrs. Racanelli!" he said. "Frank Racanelli's widow lives on Aiken and Ward Street. I know she takes in children. The word is that she's competent. My sister is a schoolteacher, and there is a little boy in her class who lives there. She says he comes to school neat and clean and seems well-fed. You could talk to her."

Mike was filled with hope. "Thank you so much. God bless you. You are a good man," he said with a catch in his throat. Instead of walking home, Mike and his daughters walked straight to Mrs. Racanelli's house. He looked around at the grounds while knocking on the door. The house was big, with a large front porch and spacious property surrounding it.

"Yes?" said a very round woman as she opened the door.

"I've come to talk with you about boarding my children with you," Mike said.

"Are these the children?" Mrs. Racanelli asked. "They are lovely. Come on in, my dears."

The girls looked longingly at the swing in the spacious backyard with a sandbox in one corner. Inside was a room with a large table, books, and a few playthings. The girls were impressed by the surroundings but waited for their father's signal before touching anything.

"I run a very clean boardinghouse," said Mrs. Racanelli. "The girls will be fed, bathed, sleep, and go to school from here. I already have three other children I have taken in. They have to behave for me and do as I tell them. But because I have a daughter of my own who has a chronic illness, I don't have enough room to sleep four more; I can take only three of them."

"How much do you charge?" Mike asked, feeling certain it would be more than he could pay.

"It will cost you three dollars a week because the little one will be extra work."

He did a quick mental calculation. If she would take the youngest three, perhaps Rosie could stay with John and Antonietta. Rosie was already a great little helper; he thought Antonietta would appreciate having her.

If I can do this for a little while until I get on my feet, the state can't take them away, Mike thought.

"You can visit them every day if you like," the woman said. "On weekends, you can even take them home for a day or so, but I still charge the same."

They stood there in a very long silence. Mrs. Racanelli broke it. "If you want me to take over their care, bring them back tonight with all their clothes."

"No, not tonight. We will start next week," he said.

After they walked home, Mike spent the rest of the afternoon and evening playing games with the girls and listening to music on the radio. He made them dinner and ensured they cleaned up before going to bed. Then he sat with them as they said their prayers, and afterward he tucked them in.

Once they had fallen asleep, he also made his way into bed. It had been an exhausting three days. Before falling asleep, he crossed himself and prayed aloud, "Thank you, God, for sending me Mrs. Racanelli. I promise to take good care of my girls."

8

A PICTURE IS WORTH A THOUSAND WORDS

Godfrey Street, spring 1929

It was a spectacular Saturday morning in April, two weeks after Easter. Mike watched his girls play on the street with some of the younger neighborhood kids. Whenever they were outside, the girls were like honey; they attracted a swarm of bees. There were as many as a dozen kids with them most of the time. They seemed to have endless energy playing tag, hide-and-seek, and hopscotch.

He looked on and felt a glow of goodness wash over him as he relived the miracle of having them all together under one roof again. He had felt that way almost every day since they had come home. Rosie had been his comfort. She had pretty much been home with him all along, except for the first few months after their mother died, when she had stayed with Raffaela's brother John and his wife, Antonietta. As the oldest, Rosie was a great help to him. With her tiny body, hazel eyes, and sweet smile, she was like a little doll. But most of all, she was very well behaved, industrious, always pleasant and cheerful, and wise beyond her years. His oldest daughter had kept Mike sane through his most difficult struggles.

The three younger girls had remained at Mrs. Racanelli's until this past November, when an unexpected event caused him to take them home. He had planned to bring Lena, Connie, and Antonietta back home when Antonietta turned five on May 28 of this year. However, by the time he took them home, they had been at the foster home for fourteen months. Mrs. Racanelli had kept them safe and clean while he worked during that time.

Mrs. Racanelli's foster care was not cheap. He was trying to keep up the house payments, and work had been sporadic for him after Raffaela died. He had cried aloud one night when, despite his efforts, he found he did not have enough money to buy the children even a small doll for Christmas. He still couldn't afford a headstone marker for their mother's grave.

Their mother had been so talented. Her hands wove magic with bits of fabric and her tiny, neat stitches. She had sewn the girls' lovely dresses and homemade dolls and always seemed to bake a little delight for them.

The City's Children's Fund, however, had saved the day, stopping at Mrs. Racanelli's and delivering toys wrapped in bright paper. Mike held Mrs. Racanelli in very high regard. However, his second oldest, Lena, often complained because she was strict with them, but Mike realized the woman was not without a kind heart. He was most grateful to her. He was most appreciative that Mrs. Racanelli had never broken her promise not to lay a hand on them.

"If they are bad, you talk to me," he had emphasized. "You no hitta my girls."

She had been faithful to her word. She had never struck them, in an era when adults often administered corporal punishment to kids. Every Sunday he visited, he would bring some hard candy and take them for a walk. He would get the full report about everything from the past week without making them aware of what he was doing.

"She's so mean," Lena had said with her little hands on her hips.

"How's she mean?" he had questioned.

"Well, she's always saying, you come right back from school, and don't do this; do that. You all stay together when you walk to school. Do not dawdle. Come right home. Only walk on the sidewalk. Oooo, she's so bossy." Lena had mimicked her voice and her stance.

The girls were too young to understand, but Mike knew that Mrs. Racanelli was doing all she could to keep things going by raising foster children to keep up the payments and taxes on the property that her husband had purchased before he died. She had raised two kids of her own by keeping children for the state and others for several years.

Then, one Wednesday morning in November, Mrs. Racanelli's chronically ill daughter, Grace, committed suicide by plunging to her death in Healy's Pond near Aiken Street.

When police arrived to tell her what had happened, Mrs. Racanelli had become so distraught she fainted and collapsed in her dining room. Her face and nose were all smashed up, and she had trouble keeping her balance. When Mike heard the news, he went right away to swoop up his girls, whom some kind neighbors had taken into their home. The girls peppered their father with questions, but despite the tragedy, the best part was that they were going home together.

For every black cloud, a little sunshine pierces through. Mike and the girls had Christmas in their home on Godfrey Street. Right in the room where Connie and Antonietta had been born and where their mother had died. The Children's Christmas Fund had again brought presents, but this time, Mike had a little money to buy each of them a small token gift. He also shamed his brother-in-law Sal into purchasing a few new things for his little nieces.

Then, just after the New Year, Mike took them all to the photographer's studio, where they had their family photo taken. It was important to Mike that they record events in their lives because he had never ceased to wish he had even a photograph of his father to see what the man's face and eyes looked like.

During the photo sitting, Antonietta wanted to sit on his knee as she often did at home. So he let her climb up. She felt extra special because she was the baby. Connie, daughter number three, was very proud of her Mary Jane shoes: they were more stylish than her sisters' tie-ups. The two older girls huddled around, knowing he loved them all. He told them they were all beautiful no matter what they wore; he was happy they were delighted.

The last time he had had a photo taken was when Raffaela was alive. Then, they had just the two older girls, and she was expecting Connie. He loved reliving the short nine years he'd with his loving wife.

9

A BRUTAL SLAP

December 1930

Mike fought hard to tamp down his rage as he fled the rectory on West Avenue at almost a run toward Wall Street. He swallowed hard. He began thinking about what to do about his problem. Fleeting thoughts came and went. When the wisp of a solution appeared, his anger at the priest whom he addressed as Monsignor crowded it out.

As Mike descended toward Wall Street, a whipping frigid wind cut at his face and bare head. His thin jacket was suitable for early October, but it was no match for the arctic-like temperatures in Connecticut in December.

He realized he was angrier with himself than with the Irish priest. He should have known better. Nevertheless, his friend Jim, the local undertaker, had lulled him into thinking this was a workable option. Mike had tremendous respect and affection for his friend, so he acted on his guidance.

However, Mike had told Monsignor Finn in no uncertain terms that he would never set foot in his church again. Though delivered in a quiet voice, he felt the tugs of regret at his outburst.

Mike and his family had found St. Mary's, the second-oldest parish in the Bridgeport diocese, a comforting place. Since moving to Norwalk from South Norwalk in 1916, Mike had enjoyed the big organ and the beautiful stained-glass windows of the Irish-immigrant-built, Gothic-revival-style cathedral.

When he and Raffaela had planned to marry, it had been Mike's choice to leave South Norwalk, where most of the Italians in the area were ensconced, to move to an area of town and a church that he knew was an Irish domain. Despite horror stories he'd heard, he found several Irishmen who had been sincere and kind to him, so he accepted Jim's recommendation as valid for Italians and the Irish. Each of the four girls had been baptized at St. Mary's, even though most of the baptisms on any given month were Irish babies. And it sure was a beautiful church.

He struggled to remember what brought him to humble himself as he had this morning. The economic depression that made finding work nearly impossible was the world's doing, not theirs. Yet these innocent little girls were facing a winter without shoes. Mike had put cardboard in each of the four pairs twice. Now, there wasn't anything left to hold the cardboard in place, the soles almost gone. Antonietta's shoes were too small, and he continued to shove her feet into them. Her sisters were close to outgrowing theirs. He had hoped for more for his children than he had had, and he would be damned if they would ever go barefoot. He never let them, even in summer, though they complained at his insistence that they keep their shoes on.

Mike had overheard snippets of conversations among several men, all referencing the church's generosity, as he waited in line after line to inquire about possible jobs. Then he had confided in his friend Jim that he had no idea what he would do to get the girls the replacement shoes they needed.

Mike had pondered the information for weeks, hoping another solution would materialize. Then, when the thermometer took a nosedive, he mustered the courage to ask the church for money to buy his kids' shoes. Despite the odds, his determination to provide for his children was unwavering. He knew the Irish stuck together. The Irish discrimination against Italians was legendary.

He rationalized that the Irish priest would show compassion for the children he saw in the front pews at mass every Sunday. Rosie and Lena, the two oldest, had already received their First Holy Communion, The two younger ones were preparing and would receive the blessed sacrament next May. The third child, Connie, had commented that Monsignor had asked her her name a few Sundays ago. When she answered, "Concetta," he had said it was a beautiful name. Connie had remarked on how nice he was. To top it off, in Mike's mind, the church was undergoing a significant renovation during a monster economic depression; he felt sure they could spare a few dollars to help him.

He knocked at the front door, and when the housekeeper who opened the door asked what he wanted, he said, "I need to talk with the Monsignor." The housekeeper didn't even offer him a seat while he waited. Then, after almost thirty minutes of standing, she returned to say that Monsignor Finn would see him now.

The frail-looking clergyman asked him to sit in a wooden chair available for visitors. He wore a simple black cassock with a big cross hanging from his neck. He had a ring on one finger with a large red stone set high. The man's hands looked soft and delicate. The office had two walls with shelves filled with books. Mike thought about how wonderful it would be to read what was inside. The pastor sat behind an impressive desk made from solid wood. A crucifix hung on the wall facing Mike, reminding him that this wasn't the office of a vital businessman but rather the office of a man of God.

The Monsignor had seemed impatient as Mike tried to relay his predicament.

"Monsignor, my friend Jim Magner tells me you are a generous man who helps those in need," said Mike. He had decided he would not say anything about his arm, as the clergyman could see the empty sleeve on his jacket for himself. Mike didn't want anyone to feel sorry for him. He wanted something for his children. Something significant. He provided food for them in every way he knew how and a safe roof over their heads, but the shoes were eluding him. It was a terrible time.

Mike never got very far in his planned statement. Instead, the priest cut him off, saying in a heavy Irish brogue, "You got it wrong. I have no money to help you or your children with shoes, food, or anything else." The weight of the rejection hung like an albatross in the air, a stark reminder of the injustice Mike faced.

Stunned by the heartless manner in which the clergyman had delivered the words. Standing, Mike said, "You help those you want to help. God is watching, and he knows your sins."

The Monsignor responded, "You'd better leave now," perhaps afraid his visitor might strike him.

As he turned to go, Mike said, "You'll never see me set foot in your church again."

Now, embarrassed, angry, and humbled, he still had to figure out how to get four pairs of shoes for his girls. Anyone else besides Monsignor would have empathized with the four motherless girls and helped their father get the shoes they needed. Misgivings swirled in Mike's brain about not allowing Antonietta and Concetta to be adopted; he brushed the thoughts aside as quickly as they came. He couldn't bear the crushing thoughts that they might all have been separated.

But he could not buy them shoes. What kind of a father was he? During his fifteen-minute walk home, he figured out a plan. It, too, would involve asking for something, but it wouldn't be charity. He didn't want charity. He had made a mistake in coming to the church and was determined to rectify it on his terms.

The following Sunday, he walked the girls to church but didn't go in with them. He had said his prayers that morning and that night before going to sleep as he always did, but he had told God he couldn't go in and honor that sinful man who was posing as a man of God. Then, he asked for God's forgiveness.

10

A PUSHCART SAVES THE DAY

Springtime 1933

"Chocolate pop a nickel," hawked Mike right after he blew the squawk horn.

It got people's attention. He had parked himself near the baseball field on New Canaan Avenue. It had been a little more than two years since he had been performing the five-nights-a-week, Saturday- and Sunday-afternoon ritual of selling ice cream pops, gum, candy, and cigarettes at all the sports events at the fields in the Broad River section of town.

He had asked his brother-in-law John, the cobbler, to fashion a leather shoulder strap attached to the pushcart's right handle; he would sling it over his right shoulder when he needed to push the cart with his left hand. The wooden peddler's cart had two large front wheels with wire spokes and two sturdy wooden peg legs in the back. Inquiring at the bus depot, he had secured a coin machine like those worn by the bus drivers and strapped it to his waist.

Each afternoon during the warmer months, Mike would push his cart laden with sundry items down Godfrey Street to the Crystal Ice House on Crescent. After loading ice, he would walk up Commerce Street, over to Wall Street, then to Knight Street, where he bought ice cream from a Sealtest-owned company called Fro-Joy, forever linked with baseball because of its advertising in the late 1920s featuring Babe Ruth. Mike could cover the one-mile distance pretty quickly. Still, the real work was wheeling the weighty cart to his choice location on New Canaan Avenue. The walk was one and a half miles and took him forty minutes. Once he arrived, he unhooked the strap from his right shoulder and used his left arm to do all his work. With that one sturdy left hand, he served mothers, fathers, and kids the tasty chocolate-covered ice cream pops on a stick, kept firm by the ice he picked up each afternoon at Crystal Ice.

Alas, the games often went on until well after nine. By the time Mike walked home, pushing the cart up the hill, he would find the girls had gone to bed as he had instructed. On the nights he didn't sell all his creamy treats, he would wake them up. "Hurry, you gotta eat the ice cream before it melts."

Bleary-eyed, the girls would comply; they never ceased to enjoy it even though it was delivered a good hour after they had been asleep. They sat up and ate, sometimes more than one each. With chocolate smudges and happy faces, they went right back to sleep, their joy and contentment a warm glow in Mike's cold world.

During the winter months, he parked outside the few factories in the area—that was how he had started. Cigarettes, gum, and such were the favored items of those workers. On the winter days, he brought home enough to cover his expenses, some for groceries and a little something for the girls' needs—like shoes.

In better weather, his ice cream sales helped raise enough money to pay some of the utility bills and put toward the mortgage payments, which were his most considerable burden.

Mike recalled the day Monsignor Finn turned down his request for help getting shoes for his daughters. Dejected, he had begged God's help when the idea for the pushcart hit him like a thunderbolt. It was a moment of inspiration that changed his life. God had answered his request, telling him he had to be resourceful when things were bad.

He was doing okay since he put the pieces together, got the required food peddler's license, and paid back the cost of the cart made for him by the carriage house people. As a peddler at night, he could get work during the day on most days during the spring and summer. This spring, things were picking up. Each morning, he'd walk to the corner of Main and Wall streets and wait with a dozen other men for the job callouts. He often got assignments as a laborer.

He heard about President Roosevelt's New Deal Program on the radio. The president promised to get the country out of the depression by reforming banking laws and creating emergency work relief programs. The entire effort would bring jobs. For Norwalk, it meant new schools and a post office building, among other projects.

So far, Mike had worked on numerous projects, such as widening the sidewalks and digging ditches for the sewers and storm drains, and there was talk of more work to come. He felt sure good times were ahead.

After a long period of nothing, the work assignments were coming almost every week. Mike figured out he could manage if he worked at least two days. The workday ended at four-thirty p.m. He hustled to get all the supplies he needed for his cart and worked at least one ball game on those days. It was dark earlier in the spring and fall, and if he worked, he skipped the ice cream offering because he couldn't get the ice and the confection and get to the field in time to do any business. He would focus on the sundries. He could work several ball games on Saturday and Sunday, his most lucrative days.

He often heard shouts, "Hey, Mike," "Good to see you!" "Do you have any Fro-Joy pops today?"

"Thank you, Mister Mike," two little boys said in a chorus as they unwrapped the ice cream pops their mother had purchased.

"We missed you at last night's game," said Mrs. Ruta, the mother of a large brood of boys. He had become a well-known figure at those events. He was grateful for the cheer he seemed to bring others, and the small profits were like a treasure, assuaging his great need to provide for his four daughters.

After his upsetting encounter with the Monsignor, he swallowed his pride and visited his brother-in-law Sal. He had shamed Sal into buying all the girls their communion dresses and lending him the money for their shoes. After two months of selling the small items from his cart as the factories let out at lunchtime and for the evening, he had earned enough to repay Sal for the girls' communion shoes.

Rosie had always been a bit frail; she was often sick, and he worried about her health. He made sure to buy fresh fruit during the winter months, and his garden in the backyard, which had always been a source of enjoyment for him, was a lifeline that provided manna from heaven with fresh vegetables for them. He worked on it as much as he could, and the girls helped, but it wasn't easy to do more with the need to look for a job every day.

Despite the summer garden, there were things he could not plant, like bananas. He bought his girls fresh bananas whenever he could after the woman principal of the high school told him that growing girls needed the vitamins they contained. The girls loved them and soon discovered that not everyone had them. Bananas were an extravagance. It wasn't often that the girls had something others did not.

"We have fresh bananas" became the girls' favorite line to say aloud to their friends and acquaintances for others to overhear at school.

He kept the girls' hair very short. With the other three watching and making signs showing that it was very short, the one seated under the scissors often cried or sat petrified.

He reminded them, "*Sta sodo*—be still." He didn't want them to be unhappy, but he had to keep them all looking neat. Most of all, he had to prevent them from getting the dreaded lice bugs and being quarantined. That would be a horrible ordeal, and one sure to have the authorities look in on him to ensure he was not being negligent. He lived with the ever-present fear that they might take his children away. Lice would be a signal for the schools to send a social worker.

With his one hand and well-sharpened scissors, he trimmed their hair straight and washed their hair every day in the kitchen sink.

It had been an adjustment after losing his right arm, but he had learned to do everything, including tying his shoes, that he had done before as a right-handed person with two limbs. He felt bad because the girls were home alone quite a lot. He had admonished them never to leave the house at night and never to open the door for anyone.

He was very thankful to God that they always obeyed him.

11

THE OLD LAMPLIGHTER AND HIS LITTLE BAND OF PRINCESSES

November 1934

"Papa, we're freezing," they said at the same time as a chorus.

He looked at their bare hands, which were pink, so he said, "Just a little bit longer."

They huddled as he lifted the cap on the lamp to expose the wick, and his two oldest daughters cupped their hands around so Mike could light it. Then, he placed the cap on and set it down. When they had helped him light four lamps, he dragged the sawhorse across the road to block off half the street, then carried the wooden ladder and propped it against the first post.

Hurrying back to where the girls were, he took the two lanterns into one hand over to the post. Placing one lantern on the ground, he climbed up the ladder, holding the other lamp in his hand while holding onto the ladder at the same time. That one hung; he scurried back down the ladder, carried it across the street, set it against the post, and repeated going up the ladder with the lantern in hand. Returning to the girls, he repeated the process a few more times while they waited.

Mike had been at this lamplighter job for about five months now, and it was going well doing it alone. But on the windy nights, he would wait until the two little ones had fallen asleep and take Rosie and Lena with him. Then, they would lock the door, alerting Mrs. Perri in the apartment downstairs that they would be out for a few hours and to keep an eye and ear out for the younger girls. He wanted to be sure she knew they were up there alone in case of a fire. On those windy evenings, Rosie and Lena helped him protect the flame from the wind, because with one hand he could not light it and shield it at the same time. Evenings like tonight were typical. After the girls had helped him keep the flame from going out, he would turn the wick up with precision and proceed to hang the lanterns.

His section of responsibility was Main Avenue from the end of their street at the corner of Godfrey up to the Winnipauk section , just beyond Broad Street. When they did the lamp at the corner of Main and Broad, he would remind them in a soft voice, "Your mother is buried right back there in St. Mary's Cemetery," pointing down the road.

Mike knew that the entire state of Connecticut was converting to electricity. In Norwalk, electricity was, for the most part, used to run the trolley lines now. Still, the area's electrification was occurring at a rapid pace, and this job would be gone soon, too.

"Keep your hands in your pockets tilla I come a-back," he instructed as he hung the most recent lit lamps. Stamping their feet and jumping up and down, Lena and Rosie joked as they watched their Papa in the distance.

"What do you think, Ro? Have we had enough? Let's tell Papa we can't stand the cold any longer. He'll feel bad and let us go home," Lena said, a look of mischief on her face, her teeth chattering from the cold.

"No. We have to help. Papa can't do it alone; it's too windy. Yes, it's cold, but not that cold. Besides, we have only a little more to go, and we'll be done," came Rosie's quick retort, her voice firm and resolute.

Overhearing part of the conversation as he was walking back, Mike felt himself crumbling. They were just little girls. Why did he need their help? He accepted the job because he needed it and assured the boss he could do it. Yet he had failed to figure out how to do this job on windy nights without the girls' help.

He was determined to keep them together; he hoped they would understand when they were a little older. Work was scarce due to the terrible economic depression plaguing the entire country. He had lost all his savings in the bank run in 1930. The bank had closed where he had had his $400 in savings. It had been a devastating blow. After that bank run, job opportunities shriveled, and he found himself behind on his mortgage payments. Often, his tenants didn't have the money to pay him either. He understood. They were struggling, too.

During the worst of the past few years, Mr. Chase, from whom he had bought the house and who held his note, had been more than patient.

Mike remembered his embarrassment when he came to the house and said, "Mike, you didn't send my payment." Feeling ashamed, Mike said, "I don't have it, but I getta to you next month." He was grateful for the man's kindness when the mortgage holder said, "I know it's tough times." He agreed to wait yet another month for the bi-annual payment.

Hurrying as much as he could, he checked the color of the children's hands; he still saw pink. He checked often, and as soon as it looked like their hands were pale, he would tell them to scurry back home.

This job had been a godsend. Mike scrounged for work, doing whatever he could. Often, there were periods when he could find nothing. It was so ironic. He had saved enough, and the girls had grown up enough that he was able to get them all home again. Then the stock market crash dealt him yet another blow, setting him back.

Now, as they were getting close to finishing, he noticed that Rosie had gotten quiet. He didn't know what she was thinking, but he guessed.

As they repeated the process several times along the last stretch of Main Street, he remembered how she had seen him, head in hand, crying in the kitchen when her mother was alive after his accident. He had been pitiful. Rosie was old enough to remember the aftermath of his accident and amputation. He remembered her worried face when he watched her at lunchtime in the school yard after their mother died. She came over to him each time. He would pat her head, her eyes responding to his love.

As he turned to walk toward them, they were facing away from him, and he overheard Rosie talking to her sister.

"Lena, I won't complain to Papa about the cold anymore. After all, he doesn't complain. He could have sent all of us to the children's home," she said, sounding like an older woman with years of experience. "You know he never said so to us, but I heard the grownups talking when they came to visit after our mother died."

Lena remained quiet.

As they made their way home that night, Rosie said nothing to anyone in particular, but loud enough for her Papa and sister to hear.

"Papa, the old lamplighter, and we're his little band of princesses!"

12

ROSIE GOES OUT TO WORK

Fall 1935

It was Sunday morning, one of those bleak fall days with gray-white clouds and the sun nowhere to be found. The stump that was his right arm throbbed, so he knew it would rain at some point.

He worried about Rosie. She was such a tiny creature. At sixteen, she carried the weight of the world. His oldest child was now a woman. She had stayed with him after her mother died; she was eight years old when she had to assume the role of mother for the other three, all so little. Rosie was much like her mother; she was not very social and outgoing but tenderhearted, organized, and thoughtful.

He had found Rosie a job in a garment factory in South Norwalk. He felt terrible that she had to leave school, but at sixteen, she could read and write better than many people with much more education. The teacher told him she also had beautiful penmanship, to which he answered: "Like her mother."

She had to help him, though. It was critical for their family's well-being and her future. He had to find a way to save up so he could someday provide for the girls' weddings.

Rosie had told him the work was hard. In some ways, she was hearty and, in others, frail. He was scared that she might fall ill or that something might happen to her. There were so many frightening stories of what went on in those factories. Each night, he pried gently so his daughter wouldn't know. He was intent on getting information on what had transpired during the day.

Today, before leaving with her sisters for mass, Rosie confessed that the factory's owners had made her uncomfortable on Friday. The boss lady had asked Rosie to model a full-length slip. The woman had told Rosie, "A man will come in and look at you to see how the sample fits because you have a model's-sized body." Seeing the distress on Rosie's face, the woman had promised that the man would not touch her or the garment in any way.

Rosie told Papa, "It was just as the woman had said; the man did not touch me or the slip, and the boss lady was there the entire time while the man checked to see how the slip fit me; he asked me to turn around for them several times. But, Papa, I was so uncomfortable to have a strange man stare at me when I was wearing just a slip!" Rosie sobbed.

Regardless of the purpose or intentions, it was apparent that this had been quite distressing for Rosie. Mike was furious. She was supposed to be boxing clothing, not modeling. He struggled with his thoughts. She was so pretty, and with her tiny, perfectly formed, full-figured body, they might call on her other times to model. He could not put his daughter in harm's way. He pondered the situation. Was it harm? Had the company owners' actions been a glimpse of bolder things to come? "Dear God, what should I do?" he gasped. "I have gotten them this far."

Now that they were sixteen, fifteen, thirteen, and eleven, he had even more to worry about. They were all now maidens and could get pregnant. How could he talk to them about such things?

After Rosie had learned the essential facts from the four girls across the street, who were just a little older than she was, she had passed them on to her sisters as their time came. Lena had been the first to get her period. She had cried aloud, screaming, "I'm bleeding to death." Rosie went to her in a flash and explained.

Mike had kept quiet. He didn't know how he was supposed to respond. Rosie thought she was keeping all this from him, but their Papa knew everything, though he never let on. Mike knew they needed their privacy despite the tiny living quarters.

Each sister had one-half of a drawer in the chest that all four shared. There would be more for them once they all went to work. Then, they could buy some nicer clothes to attract a good young man. For his part, Mike focused on keeping them safe, feeding them, and providing them with a constant in their lives—unconditional parental love. He instilled the values he knew—honesty, industriousness, being polite, and, above all, for them to do well in school; what he wouldn't have given to have gone to school.

He often said, "Someday, when my girls are all grown, I will ask the teacher on West Avenue to 'learn' me to read and write."

He dozed off with his head on his hand, and when it dropped, he awoke startled. He thought he had felt Raffaela's hand on his head. She had told him he was doing good for their children. He felt a single tear slide down his cheek. He got up and walked down the flight of stairs outside to wait for the girls to return from mass. He had made his decision, and when they arrived with the red on their cheeks like poster paint and their smiles and hair all aglow, they brightened everything despite the dismal day.

That night, he told Rosie, "You donna go to that job anymore. Tomorrow, I'll find you a new job."

Rosie was pleased but didn't reveal her elation except to say, "Yes, Papa." She had been afraid to tell him, but knew she should.

Now, she recognized that no matter what, she couldn't keep anything from Papa. She was Papa's favorite. Though he had never said so, she had always known that. Papa held her hand when she was sick. He had patted her head when she played in the school yard while she was staying with Zio Giovanni and Zia Antonietta after Mama died.

Papa would call her over and ask how they were treating her. He looked so skinny and so sad then. She wanted to tell him how awful it was to be apart from him and her sisters, but she didn't then. She knew he would keep his promise.

"I'm gonna take you home soon," he had assured her after she stayed only briefly with her aunt and uncle. "You gotta stay there because you and your sisters are little. I have to work, and no one is home to take care of you."

True to his word, Rosie came home first to be with him again. Then, after about a year, the others came home. In the interim, he had gone almost every night to check on them. While it was only about a mile and a half away, without a car and with his very late hours from watchman work and other odd jobs, he often came home well after ten p.m. During those fourteen months, on Sundays, he always took Rosie to visit her sisters.

Yes, Papa had always kept his promises. She could count on him. In the morning, they went to look for a new place for Rosie to work. Riding the bus, they exchanged very few words, but she smiled at him, and he smiled back. He was so proud of her.

13

A SHORT-LIVED GROCERY

December 1935

It had been a bleak year, even worse than the past one for work. Mike had started a small grocery store in the spring to earn money, figuring everyone needed to buy food. Right along Main Avenue, the location was perfect. In an empty storefront on the corner of Main and School streets, he'd worked out a deal with his brother-in-law, who owned the building.

Appealing to Sal's love for his sister's children, Mike had asked if he could have the space for free because it had been empty for a long time. Mike didn't see any prospects coming for it anytime soon. However, when Sal insisted on ten percent of his earnings, Mike said okay; he didn't want charity.

He also worked out a deal with a supply house for the foodstuffs. The girls helped him stock shelves and bag groceries. Everybody who came in fell in love with his four charming beauties. Things went well throughout the summer. In early September, the girls went back to school, and though it was just a hop across from the school yard, they had schoolwork to do in the afternoons. They were great helpers on Saturday. Everything was closed on Sundays following Connecticut's blue laws.

Over time, more and more people came who wanted to buy on credit. Mike felt sorry for them. Money was scarce. They appealed to him with their hungry children in line, and he was a softy. By the time November rolled around, he was in trouble. The extended credit didn't come in, and he needed to pay his supplier.

He realized those who did pay could not earn him enough to cover those who couldn't. He operated another month, saying, "Sorry, no credit." Then he remained open for one more month, until he sold everything he had, paid his debts, and shut down the small grocery store.

In mid-December, when the woman from Children and Family Services came to do a home visit, she told him she would put all the girls' names into the Children's Christmas Fund. They would all get presents, even Rosie, who was now sixteen and working. The social worker had said, "We will keep tabs until your daughters are eighteen."

He remembered the year that Rosie had learned in school that you needed to hang stockings so Santa would come. Not knowing any better, she had strung four of his large socks on a line tacked from one end of a corner of the kitchen to the other. The poor child hadn't realized the kerosene stove would set them on fire and burn in a flash. Mike's heart ached at the innocence of his daughter's mistake, a mistake born out of her pure belief in Santa.

"You're gonna burn the house down," he scolded. "What are you thinking, Rosie? You know better."

"But, Papa, they told us at school that Santa Claus will come if we hang our stockings. Santa can't come to bring us something without them," she sobbed.

Mike had pulled the stockings down while thinking that if he hadn't come home early, they would not have been able to avoid the disaster.

After removing the hazard, he found Rosie lying on her bed. He hugged her and said, "You gotta keep vigilant about fire. The stove could have burned those stockings, and the smoke could have killed you all.

"You're gonna have some presents. Santa Claus doesn't need the stockings. You are very special girls; he's a-gonna find you."

Now, with the girls asleep and the radio playing music with the volume dial set at the lowest level, he found himself weeping as he sat alone by the window, looking out at the snow-covered street. His heart was heavy with the weight of his responsibilities, and the fear of not being able to provide for his daughters was a constant companion.

He learned from a neighbor that the girls had sat by the window, playing with a candle for the past week, watching other kids out on the street below in the snow. He had told them they must remain inside when he wasn't home. Obeying his rule, they played with a lighted candle in the window—even though he told them the fire was dangerous. He feared a fire more than anything. He had watched a house off of Main Avenue burn to ashes because of a knocked-over candle not too long ago. He had told them how important it was to be sure the candle was out when they stepped away from it. His concern for their safety was palpable.

Sometimes, on Sunday afternoons in the summer, before he would head out to ply the crowd at the ball games with his pushcart, the girls would beg him for money to go to the movies. It was an extravagance; his usual first answer was, *"Lasciami stare."* The girls had gotten used to his Calabrian dialect phrase for "leave me alone."

They would keep pestering him until he gave in. "Papa, it costs less on Sunday for the early show." Then, as he put the four quarters on the kitchen table, they would grab the coins and run out, yelling, "Thank you, Papa!"

At the same time, he reminded them in a forceful voice, "Watch out for the train and always stay together!"

They were growing up so fast. Soon, they would be young ladies. He wondered who would talk with them about the things women talk about when it was time to marry, the kind of things a mother says to her daughter when the time comes. He reminded them never to go anywhere or with anyone alone and that all four needed to stay together wherever they went. He implored the neighbors to keep an eye out for them. Then, a frightening thought occurred—he needed to start thinking about when it came time for them to marry. They were beautiful, thoughtful, and engaging, and, no doubt, they would find husbands worthy of them. *Will I have the means to give them a proper wedding?* He wondered.

As worry swelled within him, he thought, *There's time enough to make it happen. There are more important matters ahead of that now. I will think about it another day.* But his love for them was unwavering, and he would do everything in his power to ensure their happiness and safety.

14

ORIGIN OF A ONE-ARMED HOUSEPAINTER

Early spring 1936

The shop was empty as Mike walked to the counter. He spotted the owner of the Brandman paint store on Main Street and waited until he caught the man's eye. Mike went late in the day, when he knew the shop would be slow.

Brandman was a good man who had seen Mike many times around town, digging and shoveling ditches or lighting lamps. The store owner had often seen the one-armed man walking into downtown Norwalk with at least a couple of his four daughters. Brandman also knew Mike because the man had run a small grocery store in the neighborhood for about a year, though it was now closed. He had stopped there several times to pick up something for his wife. He remembered the shop was not well stocked, but it did have the essentials. It was clear someone without any capital put it together to get it going.

Mike caught Brandman's eye, removed his hat, and asked, "How are you?"

"Can't complain," he responded a little petulantly.

"I've been working lots of different jobs around town with the WPA," said Mike matter-of-factly. "At one of the schools, I was the cleanup man for the guys painting the building inside. They make good money, and they work only eight hours a day.

"I think I can do this painting pretty well. After the painters went home,

I tried it on the walls they hadn't painted yet. My hand is very steady. I'm strong, but I don't know how to mix colors. I was hoping you could learn me something about it," he said with humility.

"Mike, you would do well at painting on someone's crew, but if you do this alone, you have to deal with ladders, brushes, paint cans, and the lids. There are many things involved that, with all respect, you might have trouble with," the store owner said in a compassionate tone.

"You mean because of me having one arm? I can manage the ladders and everything, but I don't know how to mix the colors. I know lots of people who need someone to paint for cheap. I don't charge much. I know I can get work."

Brandman thought for a few minutes. "Well, the colors are the least of what you need to worry about. I can help you with that. You take this card with the paint samples, and when your customer picks the color they want, you bring it to me, and we will mix it up to make it just like the sample picture here."

Mike nodded that he understood.

"The outside paint is made to resist the weather," Brandman told him. "The colors available are different. With exterior work, you sometimes have to scrape off any peeling old paint. You often have to sand it smooth, then cover that sanded finish with what's known as a primer. The primer will even everything out, and then you will apply the paint. Most often, you will need two coats for old houses. You can also price the job based on the number of coats a customer wants. If they have two coats outside and use the good paints I sell, they will not need painting again for a very long time.

"Here," he said, "these brochures are for outside paint." He handed Mike two cards with color squares ranging from two shades of white to dark blues. "You'll need paint remover for spills and splatters. I'm sure if you watched the crews at the schools, you saw how they put down a drop cloth and covered the floors. When painting the outside, you must be careful not to lean your ladder against critical items like electrical wires and windows.

"We can sell you everything you need right here. But you'll have to pay cash. With all the supplies you must buy, you will probably have to get your money up front from your customer. Otherwise, it's a pretty big cash outlay."

Mike had listened, committing all to memory, then asked, "Is the paint always here, or do I have to order ahead?"

"Except for very unusual requests, you can get everything the day before you start painting. We deliver only to huge contractors. However, when you buy your ladders and equipment, we can deliver them all for a small charge."

"Appreciate a lot," said Mike, thanking the man numerous times as he left the shop.

Once outside, he put his hat on and walked from the store to Godfrey Street. He stopped at the Bernards' home on the corner of his street to talk to them about painting their house. He had noticed it looked bad from the outside.

"Mr. Bernard," he said, "I do a good job for you."

"How much do you want?" replied the homeowner.

Mike had no idea how much to charge. "What do you think the job is worth and how much you wanna pay?" he replied. Then he went on to impart his new knowledge as if he had done this work forever.

They agreed on fifty dollars for Mike, plus the actual cost of the paint. Mike said he could start on the following Saturday, and he would stop by on Thursday and pick up the cash to buy the paint.

After showing his neighbor the color sheets, Mike said, "You and your wife look at 'em for a coupla days. Then, you tell me what color you wanna when I come to get the money to buy the paint."

He walked up the hill to his own house, thinking, *Now, I just have to figure out how far one bucket of paint goes. I don't wanna buy too much and have a lotta left over.*

It never occurred to Mike that he couldn't do the job.

15

A VERY SMART DAUGHTER QUITS SCHOOL

Summer 1938

Disappointment. It was a mild way to describe what Mike was feeling. He didn't want to force his daughters to do anything, but he had hoped that all of them would graduate from high school; he always regretted pulling Rosie out. They were all smart. The teachers had told him often that they had excellent penmanship. "Always respectful, and they do their work, and learn quickly," the principal had told him.

Connie was telling him she was not returning to school in September. With just one more year to graduation, he could not believe it. When he came home from a painting job in June on the last day of school, she shared her news with him.

"I quit," she stated nonchalantly. "Papa, the teacher made me so mad. Two months ago, Mrs. Bushnell, my economics teacher, said I could help her clean up after school 'cause I don't have to catch the bus like many other kids. I said no because it would have been dark when I walked home from West Avenue. Now, she gave me a zero as my grade! I did all the assigned work in class, and I did well. How can she do that?"

Before Mike could speak, she said, "Rosie is working, and so is Lena—I want to buy myself nice clothes. The people at Amherst Knitwear, across from the butcher shop, are looking for help and said they would hire me. I start next week!"

He couldn't fault her. She had found a job; she had a plan and was smart. He recalled how she had recited the entire Gettysburg Address that President Lincoln gave during the Civil War; she also recited for her dad the preamble to the Constitution and the Declaration of Independence, and several passages from Shakespeare. She had a keen nose for news and history, as he did. They often listened to the news together and discussed the day's topics. The only difference was that his daughter could read and write. He couldn't hold a candle to her reasoning.

He remembered the morning she went off to work for her first day. It was a beautiful June day. Connie was excited about her independence. She was a working girl now. That evening, she shared that she had reported to work early, and the owner was very impressed. She was assigned to work with the cutters, who gave her fabric all jumbled in bins. Her job was to sort them by color and bundle them together.

As summer was winding up and a few leaves were already falling, Connie confronted her father as he walked up the drive. He knew she wanted to get something off her chest, so he pulled up a chair outside and sat near the barrels he had filled with water to swell in preparation for the winemaking that would take place as soon as the grapes arrived from California. He pulled one over for her, but she didn't want to sit.

"Papa, yesterday I was thinking about the carefree time I had spent the past summers; I had so much fun those summers at the playground. I wished I were outside. I know I was daydreaming because all of a sudden, I couldn't remember the instructions about the fabric in the bins. Some days, I have to do different things with them. I did what I thought I was supposed to, just like the last few days. But when I got to work this morning, I was in trouble.

"The boss lady yelled at me, saying I had mixed up all the colors. She said she had spied on me from the back and saw me looking out the windows," Connie ran on. "I said just one thing to her, 'I guess you don't want me here anymore.' So I walked home with my face looking up to soak in the sun. I didn't like the people at Amherst anyway."

Mike looked at her and understood. But he was worried about how she had left it with the employer. Recognizing the look on her father's face, Connie added, "Papa, don't worry, I was respectful. I said, 'Thank you.'"

"Papa, I'll find another job," she emphasized.

"I know," was all he said.

Within a month, Connie worked at Frederick-Speier Footwear on Muller Street in Winnipauk, off Broad Street. "Papa, I love it. The minute I walked in, it felt like home. And Mrs. Spires is a wonderful person, and some of my friends work there, and a cute boy named Babe Rasmussen sits opposite me in the workroom. I operate the cement machine. Babe has graduated already."

Mike sat back and enjoyed the descending day and listening to his daughter. He had spent many years worried about all four of them. As he gazed out at the sky, turning a kaleidoscope of scarlet, orange, and yellow, he realized that, while they each looked, in one way or another, like their mother, they were a lot like him.

16

THE BIG BAND SOUNDS

Rowayton, Connecticut, summer 1939

The atmosphere was electric as the sounds wafting from the big structure at Roton Point served as giant magnets pulling them in. The girls had just stepped off the trolley, an investment of forty cents for the four of them. This extravagance was thrilling. They burst onto the bustling scene like gulls to a fish lying on the beach. They had arrived at the prettiest park on Long Island Sound. While less than six miles across town to the Rowayton section, it was a big deal if you didn't drive a car. They felt fortunate that the trolley ran every twenty minutes.

"Remember what Papa said," Rosie cautioned. "We have to stick together, at least two of us."

Connie turned to Antonietta and grinned. "Ann, you stick with me because I want to ride the Skylark roller coaster, and Rosie's a chicken." Making a face at their younger sister, Rosie and Lena strode off arm in arm, headed for the arcade.

During the summer months, steamers from New York City brought escapees from the city's summer heat to enjoy the beach, amusements, and music.

It was a Friday night in late August. They knew to stay away on Saturday because the park would host the Miss Connecticut pageant. Last year, 12,000 people from New York came to the pageant night. The pageant winner here would compete in the Miss America contest in Atlantic City, New Jersey, in September. The Roton pageant ticket cost was out of their reach, so the sisters consoled each other with comments about not wanting to outshine the contestants.

The boys who lived on their street said the four sisters were far prettier than any girls in the beauty contest. Lena joked that if pinching pennies, tending house, or gardening could serve as a talent, then any one of them could be a winner without a doubt, as none of the four had had any ballet, voice, or baton lessons to display during the talent portion of the competition.

Two weeks before, the girls had come on a Saturday night and walked around, played games, and listened as the sounds of Duke Ellington from the pavilion skipped across the water to their ears. They came to hear Tommy Dorsey, the Duke, and so many others who played regularly in the pavilion during the summer months.

The day had been warm, but now, with the cool breezes by the sea, the girls forgot the heat and enjoyed the music while they hoped some cute boys they had met earlier would appear as they promised.

While Lena was always meticulous about her attire, tonight she took greater care to doll up because she had met a fellow named Frank a few weeks before. He had dropped hints to suggest that he and his friends were coming to Roton Point on Friday night. Lena was tingling with anticipation.

As the pairs of sisters reunited at the concession stand after an hour of perusing and playing the amusements, someone yelled to them, "Hey, Ritzzo sisters!"

They turned, and there was the tall, handsome Frank Casavecchi with at least four other cute guys with him.

The young people spent the remainder of the evening laughing and dancing to the distant music and engaging in gentle flirting. It was clear that Lena's magnetic smile had a hypnotic effect on Frank. Of the four, she was the most into fashion and concerned about her appearance. Frank appreciated her efforts.

At ten-thirty p.m., Rosie reminded everyone they needed to catch the trolley. With a sad face, Frank said, "Guess there's too many of us for me to give you all a ride." He pecked Lena on the cheek and said, "Hope to see you again soon." Without saying a word, her enchanting smile said all he wanted to hear.

17

HERE COME THE BRIDES

April 1940

"Papa, did you get yourself fitted for the tuxedo?" asked Lena in a taut voice.

"I went last week."

"Well, don't forget you must pick up the suit on Thursday. The rehearsal at the church is on Friday night at six. You have to be there."

Mike scrutinized his second daughter with an eagle's eye. She had been terse and bossy for the past couple of weeks, but he understood her apprehension. She and Frank were getting married on Saturday. After all the preparations, the big day was less than a week away. Still, he wanted his fun-loving, smiling Lena back. He hoped her prenuptial jitters would disappear by the time of the ceremony.

Lena had met Frank in 1939 when she and Rosie worked in the factory on the third floor of the Centennial building on West Avenue. Frank had gone to the dentist located in the building where they worked. As the sisters, with a friend, waited for the bus, Frank had driven by in his brand-new '39 gray Chevy and asked them if they wanted a ride. Since they were all three together, the girls said yes.

During the ride to Godfrey Street, they asked him a million questions. Though blue-eyed, blond, tall, and fair, they discovered he was Italian, and they all thought he was cute. As he dropped them off, he asked Lena for a date.

She had said, "Only if one of my sisters comes along." He was charmed and, without a second thought, agreed. So, he brought his friend Buddy with him, and she brought her sister Connie. Together, the four had gone for a drive to watch the planes take off from West Rocks airfield.

"We had a lot of fun," announced Connie upon their return.

The relationship took off quickly after the girls met him and his friends at Roton Point; from then on, Frank took Lena and at least one of her sisters out in his new car to dances, movies, and the amusement park.

Frank was an apprentice carpenter and an industrious worker. Mike liked that. To his daughters, Mike seemed calm about Lena's impending marriage to the young man.

He had met Mr. and Mrs. Casavecchi when they became engaged. The Casavecchi family, who had emigrated from Northern Italy to America, was educated. The father, who had a humorous personality, was also a wise businessman. Because he had bought real estate, they were very comfortable despite having five daughters.

When he met with the parents, Mike did what he was supposed to do. He offered to pay for half the wedding. Italian people were big on that. He was also supposed to buy the bride's dress and pay for the cake and the band. He and his daughters had been saving for this day. The girls had all learned to save their money for the time they would get married, since they started working.

In the past few years, Mike had become significantly more financially comfortable due to his house painting business and the ability to rent his properties to tenants who could afford the rent. He still worked as hard as ever and never spent money frivolously. He didn't drink or gamble. His vices were making homemade wine and playing cards at the San Rocco Society club once a month. There, the antes were pennies, and big pots were quarters.

He was trying to imagine what life would be like with one of the four missing. Lena had been gone a lot over the past six months. She had been spending an enormous amount of time with Frank's family. Lena had become close to Frank's sisters. She had chosen only Rosie, among her sisters, to serve in her bridal party. Rosie would be the maid of honor as the oldest. The younger sisters, who also adored Lena, had understood. Still, it stung Mike that Lena had not included all of his daughters in the wedding party. Nevertheless, he kept his mouth shut. He watched the sisters' exchanges and saw it was all playing out just fine.

However, it hadn't escaped his daughters' notice that none of Frank's family ever came to their house. It seemed that neither Frank nor his sisters felt this end of town was good enough for them. His daughters thought the Casavecchis considered themselves to be of a different class.

Mike didn't quite understand that assessment. He waited for the invitation to their home to meet them; since it never came, he had invited himself to meet the parents about six months ago. Upon his return from the due diligence visit, his three other daughters, curious about their future brother-in-law's family, pressed him for details.

He shared his observation that Frank's father enjoyed his drink but was comical and pleasant. The man had joked that he would chew garlic when driving, so if the cops stopped him, they couldn't smell the liquor. Mike thought the father was a bit "old-fashioned" Italian but very nice. Frank's mother was a quiet, large, handsome woman with her hair braided at the nape of her neck in the old Italian style. He admonished his daughters for their assessment because he had found Frank's parents pleasant, down-to-earth people.

He chalked up Frank's sisters not coming to the Ritzzo home as having been indulged too much. Maybe the Casavecchi daughters didn't want to be associated with anything they felt was "*guinea*." With their father owning multiple houses and land in another town, perhaps they thought they were a landed gentry.

But, according to his daughters, who often spoke about how they missed their sister now that she spent all her time at her future in-laws' home, Lena's sisters-in-law-to-be all put on airs, and that's why only Rosie was going to be in the wedding.

Mike wasn't worried about any of it. He was sure he knew how Frank felt about his daughter. It was clear he adored her. His biggest worry was accompanying his daughter down the aisle without crying.

The morning of the wedding was exciting as the girls all helped Lena get dressed. She looked dazzling. That morning, she was acting like herself again. Suddenly, she blurted out with tears in her eyes, "I'm going to miss you all so much."

To prevent a crying fest, her sisters joked. "Oh, you'll have all the nice clothes you've always wanted; you're marrying into money. You won't miss us!"

Mike had hired a car to pick them up at the house and take them to the church. Assembled in the church's narthex, with the grandeur of the organ music, coupled with the white lilies adorning the altar, he choked up seeing Rosie, attired in her maid of honor finery, poised to process down the aisle ahead of them. As Mike moved forward with Lena on his arm, he gazed at the scene with friends and family filling the pews and realized how blessed he was. As he walked his daughter to the altar, he prayed to God and all the saints that Frank would treat his daughter well and that she would be happy.

At the altar, tears sprang into his eyes as he lifted Lena's veil and kissed her cheek. It was the beginning of a new phase in his family's life, the natural order of God's plan unfolding. He knew Lena was embarking on her path as a wife; the others would soon follow. He felt a swell of gratitude to God for everything. And, somehow, he got through this gut-wrenching ordeal of letting his child go without embarrassing himself or his daughter.

Rosie had been dating Steve Mola for a while. Steve was one of eight boys; he had just one sister. As they prepared for the November 20, 1941, marriage, Mike found dealing with his eldest daughter's fiancé's family pleasant. He had known Mr. Mola for several years. He was a barber at a shop in Norwalk, where Mike went once in a while to get his hair cut.

From the Southern Italian province of Salerno, the Molas were warm and friendly people. Steve's uncles were also barbers, and a few of Steve's older brothers also wielded the scissors. The plan was that when Rosie and Steve married, they would live in an apartment in the house on Godfrey Street.

When Rosie took Mike for his tuxedo fitting for the wedding, she shared what her sister had told them when they were last together: "Frank is wonderful, but I'm not too happy living here. I can't tell you how many times I've wanted to return home with all of you."

The Molas had been happy to have Mike pay for half of the wedding. Lena would be the matron of honor, reciprocating for Rosie standing up for her. For many years now, all the sisters called Antonietta "Ann." Connie and Ann would also be part of Rosie's bridal party.

Mike looked forward to seeing all four of his beautiful girls dressed in finery at the altar at St. Mary's Church and the big celebration party after the ceremony at St. Ann's Hall on Ely Avenue. Invitations went out to about 200 Italians for the big event. The Molas knew half the town.

Now, with the wedding day here, Rosie looked exquisite.

"Time to walka my number one daughter down the aisle," he told her.

Standing beside Rosie in the back of the cathedral, waiting to proceed down the aisle, he thought about how this tiny person, his oldest daughter, who wasn't quite five feet tall, had been a pillar of strength. At the altar, he lifted her veil and kissed his precious daughter. He saw her mother in her face, and though he intended to avoid tears, he could not control his own. He turned into the front right pew, where he sat alone, watching the tableau at the altar with all four of his gorgeous and generous daughters in finery that Mike could never have imagined when he was a boy growing up in Platania.

He made the sign of the cross with his left hand and gave thanks to God.

PART THREE

Ama a chine t'ama e rispundi a chine te chiama.
— old Platanese proverb

Love those who love you and answer those who beckon you.

1

AFTERMATH OF WAR

Norwalk, February 1946

"*Viani con me. Che fai ca. E tempo che ti diverti nu pocu. Fami compagnia. Io vio a trovarmi una mugliara,*" said Antonio Chieffalo in his most familiar dialect—a mixture of Sambrasino and Nicastrese. He implored Mike to keep him company on a trip to Italy he was planning, saying, "What you doing here? Your daughters are grown and no longer need you. It's time for you to have some fun; divert yourself."

Mike was talking with his widowed friend at a meeting of the San Rocco Society. Antonio had said that he was returning to Italy to find himself a wife. Mike responded that he did not need a wife and had not left anything in Italy for which he needed to return. What he didn't know was that Antonio hoped Mike would also find a wife.

After they parted, Mike listened to the radio news. It was a bitterly cold February, but there was good news after the heartbreaking events of the past several years, and some rebuilding of Europe was underway. It had been a long, cold, and painful war.

Since 1939, Mike had been anguished by the unfolding events in Europe, particularly in Italy. He had been devastated that Mussolini's Italy was at war with the Allies. He had his adopted sister, many cousins, and distant family there. He could only imagine how terrible the bombing, the blackouts, and the hunger had been.

Throughout the war, Mike had followed every detail on the radio. He would pick up more information at the local meetings downtown as the men discussed what they had read in the daily papers. He sometimes went to the movie theater to see the newsreel and hear and see the world reports.

At the twice-monthly San Rocco Society meetings, he would remain for the social hour, playing cards. There, he'd gleaned more news about various stages of the war. During those candid moments, he would hear personal accounts of the simmering hatred directed against his fellow Italians in America, and even in Norwalk. Italy's people suffered as Benito Mussolini joined forces with the devil; the Italians were bearing the worst fallout from that unholy alliance that opposed the Allied powers.

Mike had been heartbroken on April 13, 1945, when he heard on his kitchen radio that his beloved President Roosevelt had died the day before in Warm Springs, Georgia. Vice President Harry Truman was sworn in as the new president.

Then, less than one month later, almost without warning, a news flash on the radio said that Germany had unconditionally surrendered to the Allies. Mike's girls were so excited to learn that everyone was going to be celebrating for several days. They came to see their dad, bringing a copy of the *New York Post* with pictures of the jubilation in Times Square.

But the war still raged in the Pacific. Then, the U.S. announced that it had struck terror into Japan by dropping atomic bombs on Hiroshima on August 6 and Nagasaki on August 9.

Mike was unsure how he felt about this atomic weapon; it would change the world and not necessarily in a good way. However, it was only a short time later that the great news came across the wires that Japan had surrendered on September 2, 1945. At last, the war was over.

He was proud of his daughters' husbands, who had fought for freedom in Europe and the Pacific. He had feared for them, and the whole family was overjoyed when Rosie's and Lena's husbands finally came home, as had Connie's beau.

Ann's husband, Harold "Babe" Rasmussen, had given his life in France on December 15, 1944. The news of Babe's death had been a belly-stabbing blow. Two officials had come to City National Bank in South Norwalk, where Ann worked. Babe's unit was part of the 143rd Infantry, 34th Division, at what the news called the Battle of the Bulge. His body would be interred at the most recent established U.S. Military Cemetery in Epinal, France, not far from various battle sites and where more than 5,000 American servicemen and women were buried from the area battles. Babe was later awarded the Purple Heart.

Everyone had flocked to the Rasmussen home in Rowayton when they heard the news about Babe, who had been a football star in high school. Among the Rizzo sisters and their friends, only Ann was a wartime widow.

Thank God she and Babe did not have any children, Mike thought. Ann was an intelligent, beautiful woman. Only now, nearly a year after the end of the war, was he starting to see signs that she was moving back toward the vivacious woman he knew. She had been an excellent student at school. After graduating high school, she worked at Frederick-Speier Footwear with some of her sisters, then at the telephone company, and then on to the bank. He had often thought there wasn't anything she could not do.

"Ann could drive a Mack truck if she wanted to," he proudly told everyone who'd listen, She had been gutsy and a trooper through whatever he had asked her to do when she was young. Now, in the quiet moments, he saw and felt her heartache.

Because they had all been so close to each other, Mike had been puzzled that Ann had kept her marriage a secret from him and from her sisters until Babe died. She had married the young soldier on what seemed to Mike a whim when she had gone with Babe's mother and sister to South Carolina to see him off just before he shipped out to France.

Everyone knew and loved Babe. Though he was not Catholic and was of Danish heritage, Ann knew that neither her father nor her sisters would ever allow such things to color their opinion of the winsome young man. Mike knew her sisters were disappointed not to be at her wedding, and he still didn't understand why she hadn't entrusted them with the secret. Connie and Rosie asked him, "Why?"

Of the three, only Lena didn't have a problem with Ann's secret marriage. For her part, Lena understood that Ann wanted to make Babe happy, which is why she had agreed to his request. Babe wanted to leave, knowing Ann was waiting for him upon his return. It was something Lena would have done, faced with the same situation. When the news of Babe's death came and revealed the secret marriage, Ann confided in Mike that she had felt guilty about not having a proper wedding.

"It never felt like a real wedding," she told him. "Papa, you and my sisters weren't there; We didn't plan it, I went there to see him off, and all of a sudden, he wanted to get married; there were many other servicemen doing the same thing. His mother was there, and she wanted us to get married because that's what Babe wanted. I felt pressured; I loved Babe, but I wanted a marriage with you walking me down the aisle and my sisters standing with me."

Despite all their disappointment of learning about the marriage when she was widowed, without hesitation, they put aside their hurt and rallied around Ann, and none held it against her. For his part, Mike understood she was better comforted by her sisters than by her father. What he wanted to tell her but couldn't was that he, too, knew firsthand what it meant to lose your spouse. Though she and Babe had no children and never lived together, they had been sweethearts for several years.

He was grateful that the men in his other three daughters' lives had returned alive and intact. So many young men had returned without legs, arms, or their sanity. He well knew mutilation firsthand. He also knew that the amputation of the spirit was far worse.

2

SADNESS GIVES WAY TO JOY

Barbara Drive, Norwalk, May 1946

Mike Marotto, Connie's beau, had returned from the Pacific in December 1945, a hero also with a Purple Heart and other commendations. A handsome, fun-loving young man who was a great dancer, he had won Connie's heart before he left, but without a promise or even a letter throughout his service. When he returned, they picked up again, and they waited just six months after his return to take their vows.

The father of the bride was button-busting proud when he accompanied his third daughter to get married because it was from his new house on Barbara Drive, on June 1, 1946.

After the war, Mike's monetary situation improved, since his Godfrey Street tenants could finally pay the rent, and he built a second home. Mike was exceedingly proud of his second homeownership. The house represented for him an "arrival" of sorts. The multifamily dwelling on Godfrey Street had served them well, and he would never sell it. However, it was an old house that was in constant need of repair.

He was sorry that he was only able to build this new home for his family too late. By the time construction was complete, Connie and Antonietta were the only ones living there with him. Though Lena and Rosie lived with their in-laws while their husbands went off to serve in the war, they were frequent weekend visitors, so the house was often full of their laughter and joking, which he so loved.

It was no more than 1,200 square feet, not a large place, nor did it have anything special about it. Still, it was brand-new, and he ensured every element was of high quality. He had kept the apartment on Godfrey Street empty in case any of his girls wanted to live there with their husbands to start out. However, with the husbands going off to war, they had needed to be nearer their mothers-in-law.

So, when his good friend Antonio Chieffalo cajoled him again in late spring 1946 about joining him on a trip back to their homeland, Mike, who had never had any desire to go back, considered it. Indeed, he never shared anything with his daughters about his harsh life there. Unlike other Italians, Mike never pined away for sunny Italy. He lived in the present as much as he could make himself do so.

"There's nothing there for me," Mike had responded to the often-repeated urging to join his friend on a trip to Italy. Though he had often thought about seeing his sister Marianna again, now, for the first time, he entertained the idea before casting it aside right away. His internal struggle was clear, his heart torn between the desire to see his sister and the fear of reliving the pain, hunger, and rejection he knew in Platania as a boy.

All the same, the more he thought about it, the more the idea grew on him. He didn't want to spend time yearning for his daughters' attention. They had their own lives. He knew they all loved him as much as he loved them, but things had moved to another plane.

One Sunday afternoon at the card game, he told his friend he had decided to go with him on a trip back to Italy in September. Later that evening, he told his daughters he was going. They had all been so close. Rosie cried. Ann looked stricken, and he got a bit emotional himself. Yet, in a flash, the girls all put aside their feelings and told him how much they wanted him to enjoy his trip.

Their selflessness, their willingness to put his happiness above their own, was a testament to their love. They assured him they would all be okay. As they talked among themselves, they took pleasure in knowing he would finally do something for himself.

3

A SHOCKING VISIT TO THE OLD COUNTRY

Platania, Italy, September 1946

The ocean voyage back to Italy was much more comfortable than the initial trip he had taken over thirty years before. He was older and wiser; he knew English; he wasn't sick. Mike enjoyed the days on board the ship with his friend Antonio, talking with different people, playing cards, and watching movies. In his mind, he expected his homeland to be much improved during his absence.

The two men were jolted into reality as they disembarked in Naples and looked for transportation to the train station. Once aboard the train to Calabria, Mike spoke little. Throughout the six-hour, nonstop viewing of the burned-out landscape going south, Mike was aghast at the prominent scars of the struggles of the final years of the war, the German occupation, and the Allied bombing to root out the Nazis. He was shocked by the devastation and ravages splayed out before him. Here it was, 1946, and Southern Italy was just beginning a recuperative stage.

"*Michu, nomeno ti conscio.* Michu, I hardly recognized you," Marianna said when they met after so many years.

Mike couldn't tell her how aged she looked. He could see all that had happened on his sister's face, the result of living in fear for more than five years. Tears of joy flowed at seeing him again, and he cried, too, because of the pain of everything he saw around him.

Then Marianna introduced Mike to her two children, Maria and Domenico.

While he had known poverty and hunger growing up, he remembered the homeland as beautiful, sunny—almost majestic in its rawness. In its place, he found a gouged, desolate, scorched landscape. Poverty and hunger ran rampant. The few men left around were either old or maimed. Mussolini had sacrificed all the able-bodied young men for his vision. Those remaining had been chewed up in the aftermath of the resistance and Germany's anger at Italy's about-turn. Even the children bore the scars of bombs. Everyone had a shell-shocked appearance, made even more pronounced by the long years of not enough to eat.

Mike walked around Platania and made a quick stop at the hovel where he was born and where he stayed after his mother remarried. He could not conjure up the tiniest shred of a fond memory. There was no laughter to relive. His heartstrings were tugged only by Marianna's loving compassion. She was effusive in her gratitude for the gifts he had brought and those he had sent over the years. The cheeses, clothes, soaps, and fabric, though simple items, were treasures to her.

Mike implored Marianna to go with him to the valley to visit Petronella's sister, his cousin, Angelina Folino. While trekking down the mountain, he thought he would see his cousins for a day or two. Then, he would change his ticket to return to America in a week or so. He couldn't remain long. It was too painful.

4

TREASURES AMONG THE RUBBLE

The Chianta, in Sambiase, Calabria, 1946

Before Mike had left Connecticut, his cousin Petronella had told him all that had happened in her sister Angelina's life and what their region of Calabria had undergone during the war.

Angelina, the daughter of his uncle Luigi, had married Antonio Bonaddio; together, they had ten children. Their firstborn, Vincenzo, had been killed by a German mine during the horrors of the war. The irony of the tragedy was that it had occurred not at the front lines where he had served and been injured twice, but close to home while recuperating from the latest injury.

Italy's participation in the war had been a complex mix of disparate ideologies and politics. Coupled with antiquated weaponry, the lack of good leadership, and a clear unwillingness of the Italian soldiers to achieve Mussolini's goals, the Italian people paid with their lives for allowing the dictator to fill the vacuum in leadership. Mussolini's Fascist regime had ambitions to restore Italy to the glory of the Roman Empire. Southern Italians, who had endured a parade of invaders over the centuries, had little interest in these pursuits. However, they wanted the other promises tagged to these grandiose illusions. They wanted jobs, education, food, security, and the trains to run on time.

After almost four years of a war they did not support and were not equipped to fight, Italians wanted to move away from the wicked alliance that they felt had sold out their land to Hitler. By the summer of 1943,

Benito Mussolini had been arrested by royal order, sparking a civil war. Germans occupied the northern half of Italy. At the same time, the South was governed by the king and liberal forces, which fought for the Allied cause in the Co-belligerent Army, providing over 20,000 men for the Allies. Coupled with these were the partisans of the Italian Resistance, who fielded up to 80,000 men on the Allied side.

Angelina's son Vincenzo had been wounded as a result of Mussolini's ill-conceived campaign and defeat in North Africa in May of 1943, but he was among the lucky ones to come out of it alive. Though injured by shrapnel to his leg, he had felt at the time it was a blessing in disguise, Petronella had told Mike before he left for Italy.

The Bonaddio and Folino families had rejoiced when Vincenzo was allowed to come home after several months in a military field hospital. During the brief visit with his family before his scheduled return to the front, he had shared his disgust with the Axis Powers' plans for world domination. Vincenzo felt the war was nearing an end, and he did not want to have to return. He wanted to help rebuild the country for his family and neighbors. He hated the hunger he saw around him. He was sick with the thought that he would once again have to leave his wife and children.

It was the fall of 1943. Italy had negotiated a separate peace with the Allies; thus, changing its allegiance to the Allies. The Italians had been carrying on secret negotiations with the Allies and on September 8, 1943, the Allies released the announcement. Instead of an end to the bombing and conflict for the Southern Italians, they were faced with occupation and civil war. There were rumors of Italian troops captured by the Germans and given a choice to keep fighting with the Germans; it was rumored that about 94,000 Italians accepted, and the remaining 710,000 were deported as slave labor to Germany. No one seemed to know what was true and what was rumor.

Vincenzo's wife, Giovanna, had given birth to a son—their fifth child—two months before his short medical leave. Reveling in his children, Vincenzo had confided in his wife the tenor of a soldier with no stomach for Mussolini's vision and even less for the Fuhrer's. Italians had fought bravely and fearlessly, he had told his wife, but the Southerners didn't feel this was a fight they wanted to be a part of.

He was dealt a fatal blow when he led a small group of locals, mobilized with a cart pulled by oxen, to the next town to secure a load of rice rations for their community from the distribution center across the Amato River. The Germans had blown up the bridge over the Amato, as well as all other bridges on the retreat route, as the Allies chased them out of the area.

However, the Germans had left some souvenirs behind in the river in case there was an attempt to cross through the waters. When the Italians' cart entered the river, it tripped a German land mine, and the explosion killed them all.

Angelina, the woman with eyes the color of a cloudless sky, was exactly Mike's age. Yet when Mike reached his cousin's home in Calabria, she seemed aged and bent, wearing a coarse, black dress, the universal symbol of mourning. Though she was still in mourning for Vincenzo, gone less than three years, she believed it was God's will.

As she laid eyes on her beloved cousin Michele, aka Mike, her eyes twinkled. She screamed, squeezing him as hard as she could. She couldn't believe that almost four decades had passed since the day she had bid him a good voyage.

"When you left, we were kids, as young as fresh-made mozzarella. Now, your body is broken; you have only one arm. And I have a break in my heart that cannot mend," she said.

With almost magical telepathy, the family compound began to fill with extended family as Mike's mother's siblings entered the courtyard littered with scrawny chickens, barrels, and other agricultural paraphernalia. Each person came with a small amount of food, wrapped in a dish towel or in a tiny basket, to greet their long-lost cousin from America. They never mentioned that the gift they brought was something they had been saving for the Easter holiday months away.

Mike was offered a seat outside on a not-too-sturdy bench, while his cousin's husband, Antonio, brought out some of his homemade wine. This was unusual, as Mike had been told that Antonio had not ventured out of the house since his son was killed.

At first, the talk was subdued. Fresh tears were shed as Mike expressed his condolences at the loss of their son.

Mike noticed the marks of war on each face. There were children of every age with gaunt looks of hunger and scars. Several men had missing limbs, a hand, or a leg—all ravages of bombing air raids, mines, and stray shrapnel. Though his cousin Angelina wore a long, unadorned black dress, to him she still looked as lovely as ever.

"Vincenzo left four beautiful children," Angelina said, smiling and sobbing at the same time, and waving her hand as if to show Mike her grandchildren.

Among the many youngsters gathered there that day, Mike had noticed a handsome boy of about twelve or thirteen, somewhat short for his age, with a wary and concerned look. Mike thought the boy was asking with his eyes, *Is this one-armed man here to cause trouble?* From the moment Mike was ushered to the courtyard, the boy appeared to be gathering his younger siblings like chickens to protect them against the wolf approaching.

"This is the oldest of Vincenzo and Giovanna's children, Antonio," Angelina said as she beckoned her grandson to approach.

The boy had been a bit shy but warmed up when his paternal grandmother said, "*Questo e mio favorito cugino dell'america.* This is my favorite cousin from America." Thus, she had given her stamp of approval to this one-armed stranger, and that made it okay with him. The boy looked at Mike and gave him a hug as instructed, but said nothing.

After about an hour of visiting, talking, and determining where Mike would sleep during his visit—hotel accommodations were out of the question—it was worked out that he would sleep at the home of Angelina's brother, Mike's cousin Michele Folino. With the two houses mere steps from one another, Mike could enjoy the company of that cousin as well as Michele's twin brother, Antonio, and of course, their sister Angelina. The three siblings had almost thirty children among them.

Mike said, "Let's send someone into town to buy food for all of us."

With a sign of relief, his cousins volunteered to go. His cousin Michele had spent the past hour worried about how they could feed one more.

His wife had said, "Don't worry; God will provide." But he had not been able to shake the feeling that, having brought out their last *supressata* (homemade salami) to the gathering, they would find they had nothing to create even a meager Christmas feast. Yet his wife had been right; God, or his American cousin, was going to provide.

Mike felt an expansiveness that made him want to give every hard-earned cent of his to this loving group. His people, he could see, had suffered much during the war. The fields and the house were all in disrepair.

With an affable personality and a willingness to help his mother and grandmother, young Antonio seemed to be forever jumping up to scurry up the stairs of their home, a former fortress of the brigands, now serving as the home for three families.

The boy's mother, however, had yet to appear. Mike asked about her well-being. Without having seen her, he felt tremendous empathy for the woman. He, too, had lost his spouse and been left with four children during a terrible time when there was little to provide for them. Yet, as bad as that was, what he saw here made his own plight seem paltry. All of these children and adults were gaunt from hunger and dressed in rags.

As Angelina shared the story of her ill-fated son and his devoted wife, Mike took in the surroundings as if he had never been there before. The adjacent farmland showed signs of having been fertile and productive in better times. In addition to Angelina's own children, she told Mike that Vincenzo's widow, Giovanna, lived there with the four children.

Angelina said, "I am in mourning, but my poor daughter-in-law could be described as a member of the living dead."

5

GIOVANNA

Five days into his visit, Mike got the first glimpse of Angelina's widowed daughter-in-law, Giovanna.

She made her way down the steps from her apartment to help Antonio with the wash. She reddened when she saw Mike. She knew who he was because her son had told her.

For Mike, something happened that he never thought would happen to him again. Upon seeing Giovanna, he felt the thunderbolt. His heart had gone out to the beautiful children days before, but he had no idea that she herself was so very lovely. She looked like a lost waif with a haunted look in her very dark eyes.

He knew she had lost a two-year-old daughter, and then, the love of her life, after years of worrying and praying for him while at the front. Mike's heart leaped, feeling a kinship with her grief, and at the same time, he was captivated by her beauty.

Mike's family had told him that Giovanna Cuiuli and Vincenzo had been childhood sweethearts, whose marriage was cemented by a passionate, all-consuming love. Their youngest child, Giuseppe, had been only four months old when Vincenzo was killed.

As Mike gradually spent more time with Giovanna, she began to share some of her experiences during and since the war. He knew that she would never forget that fateful day in December when the mine exploded.

Her oldest son, Antonio, had been ten years old, and that morning, she had sent him with his father to help. At some point, Vincenzo had decided to leave the boy in the field to work, saying he would return for him that night on his way back home.

While the whole town had grown somewhat accustomed to the sounds of war, Giovanna and her daughter Angela had gone to get bread. Then, suddenly, her heart stopped and ripped open at the sound of the explosion. Even though it was obviously many miles away, she grabbed her daughter's hand, saying they must forget the bread and go right home. Giovanna had waited anxiously for the remainder of the day. Although Vincenzo and Antonio were not expected to return until very late, Giovanna knew in her heart they would not return.

Vincenzo had gone off to military service shortly after they were married because every man in Italy was required to serve. He had come home, only to have war break out. Then she prayed and worried about him being killed in Africa, in Ethiopia. When he returned wounded, she was grateful that God had spared him.

While he was at home this time, he had told his family he was tired of the fighting, the killing all around him. He believed that Italy should have allied itself with America.

Now, to have him die so close to home, as it seemed the war was ending—the irony—the pain was too much for Giovanna.

The day of the tragedy, Antonio waited patiently for his father to return to get him. An obedient boy, he did not leave the appointed spot though it had grown dark. because Antonio knew with certainty that his father was coming for him. Then, late in the night, someone found the boy and brought him home.

Despite her pain of the certain loss of Vincenzo, Giovanna was elated to see that Antonio was alive! Blessedly, Vincenzo had not taken him along to the river where the mine exploded, or Antonio could have been killed, too. Giovanna gave thanks for her son's life being spared.

After that night, her voice disappeared at Vincenzo's loss. She could not care for her children. Her milk dried up. Little Giuseppe was passed to wet nurses to keep him from dying of starvation. Her sisters-in-law, almost children themselves, cared for the kids.

A few years had passed, and Giovanna was beginning to pay attention to her children again. She faced another crisis because they had no money or a pension. Although a veteran of war, Vincenzo had been on medical leave at the time of the fatal explosion. Because he had not returned to report for duty, and the paperwork in Italy was a bureaucratic nightmare, the Italian government considered him AWOL. It took them some time to sort out the facts; meanwhile, her children languished without a pension.

When Angelina's cousin Mike came to visit, Giovanna and the children were near starvation.

On most days, her ever-faithful son Antonio urged her to get up and get dressed. He tended the younger children as best he could and worked the fields like a grown man, trying to coax a little something to grow out of the now burned-out land. His love and support, along with that of his siblings, created a warm and strong family bond that was evident to all who knew them.

6

A SURPRISING END OF THE TRIP

Calabria, winter 1947

Sometime toward the end of Mike's visit to the compound at the Chianta in Calabria, he told Angelina his intentions toward her daughter-in-law and her children.

Giovanna would hear nothing of it. In her youth, she had been an attractive and charming woman. Many had vied for her hand before she married Vincenzo. And, after she was widowed, others in her family had intervened to reason with her; a woman alone with all these children could only come to no good, they told her, as they pointed out widowers who wanted to marry her. She had held out. She was starving, but she would not marry. She and Vincenzo had promised each other that, if something happened to either of them, they would never marry.

She had the same concerns Mike had had when he was widowed; she worried that another man would mistreat her children. She did not want them to be adopted or stepfathered by anyone. She felt she did not need to marry.

Angelina urged, "Oh, you'll take my grandchildren to America; they'll be saved. We are all starving here. Mike is my cousin; he will take good care of them and treat them like his own. He raised four daughters alone and will be good to my son's children, too."

Mike had come to Italy in American clothes and bragged about how he now owned two houses. He was very proud of America and all that it held for immigrants. He told them he had arrived in America hungry, with nothing, and had taken advantage of every opportunity, and he had thrived. He shared what was in his heart and told them he felt America was the best country in the whole world. He assured Giovanna that she and her children would never have to worry about where their next meal came from.

With that plea, he began to convince her. Yet, in her heart, she felt that remarrying was disloyal; after all, she had promised Vincenzo. While she had no desire for another man, her children were starving. There was no hope in sight. Often, in the night, she sobbed, "Vincenzo, why did you leave me?"

Vincenzo had always been able to figure out everything. He had been optimistic. Playful. Even in the darkest times, he could make her smile. What was she to do but be strong and make the best choices she could for their four living children? Neither his parents nor hers could help them. The war was over, but its impact on families like hers was just beginning.

She examined her thoughts. She concluded that Michelangelo Rizzo, known as Mike to everyone, was a clean-cut, handsome man. She could sense he was a good man—after all, he was a first cousin once removed from her precious Vincenzo. Hadn't he raised four fine daughters alone? Like her, he had a place in his heart for someone he had loved. He had only one arm, an amputee. The war had created a large stock of amputees in her world circle. It didn't strike her as odd or uncomfortable.

Yet he was not the man that her late husband had been. Childhood sweethearts, they had grown up together. Vincenzo had been six feet tall and handsome beyond words. Strong. Muscular. He picked her up as if she was nothing. He adored her, constantly showering her with affection. They had pet names for each other and codes between them that they delivered with their eyes. Her children looked like him, in particular the boys. Antonio, now fourteen, and the others just a little younger, displayed the passion for life that was their father's.

Against her father's wishes, Giovanna agreed to marry Mike, a man eighteen years her senior. Her father's reluctance was not due to Mike's character but because Giovanna would leave them and go to America. He told her it would break his heart and her mother's if she did. The first time, Giovanna had disobeyed her father for love; in this second marriage, she would disobey him out of necessity. The weight of cultural expectations and the sacrifices she had to make for her children weighed heavily on her heart. Yet she knew she had to put her children first.

Giovanna and Mike married on February 9, 1947, at the Church of the Madonna of Mount Carmel in Sambiase, Calabria. That's when she became Mrs. Michael Rizzo.

Unfortunately, marriage didn't end Giovanna's troubles. She had just swapped one type of woe for another. Her children now had food, and she had a reliable source of income and someone to provide for them. She regained the respectability that, at that time, was only afforded to a married woman in Southern Italy.

Mike and Jennie, as he liked to call her, started a new life together in the same home where she had lived with her first husband. But they would face unexpected challenges in getting the family to America.

Mike was excited and thrilled to have such a beautiful young wife. After so many decades of being alone, he was experiencing an almost drunken joyousness. There was also his secret hope of someday having a son. Like his daughters, her children were beautiful, respectful, and affectionate. Though his daughters loved him, Mike felt they no longer needed him.

What shocked him was that the U.S. government, while embracing his naturalization and stalwart citizenship, had great difficulty accepting his new family, members of a foreign power that was, until a short time ago, an enemy state. It appeared almost impossible for his new wife to bring her children into America.

The government bureaucracy didn't recognize Jennie's children as Mike's children. He was not their father, and Jennie and Mike had decided that adoption was out of the question. She felt the children were the offspring of Vincenzo Bonaddio. Nor did Mike think it was right to change their last name. Until his dying day, he would always revere the man who had been Giovanna's first husband. Whenever Mike spoke of Vincenzo Bonaddio, his voice choked up.

Those circumstances caused Mike to leave his new bride, who was pregnant with his child, and return to the States. He left in August of 1947, only six months after their marriage, to work out the details of getting his new wife and stepchildren into the country. Upon arrival in Connecticut, he visited his congressional representative and made contacts in Washington, things he could not do from Southern Italy.

7

NEW GRANDFATHER, NEW FATHER

Norwalk, January 1948

"It's a girl," Rosie's husband, Steve, said with tears in his eyes.

They were all gathered in the Norwalk hospital lobby because husbands were considered persona non grata anywhere near their wives during a delivery at the hospital. Steve was flying high, and Mike couldn't help but think about when Rosie herself was born at home on River Street. He remembered that he was thrown out of the house by the midwife. At least he had been able to remain nearby. He heard his wife's screams and the baby's first cry from the back porch, where he had worried and waited for eight hours.

Mike thought his son-in-law Steve was a good man. But being from a family of eight brothers, Mike thought he might not be none too happy with a daughter. Yet Steve seemed full of joy and excited.

Looking at the baby through a glass panel, both men were moved to tears as the tiny bundle with a mop of dark hair squinted and made a face at them.

Mike left his daughter and her husband alone for a while, then walked into her hospital room.

"Papa, she's beautiful!" his eldest daughter said, beaming at him.

"Just like you were," he said with a catch in his voice. "Don't worry that the baby is so small; she'll grow up strong."

"We are going to name her Shirley," Rosie declared.

"What kinda name is that?"

"It's America, Papa. We don't want our daughter to have some *guinea* name," she chuckled with love at her father and added, "Grandpa!"

As Mike walked the couple of miles from Stevens Street to Godfrey, he smiled as he realized he had just become a grandfather for the second time in two years. Lena's first child and his first grandchild, Barbara, had been born while he was in Italy and was already a toddler.

In Italy, his wife would soon be giving birth to their child. He would be a grandfather and a father all in the same month. He had been disappointed that Jennie had refused to come to America in her eighth month of pregnancy. But he understood her fears. He was furious with the consulate for taking so long to expedite the papers for his new wife to join him.

To Mike, the past few years had been like a dream. He had gone back to his birthland reluctantly, yet it had changed his life. So long alone, he was totally in love with his much younger wife. He couldn't wait to have her wonderful kids with his four daughters and their children. It was the large family he had never had and always wanted.

He hoped his new baby would be a boy. Jennie had three boys and one girl; they were certain to have a boy together.

"God, forgive me for wanting a son," he prayed. "I know you sent me the very best daughters a man could ever have—sweet-souled, pretty, hardworking, polite, wonderful personality, and with a loving heart toward me. I am grateful. But I still want a son to ensure our name, Rizzo, continues. If it's wrong, I'm sorry."

He made the sign of the cross as he walked past St. Mary's Church on West Avenue.

Rosie, Steve, and little Shirley lived upstairs in the house on Godfrey Street. They were a nice little family, he thought to himself as he finished his midday meal of fried potato chunks and a cubed steak just a little more than two weeks after Shirley was born. He sat as he often did, thinking as he sipped his glass of homemade red wine. The wine had come out just so-so this year. But he wasn't going to throw it away.

Since he had returned from Italy, leaving his new wife behind, the house had a hollow quality. At one time, when he had worked so hard and long each day to raise his daughters, the house had always been abuzz with activity. Now, at fifty-two, a grandfather twice over, he was married again, with four stepchildren and a new baby on the way.

He had amassed a good bit of savings in the past eight years. He owned the house on Godfrey Street with the three apartments he rented out. Of course, he was only charging a token amount to his daughter Rosie, as he had with Lena. He had regretfully sold the house on Barbara Drive after trouble with an abusive, foul-mouthed neighbor. He had built that one-family house. It was a badge of success. It would have been a great place to take Jennie. It had a pretty yard and was just off Westport Avenue, a very desirable neighborhood. He had made a profit on the sale, though and had moved back to Godfrey Street in the largest apartment on the first floor.

Mike would have several painting jobs starting in March, but he hadn't been working much for the past several months. No one wanted to paint a kitchen or a bedroom close to the holidays. Now, with January's extreme cold, the paint fumes made people uncomfortable because they had to open windows. When he first returned from Italy, he had not sought out any work, as he had been too busy trying to wade through all the complications of getting his wife and her children to America.

He remembered the conversation with his cousin Mickey Nicholas (aka Nicolazzo, the son of Zio Pasquale and Zia Maria, who said, "Mike, we'll go talk with the congressman and he'll help us get it sorted out." Though he was reluctant to do so, Mike had sought help from Mickey. Mike had a fleeting thought that perhaps he had taken on more than he could afford. He wasn't getting any younger. Could he raise all these kids?

He pondered what the future would look like, as he sat staring out the kitchen window into a snow-filled backyard. Jennie's oldest son, Tony, would be able to go to work soon and help if needed. He brushed away the thought as soon as it came. No, he couldn't bring those kids here and expect them to go to work. He wanted them to learn and do well, like his daughters.

Then he saw a man walking up the driveway. He knocked at the door, and Mike rose from his chair to greet him. "Western Union telegram for you, Mr. *Ritzzo*," he said, giving his last name the American pronunciation.

Mike fished for a coin in his pocket to tip the young man. He said thank you and held the paper in his hands for a long time.

Then he stepped out and knocked on the door to the apartment above him where his eldest daughter lived. Rosie came down the stairs with little Shirley in her arms.

He bent over, kissed the baby, and said, "I gotta telegram; you read for me."

Rosie opened the envelope, and she almost whispered, "Papa, you have another baby girl."

8

A FULL HOUSE

New York, May 1948

The ordeal was almost over. Newly married, Mike had spent nearly ten months alone. He had never imagined the difficulty he would meet trying to bring Jennie and her children to America. He was a citizen of the United States of America. He had a document to prove it. He could not have been prouder when he'd passed his naturalization tests and been sworn in on May 7, 1936. Yet, after he married Jennie, he was astounded by the barriers that seemed to crop up at every turn. He'd felt from the beginning that U.S. citizenship should trump any of the arcane laws on the books. However, it was not to be. The worst part was that he'd found it impossible to bring Jennie and her children all together.

The Immigration Act of 1924, still in force at the time, was a significant obstacle in Mike's path. This act, which established a quota system according to national origin, severely limited the number of immigrants and refugees able to enter the U.S. It was the principal reason the waves of immigration from Italy had stopped. It was the reason Mike found himself in this predicament.

He had spent months talking to everyone who listened. He'd made inquiries and gone by bus to meet with Congressman John Davis Lodge in Westport. The man had been extremely polite and appeared to sympathize with Mike's plight, but spent a lot of time explaining why he could not do anything to hasten the process. The children would have to follow their mother. Lodge felt confident that a law then under consideration would pass in Congress soon, providing a window of opportunity for the children to enter the country as displaced persons. He said he couldn't promise when, but things were looking optimistic.

The congressman indicated that after Jennie came, he would help pave the way to bring the children into the country. Before that, they would not fit the criteria.

Several weeks after he met with Congressman Lodge, Mike was shocked to learn that Lodge's grandfather had been instrumental in passing the law that kept immigrants from certain countries out. He almost understood the bias against Italy caused by Mussolini's alliance with Hitler. What he couldn't fathom was a law that deliberately discriminated against and kept families apart.

Complicating matters further was the government's assessment of his assets, which found they were insufficient to serve as a legitimate bond for the care of his four stepchildren. The government didn't want anyone in the USA who might go on public assistance. Tempted to relay that he had maintained his home during the most profound economic depression and provided for his four motherless daughters, he had no intention of having his stepchildren accept any public aid. His stubborn self wanted to storm out of the meeting, yet he'd learned a thing or two over the years and kept his ire in check.

Instead, after he left, he appealed to his cousin Mickey Nicholas, who had changed his name from Nicolazzo to sound more American. Mickey had married again and had amassed a good amount of land. He offered to provide the bond for the children.

Mickey knew the congressman, having donated to his election campaign. The congressman's aide told them they needed to get Jennie's oldest boy, Antonio, here before he turned sixteen. The Italian government, its workforce depleted by the war, was making a serious effort to hang on to its young men by preventing those approaching sixteen from leaving, though the conscription age was nineteen.

Then, when Jennie's papers had finally come through for her to emigrate, she was too late in her pregnancy to travel.

Finally, on a gorgeous spring day in May, Mike and his family awaited the arrival of his wife and a daughter he had not yet seen. The entire family was bursting with anticipation. Mike bragged to his four daughters about how lovely Jennie was and that he was sure they'd love her. The daughters were thrilled at the prospect of gaining brothers.

He had spared no expense, buying Jennie and the baby, Raffaela, first-class passage. He wanted them to travel comfortably, knowing how grueling the trip across the Atlantic could be. He was determined to make the experience as easy as possible for Jennie, who had been through so much. It was a small gesture that spoke volumes about his love and care for her, considering the emotional turmoil of leaving her other children behind.

Built in 1926, the *Vulcania* had a long history; reconditioned in 1946, it now carried 240 first-class and 860 tourist-class passengers, running between New York, Naples, and Genoa.

Mike, his new son-in-law Lester—Ann's husband—his oldest daughter, Rosie, and her husband, Steve, all waited with anticipation near the first-class disembarkation area because those passengers came out before the tourist class. Mike had positioned himself so Jennie would see him quickly. With Rosie holding flowers, her handsome husband Steve beside her, and his tall, handsome son-in-law Lester standing beside him, they looked like a royal greeting party.

People started pouring out, but not Jennie. After the first wave of passengers had exited, Mike began to feel nervous. It had been over an hour since the disembarkation process started, and there was still no sign of his wife and baby daughter. He didn't want to leave their chosen spot, fearing Jennie might come out and feel scared if no one was there that she knew.

Mike asked, "Lester, please make your way against the crowd to speak with one of the stewards?"

Lester disappeared for a while, which only increased Mike's anxiety. He struggled to push away the troubling scenarios running through his mind, including the possibility that they had fallen ill. Mike was sure Jennie was on board because her brother, Francesco, had sent a telegram when there were issues with baby Raffaela's American passport. He sent another message when he saw the ship leaving the port in Naples.

At last, after about three hours, when all the passengers had disembarked, they found a frightened and bedraggled Jennie with a babe in arms, the last person to come off the ship.

The bursar had told Lester that the passenger he sought had not been in first class but in tourist class in a cabin with a portal below the waterline. She had been very seasick, but the baby had been even more so, and they had transferred the child to the infirmary. Lester returned to the group when Jennie appeared.

"Why weren't you in first class?" Mike asked with tears in his eyes.

She began to cry. She was so happy and relieved to see Mike. She relaxed in Rosie's embrace. Exuding warmth and affection, Rosie spoke to her in dialect. And her husband Steve did as well. And though Lester didn't speak Italian, she saw that he took charge and was very considerate of her needs. Jennie understood they would get her luggage, get her something to eat, and help her with the child. The entourage had come in two cars, and once they loaded the luggage into Lester's car, Mike, Jennie, Rosie, and Steve followed him to the designated location.

Once at the restaurant, Jennie was again bewildered by all she saw. It was like the first night on the ship all over again. Rosie helped her relax. Joking, she kept saying, "*Mangia, mangia*—eat, eat." Jennie at once understood that her eldest stepdaughter, just seven years her junior, would be her friend.

After they had eaten and Jennie breastfed the baby, Mike at last coaxed Jennie to share what had happened. She explained that she was distraught when she boarded in Naples, so much so that she wasn't thinking straight. They showed her to a stunning cabin with a balcony. Everyone around her was very well dressed and spoke impeccable Italian. She felt she didn't belong in first class; she was ill at ease and had no one to talk with. She was miserable. All she could think about was the pain and anguish of leaving her other children behind and how her brothers helped her onto the train in Nicastro.

Then, with the ordeal they met at the American Embassy in Naples, she felt she'd never make it to America. While waiting in Naples for the medical exam for her and the baby, she met some people from a town in Cosenza; they had emigrated to America decades ago but had returned to Calabria to visit family. The older woman had been very kind, holding the baby for Jennie while she entered the examining room.

Once they boarded her bags in her cabin, Jennie went to the upper deck, along with everyone else, to watch Naples recede as they sailed away. There, with tears in her eyes for all she was leaving behind, she ran into the same family. Seeing her tears and comforting her, the older woman asked Jennie what was wrong. Jennie poured out the story of the four children left behind and how embarrassed she felt, even after being in the first-class cabin for only two hours.

Full of compassion, the woman had said, "Why don't you come and be with us?"

Jennie shared how foolish she had felt; after all, she knew it must have cost Mike a lot to send her first-class passage. But when she returned to her first-class deck for dinner, she was mortified. The table had more china, silver, and crystal glasses than she had ever seen, even in the big store in Nicastro where people from the city bought their wedding table settings. Never having owned anything but basic utensils herself, she didn't know what to do with all the silverware and glasses. She watched others, but the stress was so great that she ate nothing when they started bringing out the food. The social differences were stark, and she felt like an outsider in this world of luxury and refinement.

Continuing her story, Jennie said she asked one of the women who cleaned the cabin if there was a way to find a family who was in tourist class. The maid, a woman from Abruzzo, took pity on her and directed her to the bursar. There, the maid asked if they could help Jennie find this family.

The bursar had been kind and said, "Absolutely, madam, but those in the tourist class cannot come here; however, you are welcome to visit there as much as you like."

When Jennie finally reached her new friends, she broke down. The woman's husband went to talk with someone who put Jennie in an unoccupied cabin near them. At first, Jennie had felt so much better being with people who spoke and dressed as she did, and they were so very kind. But then, when they were out at sea, both she and the baby were sick non-stop. She began to fear for the baby's life and soon she was worse off herself.

"I kept praying and worrying that my little girl was going to die," she sobbed in the restaurant. "They kept the baby in the infirmary for most of the trip."

Looking at his wife and daughter and their condition, Mike tried hard to dampen his anger, but couldn't help saying, "How could you have been so foolish to get yourself moved to tourist class?"

Lester said, "Don't worry, Pop. We'll get you reimbursed for the difference in the fare, which is tremendous, I know."

"Thank you," said Mike. He sheathed his ire and said, "I'm not mad at you, Jennie, but I'm angry that you and our daughter were so sick and uncomfortable. I wanna give you the best I can."

9

ANOTHER LOVER OF RAW CLAMS IS BORN

Norwalk, August 1955

Mike had always loved seafood. Clamming was something he could do with his one hand. He went whenever he could get someone to drive him to Calf Pasture Beach on Long Island Sound during summer. Tonight was special. His stepson, Antonio, now twenty-two and known to everyone as Tony, had said they would go fishing for *nunnata*—Calabrese for ultra-baby shiners in English—and clams when he got home from work. Mike would wrap up his painting early to be ready.

When Tony arrived, Mike and the kids piled into Tony's old Plymouth. The youngest was the son who'd finally been born to Mike and Jennie five years ago—Mike Junior, who all called Mikey. Little Mikey sat in the back seat with his sister, Raffaela, whom her sisters had renamed Marie (which everyone but her dad now called her), and Mike's younger stepson, Joey. Buckets, nets, and bait all went into the trunk.

While driving to the beach, Mike had a chance to ask Tony about work and how the plumber's apprenticeship was going. Ever the grateful and respectful young man, Tony shared how he was learning so much. Mike asked him, "Are they working you hard?"

With his iconic wry smile, Tony turned and said, "I'm so happy for the chance to learn a trade; I have no complaints." About ten minutes into the ride, Tony turned to his three younger siblings in the back seat, who seemed to be struggling to contain their excitement. Tony said, "Sit still; we are almost there. If you aren't good, I'm going to have to spank all four of you."

Marie said in her bewildered seven-year-old voice, "But, Tony, there's only three of us!" Still smiling, Tony answered with a calm yet ominous voice, "Somebody's going to get it for two." There were no more sounds from the back seat until they arrived.

Mike appreciated how Tony looked after the younger ones. He knew that spanking was not something Tony would ever do, but he appreciated that he let them know misbehaving might have consequences. He always basked in his oldest stepson's company; he could not have loved the boy any more if he had been his own.

Upon arrival, Joey jumped out first to help his older brother remove the nets, the buckets, and other paraphernalia. At twelve years old, Joey emulated his brother in being a man. Both deferred to Mike by calling him Papa. Mike often remarked how their mother had done a great job instilling in the children the importance of respecting their stepfather and elders. They were all very polite. It was something Mike prized.

Joey set up the net. He and Mike took one side of the pole, and Tony took the other. The tiny *nunnata,* ultra-baby smelts, were perfect this time of year. Jennie would make a delicious batter to drop the tiny, silvery creatures —less than an inch long—into, and fry up the patties, which were a delicacy. On their first drag, their catch filled the bucket halfway.

The two younger children, busy playing at the water's edge, were fascinated with the catch as Mike and Tony dumped it into the bucket and cleaned the net of some of the stowaways like crabs that they picked out and threw back into the sound. For the second drag, Joey announced that he could manage the second pole alone and that Papa should rest.

Instead of resting, Mike went out to dig clams. He waded into the shallow water, leaving the two youngsters to "guard" the catch; he used his hand to dig into the muddy bottom along the rocky breakwater. As he pulled out a couple of clams, he put them in the pockets of his bathing trunks; then, when Mike had four, he'd wade in and dump them one at a time into his zinc bucket containing a little seawater in the bottom. He made that trip back and forth quite a number of times.

As he unloaded his last haul, Tony and Joey finished their second catch. Mike had dug more than two dozen clams while the brothers had filled their bucket with the tiny smelts. Mikey and Marie were all aglow with the process and the catch.

They loaded everything and headed home, where they all knew Mama would be waiting with batter ready and a pot boiling to steam the clams, and they would all eat dinner.

Once home, Joey and Tony set out to clean the net and buckets after they deposited the clams and the tiny fish into their mother's care. Jennie flew into production mode. She had a family to feed, and everything else was ready, just waiting for the catch.

Standing over the sink inspecting the catch, Mike was thrilled that he had gotten eight blue mussels and a dozen cherrystone clams, which were his favorites. He knew Jennie did not like clams, though she loved the *nunnata*, and that had her attention now. She had already steamed the clams slightly so they would open up. The rest of the job was his. He began the meticulous process of cleaning out all of the bad stuff in the clams. Then he would squeeze a lemon into the open clam and then suck it down.

"Delicious!" he announced.

His young daughter watched with big eyes. He cleaned another, squeezed the lemon, and put the clam to her lips.

"You suck it up," he said with a twinkle.

Jennie admonished him, "Don't give that to her; she won't like it."

Nevertheless, the child did as he said. Her face lit up as she felt the texture of salty sand and lemony taste.

"Papa, that was delicious! I want another one." Then, turning to her mother, "It's too bad you don't like them, Mama; they are so good!"

Mike was ecstatic; at last, he had one child who shared his love of raw clams.

10

THE NEXT GENERATION

Norwalk, October 1958

In mid-October, southwestern Connecticut can be warm and colorful, with leaves turning vibrant shades of yellow, red, and orange. However, the evenings were getting cooler, and on that Saturday morning, the temperature was a brisk forty-six degrees, signaling winter's approach.

It was October 4, and the new school year had settled in. Mike was walking down Main Avenue with his eight-and-a-half-year-old son, Mikey Jr. As they turned onto Wall Street, Mikey asked, "Papa, where are we going? I was playing baseball with my friends. We have just a few weeks left before it gets too cold. I have to get back to watch the World Series at a quarter to three. The Yankees are playing Milwaukee."

"Be patient; you'll see," Mike replied.

He did not want to tell Mikey where they were going. He was proud of his little boy, a handsome, joyful lad, the only male heir to his family's name; he wanted him to appreciate the importance of buying something of quality. He had noticed his son's shoes had the tongue flapping out for several days.

Jennie was home with her usual Saturday morning chores; though not at the factory that day, she had no time to waste. *She works hard*, he thought. She'd bought Mikey the shoes he was wearing at Woolworth's in South Norwalk on her way home from the factory where she worked as a sewing machine operator. They hadn't lasted long. It was too bad; Jennie did not understand that because the item was cheaper, it didn't make it a good deal.

Mike had rounded up Mikey, who was already playing with his friends in the schoolyard behind the house, when he woke from his short rest period each day after returning from his night watchman job at eight o'clock each morning. On most weekdays, he had a painting job he went to around midday; during the longer days, he could get in six hours once he set up the job. Between painting jobs, Mike just finished a big house on West Avenue.

Joey was a hard worker and proved to be a great help with most of Mike's painting work during the summer. With Joey's help, Mike was taking on work that he would have had to turn down before. During the summers, while Jennie was at work, Joey kept an eye on Marie and Mikey. All three children had chores their mother expected them to do daily.

Marie was a great help with household chores and very good in school. When not in the kitchen, she was engrossed in library books. In fact, the three younger children walked to the public library on Belden Avenue at least twice a week during the summer. Mikey had few assigned jobs; the youngest enjoyed playing baseball.

Mike felt he had some lessons he wanted to impart to his son, but it wasn't easy, given the hours he worked and the kids being in school and playing with friends. He took every chance he could. He was grateful; they were all good kids.

Tony, his oldest stepson, had married in April. Mike's cousins from Bridgeport had all come, and he and Jennie had basked in the gathering of so many friends and family. The bride was a gorgeous woman with raven hair, and he and Jennie enjoyed the company of her parents and their other children. Mike's pride in Tony was enormous; Tony had completed his apprenticeship and was now a journeyman plumber. He had earned the respect of all who met him through his good manners, industriousness, and integrity.

As they walked, Mike thought about his other two stepchildren, Frank and Angelina. Jennie's worry for all her children was constant, but in particular she worried most about Frank and Angelina. Angelina—Angie—had had a difficult time. She was the last of Jennie's children to come to America. She had been turned back at the port of Naples because in her physical exam, the doctor who examined her stated she had tuberculosis. Instead of arriving with her brothers Joe and Frank, the twelve-year-old was sent back to Calabria.

Jennie almost had a nervous breakdown when her brother's telegram arrived with the news; she envisioned she would never see her daughter again. However, when back in Calabria, the doctors diagnosed bronchitis and treated the girl. She was able to come eight months after her younger brothers. Tony had come six months after Jennie and Raffaela. In all, it had taken them twenty-two months to get all of Jennie's children to the USA.

More recently, Angie's marriage had been tumultuous. Who would have known the man was illegal and would be deported? Now twenty-two years old, Angie was living in one of their apartments upstairs from Mike and Jenny on Godfrey Street. Mike had found her a job at O'Brien Press, where she worked in the composing room. She was beautiful, intelligent, and hardworking, but she and her mother tangled frequently.

Meanwhile, Frank, now called Frankie, was a senior at Notre Dame Catholic High School in Bridgeport. Living with Mike's cousin, Mickey, and his wife, Doreen, since right after he arrived in America, Frankie seemed to thrive in the environment that his wealthy cousin provided. Frankie had a great attitude; he was easygoing and amiable.

Despite the lavish home Frankie lived in, Mike was concerned about the lad's future. "Uncle Mike," as the kids all called his cousin Mickey, was pushing hard for Frankie to go to college. Frankie, although smart, did not want to go to college; he had confided in his mother when he had come for an extended visit during the summer.

He thought about how gracious Jennie was with his older four daughters and how they all got along so well. Those daughters were married and living with their husbands and children; all except one of them lived in Norwalk. He always enjoyed his time with them. Rosie and Steve would come to visit tonight as they did most weekends. Lena had come to visit this week. He spoke with Connie on the phone and was glad to hear that she and the three children were doing well. Ann had come to visit from Meriden two weeks ago with her husband, Lester, and their two girls. Linda, their oldest, was the same age as his boy, Mikey. It seemed that all was going well for his four daughters.

During their fifteen-minute walk, Mikey had interrupted his father's thoughts a few times early on but had been quiet in the last ten minutes. Mike liked to think; it was something his little boy seemed to be getting used to about him. As they turned onto Wall Street and passed the bank, the boy got his hopes up. He thought they might be headed to the Fanny Farmer candy shop. It was not that anyone from his family had ever gone in there. Still, it was a great place to look in the window while the chocolate aromas wafted onto the sidewalk. Instead, Mike stopped in front of the Stuart Shoe Store.

Then, Mikey got excited. "Oh boy! Are you going to buy me new shoes, Papa?" He stood at the window and pointed, "I want those."

"*Sta sodo,*" Mike shushed him with a dialect word he used often, communicating for his son to be still and quiet. They stepped into the small shop. Sitting at Mike's left, Mikey lifted his pants leg to display the destroyed cheap shoes.

Mike said to the salesman, "You measure his foot and get a good, strong pair of shoes."

Mikey enthused, "I like the loafers in the window."

"You bring some sturdy ones to try on so his feet grow good," his father instructed the salesman.

The young salesman brought both the Buster Brown-style shoes and the loafers. Mikey tried on both. The stylish ones cost five dollars, and the Buster Brown tie shoes cost three-fifty.

Mike examined the loafer with care and pronounced, "I don't think these are built too good. See these seams; they're gonna pull apart and gonna break quick like the ones you got on. They have no support for your feet. You have to buy good shoes; it's important."

Mikey looked at the combat-like shoes his father favored. They had round toes with laces. He squirmed and said, "But, Papa, I like the other ones."

"*Stati zitto,*" Mike answered, telling him to be quiet.

The shopkeeper said, "You had better listen to Grandpa; he knows best."

"Whatta you mean?" Affronted by the mistake this whippersnapper of a clerk made, Mike asserted, "This is my son!"

"Oh! I'm sorry."

Mike stood up. "We buy these."

He saw the disappointed look on his son's face as they walked to the front to pay but knew the shoes with the laces were the best choice. Beyond the disappointment of the style, Mike realized that his son had just become aware that his father was old. He hoped that someday he would understand his choice of shoes and appreciate the importance of buying quality and sturdy footwear. Mike wanted to tell his son that he had had no shoes—nor a father, old or otherwise—that he could remember. His heart burst to share so much with the boy, but he kept quiet.

With their purchase in hand, they walked to the Army/Navy surplus store, where the shopkeeper, an older woman, greeted Mike warmly. They had known each other for years. Mike bought his son a few pairs of sturdy pants and a couple of basic shirts. Then, on the way back home, they stopped at Sip and Sizzle on Main Avenue, and Mike bought his son a Coca-Cola. The boy guzzled it down.

"That was so good, Papa. Thank you!"

As they got closer to home, Mikey got antsy.

"Papa, the World Series is gonna start soon."

"Not too long, we gonna be home," he assured his son.

Mikey knew not to say anything else.

Then, Mike made a familiar stop at the Brass Rail Tavern. Telling Mikey to sit at one of the tables off to the right side of the tavern where they served food in the evenings, Mike stood at the bar and ordered a beer. Knowing the routine, the bartender drew a Pabst Blue Ribbon with a fine head and handed it to Mike.

Then he walked around from behind the bar to the tables where the boy sat. He turned on the TV, saying, "Gotta root for those Yanks." The smile on Mikey's face said it all.

Leaning on the bar, Mike watched his boy glued to the World Series, a game he was disinterested in.

"The boy's growing up," said the bartender. "I remember when he was born; I kidded you about being around to see him grow up."

Smiling, Mike said, "I felt young then—now I'm not so sure." As he nursed his beer, he said, "Almost lost him when he was born because of a breathing problem. Then, again, when he was five, when he and my stepson Joey were on the swing that we rigged to the maple tree in our driveway. We never knew whether his hand slipped, or whether the boys decided to jump, but Mikey hit his eyebrow on the edge of a cement block. The blood was everywhere," he said.

"Jennie went crazy; it tooka only a few stitches to close the cut over his eye. But I wasa scared he may have damage to the brain. It was swollen and ugly for about three weeks, but thanks to God, it healed okay."

"Mike, the boy seems sharp and smart. I guess there is no lasting harm from that. I can hardly see that small scar above his eye," the bartender reassured him.

Mike turned and watched his boy engrossed in the TV. *Yes,* he thought, *I am grateful there was no lasting injury from that fall.*

What Mike didn't know, and Mikey couldn't express, was that the boy was blind in that eye.

11

BUSINESS LESSONS FOR A FIFTH-GRADER

Norwalk, 1959

"Hey, Mike! How are you?"

"Not too bad."

"How's your wife? What did the doctor say?"

"She's got a growth on her arm; they are taking care of it, though. Doctor said it's not going to be a problem."

Mike walked a little farther with his youngest daughter, Raffaela Marie, in tow.

"Beautiful evening," he said, stating the obvious as they walked past the men's shoe store.

"What's happening with the grapes, Mike? Is there any news from Cocchia? You making wine this year?"

Mike moved closer to Mr. Mola, the barber, standing at his storefront to share what he knew.

"It's been dry; they should be pickin' 'em next week. I heard it's a good grape season this year in California. The wine should be good. I ordered eighteen boxes of Elegantè Bouche and two boxes of Zinfandel. I'm a gonna blendem and make a good glass of wine," said Mike.

"Last year, I did that, too," said the barber, "but I mixed in too much Zinfandel."

Mike interjected, "This year, I cut back on the Zinfandel. I put the barrels outside. I fill 'em with water already. They're swelling. They should be ready in about another two weeks. How about you? What are you doing this year—same grape mix you did before?"

"No way. I am out of the winemaking this year. The cost of the grapes went up too much, and I lost all of my wine last year to the *Amuffa*. Once the mold sets in, you can't use those barrels. I have to get new ones and can't afford that this year," lamented the barber.

"Whatta ya mean? You make a tonna money here," joked Mike.

"Yeah, but my wife has plans for it. Business is okay, but it could be better," the barber sighed.

The conversation then turned to local news and politics. Mike noticed his youngest daughter was getting fidgety. With a smile, he announced, "I gotta go to the bank before it closes. See you again."

Putting his hat back on, he took his daughter's hand, and they walked on. A few steps further toward the bank, Mr. Kydes, the owner of Champion Shoe Repair, was outside his shop and said, "Good evening, Mike. Are you busy?"

"Heading to the bank and then on to the A&P to get a few groceries for my wife."

"You still working?"

"I got small kids, I'm gonna work till I die."

"Come see me next week. The shop needs painting, and my wife wants the kitchen painted, too. Stop by and give me a price."

"You know I work cheap," Mike said with a smile. "I comma Tuesday afternoon 'bout four o'clock. You be home?" Seeing a nod, he moved on.

Walking across the Norwalk River, he realized that these walks into town might be tiring for Raffaela, whom he could never bring himself to call Marie, as everyone else did. Now eleven years old, she was quiet and very smart. She never gave him trouble; she was a tremendous help to her mother at home. On these weekly trips, she said nothing, though, to be fair, he was pretty quiet himself. Walking into town always made him feel good. He loved the newly installed streetlights; he got to see people he knew, liked, and respected, and they appeared to respect him. His child was a comfort, and he felt proud of who he was in this thriving community.

Ever since she was very little, Raffaela Marie had gone with him on his Friday night jaunts into town. Often, he was delayed quite a bit. She seemed patient, always watching everything around her. She was more than a bit shy. He was trying to help her be more outgoing.

As they crossed the bridge, he slowed down. She always liked looking down at the water. Since the flood five years earlier, the river was more exposed at the Main and Wall Street Bridge. The devastating flood took out two of the largest buildings and changed the appearance of the town forever.

As he thought of his adopted hometown of Norwalk, he got a bit choked up. It was getting close to fifty years since he had arrived. Much had changed since then; it was so long ago. For one thing, the town had grown considerably from the 25,000 or so residents to more than 60,000 who lived there now.

Sitting on Long Island Sound, it was only forty-one miles from 42nd Street in New York City's center. The thirty daily trains each way, and the hour commute, had turned Norwalk into a bedroom community to the metropolis, despite its own commercial manufacturing and oyster fishing. New people moved from New York more and more to escape the crowds. They also came to Norwalk for the public schools, lovely beaches, rolling hills, and the appealing countryside. He envisioned it changing even more over the next decade as city escapees would build or buy much bigger houses with a yard and live a quiet life on the weekends, commuting into the big city Monday to Friday.

At sixty-three, he had an eleven-year-old daughter and a nine-year-old son. While it meant he would be working for a long time, he was proud of his son and his youngest girl.

When father and daughter finally arrived at the bank, a couple of men he knew were standing outside. As was typical on Friday evenings, the bank remained open until eight p.m. and the A&P on Belden Avenue stayed open until nine.

"Mike, you gonna come to St. Rocco's Sunday afternoon? We're planning an extra good time with a tournament of *briscola* and some new card games. Haven't seen you for the past couple of weeks," said one fellow club member, of whom he wasn't especially fond.

"My wife's been sick. I'm gonna come this Sunday though."

"Who is that with you, your granddaughter?" the man asked.

"No. It's my youngest daughter. I brought her from the old country. I gotta boy a little younger."

The response elicited a whistle from the fellow's sidekick, a small, wiry-looking man whom Mike knew only as Pasquale, who sometimes played cards with them. "Mike, all these years I've been playing cards with you at the club, I never knew what a sly dog you were," Pasquale joked.

Raffaela was looking at the man closely. As he spoke, she looked down.

Mike was a little miffed at the way the man had spoken in front of his little girl, but he let it go with the thought that some men are just rude. He excused himself and moved on into the bank.

During his walk into downtown, only one other person had acknowledged the child was even there. She had mostly hidden behind him as people talked with him. Entering the stately building, Mike removed his hat.

As he walked into the lobby, he glanced to the right. He told his daughter in a gentle tone, "Pick your head up and say hello to people at the bank."

The office on the right was unoccupied except for a woman sitting behind a huge mahogany desk. Mike took a step to the entrance as she beckoned him in. The executive vice president rose and extended her hand.

"Mr. Ritzzo," she said brightly. "How lovely to see you." She shook his hand. "How have you been? "

"Things izza good, though my wife's been sick. She is going to work on Monday though." With an almost reverent tone he asked, "How are you? It's busy here tonight."

"Oh, it's been a very busy day. We can't complain though, lots of customers. That's a very good thing. Big thanks to you for much of this, Mr. Ritzzo. Every one of the customers you have recommended has always paid their mortgage on time, and many make weekly deposits into their savings accounts. We rely heavily on the immigrants' business. They are the backbone of our bank. I don't know if I have ever thanked you for all the people you have brought into us."

"You all been very good to me. I know you gonna treat 'em good, with the best rates."

Then Mrs. Raymond turned her attention to the shy child hiding behind her father. "Please sit, Mr. Ritzzo." She pointed to the two chairs. "And you, too, young lady."

Mortified that the important lady had spoken to her directly, Raffaela looked up. It was a kind and pleasant face. The woman was dressed in what the girl thought were "old lady" clothes. Nevertheless, she was tall, and her hair was wrapped in a bun at the nape of her neck. She looked elegant in a classic kind of way. Raffaela sat at the edge of the chair, hardly breathing. Suddenly, she found herself at the center of attention, something she dreaded.

"What grade are you in at school?" the bank executive asked.

"Fifth."

"Is that at Tracey?"

"Yes, m-ma'am."

"Do you like school?"

The response came quickly before she could think about it. "I love to go to school."

"I'll bet you are a good student."

To that statement, Mike replied, "The teachers say she's very good."

The woman stood, signaling her need to address other business.

As they left the bank and headed past Woolworth, Genung, and Tristam & Fuller department stores, Mike looked down at his little girl and decided she was old enough for him to share some of his hard-learned wisdom.

He said in a soft voice, "When you are older, you go to the bank, and you always ask to talk with the head person. You say hello and ask them how they are. You save your money every week at the bank, and you'll be good. You gotta be polite and talk to people. Never talk fresh.

"Remember, when you talk to people, you look 'em in the face and eyes. When you say you gonna do something, you do it. You only have your good name. Nothing else. Take good care of it."

Then he smiled at her. She looked at him and smiled back. And he knew she would be all right.

12

EULOGY TO A HAT

New York City, 1960

It was the dawn of a new decade, 1960. American business was at its peak, relying on the United States Postal Service and the sheer power of its people to expedite work orders and communicate vital information.

Only the most trusted and reliable individuals were entrusted with the crucial task of carrying official signed work orders for print jobs or ad space placement. These human couriers were the backbone of business expediency, their reliability unquestionable.

Armed with a leather briefcase under the stub of what remained of his right arm, Mike shuffled off the crowded Lexington Avenue subway at Blecker Street one November morning. He knew what street number he had to look for, and he knew his numbers. His eyes were heavy from his tour of watchman's duty from midnight to eight a.m.

As he did every Monday and Thursday after the eight-hour evening shift, he had trudged the two-minute walk up the small hill from O'Brien Suburban Press, where he had worked since the 1950s, on Main Avenue, perpendicular to Godfrey Street. The company employed about 200 pressmen and other people and printed publications for other media outlets, as well as printing and selling their own products. Most of the $1.6 million worth of work was generated out of business orders from other companies in New York City.

The Rizzos now lived in four rooms on the first floor in the house Mike had bought with his first wife in 1919. Tenants occupied the two-room apartment, also on the first floor, as well as the other three-room apartments on the second floor. Altogether, four families lived in the box-shaped house, built long before indoor plumbing and heating were even a figment of an idea.

Mike would clean up after his night job and then dress in his one good suit, buttoned shirt, and a fashionable tie and head back down the hill to catch the eight a.m. bus for South Norwalk, where he would take the New Haven Line Commuter Train into New York City. Once there, he would go downstairs within Grand Central Terminal, and take the Lexington Avenue subway downtown, then walk to whatever office he needed to go to among a handful of small and large publishing companies whose print jobs O'Brien Press depended upon. There were a few in the midtown area to which Mike could easily walk.

Once at one of these customers, Mike would buzz at the door at street level, and someone would let him into the building. He would take an elevator up to the appropriate floor and get out at a small reception area of the appropriate office. There, he exchanged a sheaf of paper with the receptionist, who always asked him to wait. Sometimes, he had nothing to give them; he would only receive orders that he would bring back to his employer. In most cases, he would wait about an hour; then he would receive a small piece of paper that was a carbon copy with several numbers on it. The important thing he knew to look for was the signature at the bottom. Sometimes, he might get a large manila envelope sealed shut with checks inside. Armed with the paper or envelope, he would reverse his route.

It was an important job for a night watchman to serve as the messenger into New York City. They chose him because he was known as reliable and honest. They didn't know he could not read or write. He appeared intelligent, knowledgeable, and worldly. And, when they had asked if he knew how to get around New York City, he answered, "Of course." He had never lived in New York City. He'd gone with friends to the Bronx to buy Italian oils and cheeses. He had gone once or twice with friends by train to the famed San Gennaro Festival, held each year in September and centered around Mulberry Street in Little Italy.

Once he had landed these added responsibilities to his job that increased his weekly pay, he asked someone he knew to show him around and help him sort out the subway system. Mike looked like a businessman because he had always felt it essential to buy a good suit, a smart, high-quality hat, and a good pair of shoes. *Nothing makes a person take a man more seriously than good manners and being well-groomed,* he thought. His suit, bought about once every five years, always came from Ed Mitchell's clothing in Westport, a respected fine men's clothier.

Mike's dedication to his job was evident in his daily routine. The commuter train ride into the city usually took about an hour. But before the train, there was a bus ride from the stop at the foot of the hill of his street. Twice a week, he dropped a token into the coin collector's slot as he greeted the bus driver with a hearty, pleasant good morning. About thirty minutes later, he would stride confidently into the South Norwalk train station and line up at the ticket counter to buy a ticket on the New Haven line train into Manhattan at Grand Central Terminal. His commitment to his job was unwavering, and he approached each day with the same enthusiasm and dedication.

The train into the city was often crowded; he stood with his hat gripped between his thumb and index finger, and he wrapped his other three fingers around the pole. Although he knew there was a risk of leaving his hat on a bus or subway, he promptly removed it as soon as he got on, because he knew it was the polite thing to do. He tucked the all-important briefcase under the stub of his right arm. He was illiterate, but intelligent. He was very clean of body, mouth, and mind. Dressed in his one good suit, he was, after all, a gentleman.

Returning to Grand Central in the afternoon, he became part of the throngs of commuters who pounded the pavement like troops marching on a battlefield, all moving to a harmonious crescendo. He took the stairs to the lower level and the subway. It had been an uneventful trip to the publishing company's offices today, and they had been a little quicker than usual in their turnaround.

And now here he was, heading back to Norwalk again. With orders in hand, he knew he had the important paper with a signature confirming that the factory would have work for its employees next week. Although he couldn't read the documents, he knew of their value.

Tonight, as the subway rumbled along toward Grand Central Terminal for his ride home on the New Haven line, he dozed as he often did. When the subway came to its stop, there was no time to dally. He always raced to re-seat his felt hat on his head with his huge left hand. Then he would rise, grabbing the briefcase that held the all-important work orders, and tuck the briefcase under his stub.

He was a bit excited because, if all went well, he'd be home by eight-fifteen or so instead of his usual nine or nine-thirty. He might even be able to catch an hour's nap before starting his watchman midnight shift.

He had beamed when the publisher's receptionist commented on his new hat. It cost quite a bit, but it was a dark gray, almost velvet-feeling fedora with a leather band and silk lining. It was the well-known Bostonian brand. The train didn't have room for it, so he had to place it in the luggage rack above him.

Suddenly, the subway car lurched. Had he overslept at his stop? His reactions were slow, and the door was beginning to close. He gathered himself in the nick of time and jumped through the doors as they were about to close in on him. He was off the subway and could make his train with ease.

As he watched the subway zoom like a flash to its next mission, he remembered his new hat stowed on the rack above his seat, now halfway to what might have been another world. He swallowed hard, clutched the briefcase with the valuable contents, and stood straight up. He walked to the information booth and gave the details of his lost property. They asked for his phone number in Norwalk, but the man behind the glass didn't want to give him any false hopes.

Mike wiped the pit of disappointment from his mind and made a hasty beeline to the lower level to the correct track to catch his train back to Connecticut. With no hat to keep him from the cold November winds, he shivered as he walked from the train station in South Norwalk to the bus stop a few hundred yards off. As he boarded the bus, his good-evening greeting to the bus driver hid his emotions.

When the driver asked him how he was this evening, Mike said with a voice of reverence, "I forgot my new hat on the subway in New York." The driver seemed to understand the significance of this loss and remained quiet out of respect.

Stepping off the bus at the foot of the hill, he trudged up Godfrey Street. When he came in, his daughter Raffaela was in the kitchen setting the lone place for his dinner because the family always ate without him on Monday and Thursday nights, keeping his food warm on the stove. Jennie was in the cellar, tending to laundry.

As his daughter started to lay out the food, he plodded into the bathroom to wash up. He went into the bedroom to change from his suit into his midnight-watchman work attire: tan chinos and a tan pullover shirt with a soft collar and a red panel in front that formed a vee along the three-button placket. Then he sat down at the table.

As he looked up, he said to his youngest daughter in a voice that might be used to convey the news of the death of a good friend. "I left my hat on the subway train in New York."

He bowed and gave a silent prayer of thanks for his food. Then he looked up again and began to eat in the slow, pensive fashion that was his trademark. His daughter stared, saying nothing. She seemed to understand. The entire kitchen seemed to be in mourning.

PART FOUR

Megghiu namicu ca centu ducati.
~ old Platanese proverb

Better to have a friend than one hundred coins.

1

TREASURES BETTER THAN GOLD

Norwalk, 1962

"Mike, you didn't punch all the clocks last night. Did you fall asleep or go home?" asked the foreman in a kind tone.

"No. I've been working here for a long time. I never leave my post. I must have forgotten one. It won't happen again," he said, humiliated.

It had been a while now that he'd felt the night duties as a serious weight. His stump throbbed, and his shoulders ached. The fingers on his left hand were gnarled and swollen. He was painting less and less, but the night watchman work was more than he could handle even when he took a small paint job. It was all getting more and more difficult. Walking through the factory, checking all the areas, punching the clocks used to be a snap. Now, it was a sentence. He didn't know how much longer he could keep it up.

He had hoped to work until about seventy. Raffaela and Mikey were still children, the girl fourteen and the boy twelve. It would be a while before he felt his son had enough money to get married, and he wanted to help the boy get started in life. Mike could collect Social Security now, but he was trying to wait as long as he could because he had been told he'd get more money if he waited. But going on sixty-seven, he didn't think he could delay any longer.

Jennie had stopped working after a fall caused by slipping on the ice on her way to work the previous winter. The black ice was invisible on the front walk. She seemed never to recover from the concussion that left her without her sense of smell and chronically dizzy and off balance. It had had a traumatic effect on her. He wasn't sure if she would ever be able to work again.

It had never been his intention for her to go to work in those sweatshops anyway. But she had insisted that she needed the money. It began when she wanted to send money and packages to all her family in Italy. Then she found his money didn't allow for the little extras she craved. For his part, this was the first time he was experiencing a menopausal woman. He had talked with the doctor about her anxiety and nervousness. The doctor explained that patience was critical during this time. Sometimes he had it, and often he didn't. Now, it was affecting his ability to work.

He'd been respected at O'Brien Suburban Press. He had been working there for decades and had been their trusted messenger into New York for many years. To have this young foreman question his integrity was demeaning. But if he had failed to punch a clock, it was a serious oversight. He would have to be sure to get more sleep during the day.

This weekend, there would be lots of company at home. Jennie liked to have people over. When she was not feeling well, she liked to surround herself with distractions. When she was well, she just liked the fellowship. No matter how you sliced it, there was no time when the house was quiet enough so he could rest. He felt himself on edge and testy. He didn't like himself when he was like that.

He clocked out at seven a.m., left the factory, crossed the street, and trudged up the hill to his house. The children had gone to school, and Jennie was resting on the couch when he came in.

Before he could say a word, she lit into him. "The furnace broke; you gotta call someone to come and fix it."

"Leave me alone," he responded before he could even think about it.

"That's all you ever say. Now, you gonna go to sleep and later you won't be able to find anyone. The house has already gotten cold."

As he fixed himself some breakfast, he found that she was right; it was already getting cold in the house. At about nine a.m., he called the heating company and asked them to send someone to fix the burner. Then, after getting washed up, he went to bed.

About two hours later, he was awakened by a slamming of the cellar hatch door. The furnace repairman had arrived. He knew Jennie wouldn't deal with repairmen, so he dragged himself out of bed, pulled on his clothes, and went out and into the cellar.

"Good morning, Mr. Ritzzo."

"Morning, Bill. How you? What's it looka like?"

"Well, I haven't had a chance to look at it too close yet, but it won't fire up. You have plenty of oil."

Mike sat himself down on a little bench and watched as Bill Santaniello, brother of the probate judge, pulled apart the furnace.

He felt himself dozing when Bill said, "Sorry to say, Mr. Ritzzo, you're going to need a new burner. This one is shot."

Mike sighed. "I figured it was going to be time soon. That one izza 'bout ten years old. How much do they cost now?" When Bill told him the price, Mike sat in silence digesting the figure. Then, he asked, "Can you wait until next month to get paid?"

"I'm gonna need twenty-five percent of it now, so I can get the parts. Regarding my labor, I can wait up to sixty days for you, Mr. Ritzzo, but please don't let anyone else know. I got little kids, too."

Mike sat there feeling bad. Tired, dejected, and ashamed, he couldn't pay the man who he knew worked extremely hard. Fifteen years earlier, he'd thought all his money troubles were behind him. He owned two houses and had $2,000 in the bank. Now, a year past retirement age, he was working two jobs, and he didn't have the money he needed for necessities. How did he get into this position?

He went back upstairs. Jennie asked how much, and he said, "Never mind." He was depressed.

He went back to bed, but sleep wouldn't come. He knew Jennie was unhappy, yet he couldn't do anything about it. He was unhappy, too, but didn't know what to do about it. He tried to focus on his kids. He had two adorable children with Jennie. And he loved his stepchildren. The oldest, Tony, was a godsend, and he had two beautiful little children. Mike appreciated his stepson's sense of humor and his respectful manner. Tony's wife was also respectful to him.

His other stepchildren were also wonderful to him. Angie and her husband and children were always around. Joey often helped him with house repairs. Mike enjoyed playing cards with Joey and his other stepson, Frankie. Now grown and married, all of them stopped by often and invited him and Jennie to their homes for dinner on a regular basis. He always enjoyed going to their homes for birthdays, holidays, and other occasions. The stepchildren often came to pick them up and drove them back home.

His older daughters all had their own lives with teen and pre-teen children. His oldest daughter, Rosie, and her husband came to visit every week. Lena and Connie stopped in frequently for lunch, and Ann came at least once a month from Meriden. Jennie gathered them all for dinner about once or twice a year, though it was a tremendous job for her.

He counted them all up. He realized he had gone from no family to an extended family that was the envy of others. Every one of them was good-looking, hardworking, honest, and smart, he thought. They were all clean and respectful. So why was he depressed?

He needed to find a way to relieve his money pressures. If he did that, he felt certain he would feel better. He was getting old. If he died while his two youngest were still in school, who would care for them? He needed to be sure to leave a little money for them. He felt himself falling asleep.

In his dream, he was on a search. But he couldn't seem to find what he was looking for. He knew he was getting close, then it was snatched away. He awoke in a cold sweat. He felt sick, and he had a searing pain in his belly. He tried to get up but couldn't. He yelled out for his wife.

She looked at him and called an ambulance. Then, she dialed each of Mike's daughters' phone numbers from memory. Everyone except Lena was at work. Lena arrived to pick up Jennie, and they headed to the hospital.

Marie was the first to arrive home from school. She found it unusual that both Mama and Papa were gone. Within moments of her arrival, Mrs. Salvato, the next-door neighbor, came.

"They took your father to the hospital in an ambulance. I don't know what the matter was."

As she pondered what to do, the phone rang. It was Lena.

"Marie, Papa is having a heart attack!"

Young Marie waited for Mikey to get home from school, then asked him to go to his friend Billy's house. She locked the door and walked to the hospital. Once she arrived, she found her way to the ward her father was in.

The nurse on duty told her, "Your father is resting comfortably. We'll be running more tests; but we have ruled out a heart attack. At this time, the doctor believes he has an exceptionally large kidney stone. Once it's confirmed, he will go right into the operating suite; it will require major surgery."

Lena brought Jennie home, and Marie remained at the hospital. Once Mike was out of surgery, they made her go home, too.

At the house, Jennie prayed the rosary. The phone rang every few minutes, and people were inquiring about Mike's condition.

The next day, after school got out, Marie walked straight to the hospital again. She found her father awake. He said Lena and her mother had just left. He was in a great deal of pain. She then did what he had always done for her during her hospital stays when she'd had her tonsils out and a cyst removed from the base of her spine; she held his hand and sat with him without saying a word.

Then, she noticed on the bedstead table next to Mike a clear jar with a beautiful, orange-colored, oval-shaped stone the size of a golf ball inside it. She stared at it and then asked, "I wonder how our bodies can make such a thing."

Mike wished he had the strength to answer her. He took a few sips from the cup of water she held up to his lips. His left arm was wrapped to a board and two intravenous needles inserted in the veins of his hand, making it useless.

"How are you feeling, Papa? Are you going to be okay?" she asked him, her face a mask of concern.

"Not too good now, but I'm gonna be okay now that they take that stone out," he whispered.

"How did it get in there?"

"My body made it."

"I'm gonna stay here with you tonight."

"You go home. Do your schoolwork. You come again tomorrow."

"Not yet, Papa."

He dozed.

After a while, a woman in a gray uniform arrived with a food tray. Lifting all the lids, Marie found green Jell-O, a cup of clear broth, and hot water for tea.

When he woke, Marie said, "Papa, you should try to eat some of this. It says on the paper a clear diet." She spooned up the Jell-O. He ate most of it.

He sipped the broth and grimaced at once. "Too salty," he said. He didn't want the tea.

He lay back exhausted as if he had run a marathon. His daughter sat next to him in silence, holding his hand. Mike started to think back to the day before, recalling his sense of despair. He knew his hospital bill would add to his money woes. But as he watched this little waif of a daughter with the worried look on her face and her attentive behavior, he was flooded with a sense of peace.

Then he heard voices and realized that Rosie and her husband, Steve, had arrived. Then he thought he heard his stepson Tony's voice, along with others. They all sounded so distant. In the fog, he realized he didn't need money. He had treasures worth more than gold. He had children who loved him, people who cared. As he drifted off to sleep, he felt certain God would take care of the rest.

2

ONE GIANT STEP

Summer 1969

After an almost fifty-year love affair with his radio news, Mike looked to Walter Cronkite on CBS each day for his update on the world. Mike had grown to trust Mr. Cronkite. He liked his demeanor and his respectful manner. Despite that move from radio to TV for his world update, ever the news junkie, Mike never failed to turn on the radio at nine, noon, and three with his knotted, clubbed index finger and the thumb of his only hand to catch the WNLK Norwalk news.

He didn't want to miss any essential happenings in Norwalk or the greater New York and Connecticut area. And he didn't mind hearing the world updates according to the local broadcaster, whose voice he had come to depend on for decades. There was always something of interest in those reports that Mr. Cronkite would not cover.

Like much of the world, Mike watched and paid close attention to all the intense coverage leading up to July 16, 1969, reporting about the United States launch of Apollo 11 via a Saturn V rocket from the Kennedy Space Center in Merritt Island, Florida. The U.S. space program went full throttle in 1961, when President John F. Kennedy challenged the nation to claim a leadership role in space, land a man on the moon, and return him to Earth before the decade's end.

By the end of the 1950s, the Soviet Union, America's Cold War rival, had surged ahead of the U.S. with spectacular achievements in space that struck fear into the hearts of many Americans, Mike included. The Soviets had used these accomplishments as a testament to Communism.

Now, America was within striking distance. Mike said little as the world listened and watched the events unfold like an epic movie. The Apollo spacecraft launched that July, unlike the previous Apollo missions, had a cabin for three astronauts, a lunar landing module, and a return booster to get the astronauts back to Earth.

For four days, Mike had been ultra-quiet, wearing a look of worry. Jennie, never liking silence, kept cajoling him to converse with her. As was customary for their daughter, Marie stopped by each afternoon before heading home to prepare dinner. Her child was just two years old and a bit mischievous, so over the past several months, she came just for a quick visit, worrying that the toddler was too much for Mike, now seventy-three years old.

Jennie phoned Marie after she returned home on the afternoon of July 20 and complained again about Mike's lack of responsiveness. He overheard the conversation. She was worried that he looked worried. Jennie and her daughter discussed whether Mike—never one to complain—might be sick and not telling them.

The mother and daughter decided to keep an eye on him, and if he wasn't better the next day or so, they would make an appointment with Dr. Andrews and have him checked out. On the night of the 20th, most of the world remained glued to television broadcasts. Marie had said she was staying up to watch as Neil Armstrong took one step on the moon at four minutes to eleven p.m. EST. Along with almost half a billion viewers, all recognized the enormous event as a defining moment in history.

At twenty-one, Mike's daughter, much like himself, was prepared for a brave new world of adventure and other-worldly happenings. She was taking it in stride, as something that would happen without anxiety or any thoughts that it might fail. Her comment was, "We are America." Her youth led her to think there was nothing America couldn't do well.

The following morning, concerned about her father, Marie came for lunch. Mike, ever the quiet one, sat with his daughter as they devoured her mama's gourmet meal: homemade chicken soup with broken pieces of linguini floating in the bowl. The fresh garden basil made it aromatic and delicious. Together, they enjoyed a salad of Mike's vine-ripened tomatoes with his crispy cucumbers. Jennie had a way of tossing them together with a light vinegar-and-oil dressing. They used the crusty Italian bread to sop up the juices left by the tomatoes in the dressing. They reveled in the amazing flavors and Jennie's culinary talents.

As they finished eating, Mike said to Marie, in almost a whisper, "I never thought I'd live to see it."

It all became clear to his daughter in that moment. Mike, a man of few words, knew she would understand. For her part, Marie grasped it at once. Her father had been apprehensive that something might go wrong, that the moon landing might be jeopardized by a malfunction, or that the astronauts might be injured or worse.

He had followed the space program with unwavering attention, viewing each success as a shining example of America's greatness. He had feared that he might not live to see the historic event. Marie had never realized the extent of his anticipation until that moment. His voice and demeanor revealed his awe and gratitude at having lived to witness such a monumental achievement.

Mike had developed a deep admiration for the brave astronauts, reveling in every display of American ingenuity and success. He had always embraced change and never agreed with the naysayers who predicted failure or disaster. He saw the Apollo 11 mission as a confirmation of the lofty dreams of the late President Kennedy, whom he had always admired.

He had come from being a barefoot Italian hillbilly with an empty belly to experience the wonders of the telephone, see the horse and buggy acquiesce to the automobile, watch radio give way to television, and now he watched a man make his way from Earth to the great unknown of space and the moon. He had seen countless changes, and he felt they were all ways of advancing Americans.

They sat together for a bit longer. Then, he said to Jennie, "The soup was delicious!"

3

ONE LAST TRIP TO THE HOMELAND

Calabria, 1970

It was right after Labor Day when Mike and his twenty-year-old son, Mike Jr., left on a night flight from New York's John F. Kennedy airport via Alitalia Airlines to Rome. Boarding just after nine p.m., the packed flight had nary a seat to spare. This trip was not just a vacation, but a journey to help Mike's American-born son connect with his Italian peasant roots, to visit the town where he and Mikey's mom were born, and to allow some curative baths for Mike's arthritis.

During the flight across the Atlantic, Mikey thought his Papa was extra quiet. That he didn't say very much wasn't unusual, but he seemed ultra-pensive this time. Once the flight took off, Mike told his son he was cold. Being a dutiful son, Mikey asked the stewardess if he could get a blanket for his father. The attendant wasn't keen on tending to the coach cabin as she was normally assigned to first class. With a grudging manner, she found a blanket and tossed it off-handedly into Mike's lap. Mikey was shocked at the rude behavior.

However, when Papa grabbed the tossed blanket, she at once became aware the man had only one arm. Never one to allow rudeness to dictate his behavior, Mike showed his appreciation, saying "Thank you very much." The stewardess looked embarrassed by her actions and apologized.

During the flight, both father and son slept a bit. Mikey wondered what they would do once they arrived, and hoped Papa knew where he was going because he sure didn't. He worried that his Italian dialect was rudimentary at best. Would he be able to communicate? He knew his Papa hadn't been back to Italy in twenty-three years.

As his father sat in silence, Mikey kept wondering what was happening, because it was unusual for Papa not to engage the people near him in even a short conversation. It dawned on Mikey that Papa might be harboring apprehension about the trip. Throughout the nine-hour flight, Papa never once voiced a complaint, despite his excruciating arthritic pain.

One of the main reasons for this journey was for Papa to experience the legendary cures of Caronte's sulfur springs, at the base of Monte Reventino in Lamezia Terme, the town Mikey's mother and paternal grandmother were from. Then, Mikey caught his first glimpse of Rome from above, filling him with excitement.

Once they landed in Rome and navigated through customs and Italian immigration, Mikey couldn't contain his curiosity. "Do you know where you're going, Papa?" he asked, his eyes darting around the signs written in Italian.

Papa's gravelly voice replied, "Youa no worry; we gonna catch the *Rapido.*" Mikey noticed that once on *terra firma,* Papa appeared in command. Mikey felt a huge worry lifted.

It hadn't occurred to him that Papa had come by ship out of Vibo Valente and into Naples on his initial voyage to cross the Atlantic. On his second trip he had gone from New York City to Naples and again returned by ship after a year. But this was Papa's first trip to Rome. To top it off, Mikey thought his father had had no experience with planes and airports. And yet Mikey also had failed to grasp one important fact: Papa had done what he always did when faced with the unknown—his homework.

He had inquired from people he respected about plane rides, the airports, and how to catch a train from the airport to Calabria, which train was best, and much more. He had ferreted everything he needed to know to ensure they arrived safely to his hometown. Just as he had mastered New York City for his messenger service job, he employed his manners and internal antennae.

He cast a knowing eye, walked without hesitation with his son in tow to an information counter, and asked about the train station. They went via shuttle from the Fiumicino Airport to the rail terminus. Once in the massive Roma Termini station in the heart of the eternal city, Papa said, "*Due biglietti sul rapido per Nicastro, provencia di Catanzaro.* Two tickets on the rapid train for Nicastro, in the province of Catanzaro."

Handing the agent thousands of lire for the two tickets, he then asked, "*Che tracca?* What track?"

The man at the window answered with what sounded to Mikey like proper Italian, "*Benario dodici*"—using the proper Italian word for track but knowing very well that *tracca* was dialect for *benario* in most Southern towns. Unbeknownst to them, the ticket agent was a Southerner, like hundreds who went north to work supporting a family somewhere in Calabria or Abruzzo. His polished language skills were the result of a family that had kept him in school—though they, like most Calabrese, could ill afford to do so—with the desire that their son could secure a good work post. These jobs were considered plums for the Southerners, though most Romans considered these positions beneath them.

With tickets in hand, the track identified, and a two-hour wait ahead of them, they bought something to eat and drink at a little stand within the station to fortify them before boarding the train for the long trip south. Mikey tried to order by himself and managed to communicate the need for coffee and a sandwich, which he learned was called a *panino*. He listened to the buzz of voices and found that while he understood a lot of what he heard, the Italians spoke a language that was very different from the amalgamation of part-English and part-Italian hillbilly dialect of Platanese, Nicastrese, and Sambrasino that he was accustomed to hearing in America. Somehow, though, he and his Papa made themselves understood.

Mikey found the eight-hour train ride quite interesting. He enjoyed watching the various towns and countryside fly by. The orange tile rooftops and the stucco houses fascinated him. Everything seemed crowded. At one point, after the train stopped in Naples, Mikey was mesmerized by the blue waters of the Mediterranean off to the right from the train's perch atop the steep cliffs. He had never seen a more beautiful place.

They got into Nicastro close to nine at night.

Jennie's niece's husband, Giuseppe Mercuri, as if by magic, was there to pick them up at the Nicastro train station. They planned to stay at Giuseppe and Peppina's house for their visit. Peppina's other sisters—Maria and Franca—were as excited as little children to learn what Zia Giovanna had sent them from America. Knowing her penchant for generous giving, they waited with anticipation for their uncle's arrival because he would bring gifts from America. Sure enough, Zia Giovanna did not disappoint them. Jennie had sent thoughtful gifts for everyone in the family.

To Mikey, it seemed everyone treated Papa like an elder statesman. *It's just like in Norwalk, where everyone knows my father*, he thought. Mike and Mikey went to visit all of Mike's cousins and had dinner with a different family every night. Papa's cousins—the Folinos—Mama's in laws Zio Michele Bonaddio, Zia Carolina Bonaddio, and so many others.

A distant relative, Frank Torcasio, who now lived in Norwalk, had come to visit from America at the same time as Mike and Mikey. And both were grateful for someone who spoke English. Father and son went with Frank to the area his family was from, St. Eufemia, and he also drove them both to Papa's hometown of Platania in the mountains above Nicastro.

Months later, when talking with his sister Marie, Mikey expressed his awe at their father's celebrity.

"Papa arranged for the two of us to spend a lot of time with his old and dearest friend, *Compare* Antonio Chieffalo," he told his sister. She reminded Mikey that it was *Compare* (godfather) Antonio who had been responsible for Papa returning to Italy, on the trip when he'd met their mother. *Compare* Antonio had served as best man at their wedding, hence the *"compare"* title of respect bestowed to people involved in sacramental occasions, such as best men, maid of honor, baptisms and confirmation. *If not for him*, thought Mikey, *I would never have been born.* Antonio's son Franco and his grandson became constant companions to Mike and Mikey. Having grown up in America, they all spoke English, Mikey was ecstatic about that ease to communicate.

Mikey found it amazing that in every home, everything in Italy was made of marble, including the bathrooms, foyers, and hallways. In his experience back home in America, marble almost never appeared in ordinary homes and was equated with wealth.

The pair also visited Jennie's oldest sister, Angela Cuiuli Talarico, living in the very rural countryside on her husband's family farm. Mikey was struck by her beauty. Though an old woman, she was tall, fair-haired and blue-eyed. In a letter to his sister back in Connecticut, Mikey remarked, "Our Aunt Angela's features are just like our mother's despite the difference in height and coloring." She seemed pleased that this American-born nephew had come to find her. "She gave me a beautiful, happy smile. Later, I learned that she almost never smiled, so I know I was special to her."

Mike and Mikey received warm receptions wherever they went. Distant relatives and friends of friends rolled out the red carpet, prepared food, and shared their wine. It never occurred to young Mikey that for many of these relatives, the food they shared was all they had.

Father and son traveled from Sambiase and Nicastro up the mountain to Platania. They made several trips there during their stay in Calabria.

Mike shared with his son that he had walked up and down that mountain more times than he could count. "I was young and strong then."

"On the first day visiting there, Papa didn't say too much," Mikey wrote in his letters back home. "The Rizzo house was down past the church of St. Michael the Archangel. To get there, we needed to go off the road, we walked down another quarter mile to the left. We got close enough—Papa said his house had been around the bend and down a very steep incline. We had a glimpse of the loose stone structure; it was little more than a hut. There were only a couple of stucco houses closer to the road, but not much of anything else in the area. Where the Rizzos lived was still very remote.

"We couldn't get any closer; the three-wheeled truck we came in wouldn't be able to keep its balance there. And, for Papa, it was too steep a climb with his bad arthritis, " wrote Mikey to his sister.

At seventy-four, Mike had wanted to show his son where he had lived. Mike reminisced to his son that in the last couple of years before he left for America, he had had a cow and chickens. "I trekked down the mountain to Nicastro to sell the eggs; I only kept eggs for ourselves on holidays." Mike was touched and felt proud that his only son was interested in his past.

Mikey was struck by the distance from Platania to the valley of Nicastro; with all the switchbacks and hairpin turns, it had taken an hour in the car to get from the valley up the mountain to Platania. When at last in the town center, Mikey asked his father, "You walked this entire way when you were a kid? How did you do it?"

Mike replied, "Hunger drives you to do whatever you need to do."

The next time father and son went back to Platania, they went on the feast day of St. Michael, September 29. It was the biggest day of the year in the small mountain town, as St. Michael the Archangel was the town's patron saint.

Mike was thrilled to see that his hometown still practiced the feast day in much the same way as when he was a boy. Now, his son Mikey learned and experienced how each year, this parish honored their patron and protector with faith and pride. With his father, Mikey watched the procession through the streets, the statue of San Michele Arcangelo held high, while followers showed their reverence with songs and prayers. Then, the parish priest and the congregation recited the rosary, followed by the celebration of the Holy Mass. The prayers of the faithful were addressed to the patron saint so he might turn his eyes to the suffering and hardship of the people. At the end of the celebration there was a feast with food and vendors that took three days to prepare, and finally, a spectacular fireworks display. The events of the day were so familiar to his father that Mikey wondered if his father's faith had been honed here at this annual demonstration of love, reverence, and hope.

The next day, Mikey wanted to return to Platania because he had spotted a cute girl he hoped to talk with, plus he had such a great day there with his dad. But his father responded, "No, you go."

Though Mikey tried to cajole him to come, Mike didn't want to go back to Platania again. He had had his fill of Platania. Despite the pleasant day and his pleasure at showing his son where he was from, the bad memories still haunted him.

He shared with Mikey that he had worked all the time when he was a boy. He had tended the cow, and then he went somewhere else a good distance from home to tend the chickens, dig potatoes and gather firewood. He told Mikey, "My life and my best memories are in America. I enjoyed my relatives and friends in Italy. And I much appreciate their hospitality and loving attention, but this is no longer my place. I belong on Godfrey Street in Norwalk, Connecticut, in the United States of America with my wife, Jennie, your mother."

While his son went back the next day to search for the cute girl, Mike went to visit his Folino cousins. The previous week, the pair had been at the same cousins' home when the Folinos were making the wine. Mike looked forward to making his own wine when he returned home. The harvest in California would have started already.

Mikey returned, saying he had another great day but failed to see the cute girl with whom he had made eye contact.

While his son went out with the cousins, Mike often went to the sulfur baths at Caronte to help ease his terrible arthritic pain.

Three days after the feast in Platania, Mike and Mikey went to revisit the Folino cousins and stayed the entire day. There, Mikey was given a pair of slick rubber boots, and all the young men stomped the grapes on the cement floor, which had a big hole with huge oak boards around the perimeter. Once that chore was done, they feasted on cheese and fruit and drank the old wine. They reveled in the sweet fragrance of the ripened grapes and the musty smells that followed.

Mikey told his father how much he enjoyed Zia Carolina Arzente's sons. Fun-loving and pleasant, they had never been to America and desperately wanted to visit. Together, the young men went to restaurants and gatherings of young people. "I didn't think I'd like it here, but I'm having a lot of fun, Papa," he confided.

Early in October, Mikey, his cousin Mimo Arzente, and friend Frank Torcasio, went to another town in the province called Cosenza. There, they ate *fice d'india*, or cactus pears. Then, they traveled on to Tropea, to the Church Santa Maria dell Isola, where it felt like a million steps to the top. Mike sat it out in the square, but the young men climbed to the sanctuary, going to each landing, then another and another. People came and went up and down.

Mikey remarked to his companions, "It seems as if Italians have no trouble with the steep stairs. Me, on the other hand, I can just about do this."

After watching a Clint Eastwood movie dubbed in Italian one evening back in Nicastro, they all went to get pizza, and then on to the *passeggio* on the *corso,* a fascinating custom, Mikey thought. It seemed every evening the entire town came out; they walked along arm and arm, stopping for espresso or gelato, visiting with friends, chatting, all wearing their best clothes. For the young men it was a great opportunity to see the eligible young women; for the young women, it was an opportunity—under the watchful eye of mothers, sisters, fathers, and brothers—to pretend to ignore them.

The next day, Frank took Mikey to one of the many beautiful beaches in the area, for an entire day; on his prior visits, they had visited the churches and sites. Now, as he lay on the white sand enjoying the deep blue water, Mikey's eyes almost popped out; there, right in front of him, he saw many women bathing topless. He had always thought that Southern Italian women were straitlaced and modest, based on the tales of Arab invaders in previous centuries. Now, he saw their buxomness in full display.

Father and son spent a lot of time in the area where the Folino and Bonaddio families lived, an area the locals called La Chianta, playing the card game *briscola.* They played a version called "boss," to control the distribution of the beer or wine. Then it happened. Someone came to talk to Mike about a daughter; they wanted to do some matchmaking with Mikey. Mike talked to his son about it, but it was clear that he did not want Mikey to do anything he did not want to do.

"I no force you," he said, and his son was grateful.

After an enjoyable two-month stay, Mike said matter-of-factly, "We're leaving day after tomorrow. It's time to go back."

Taken by surprise, Mikey did not know what prompted his father's decision. Mike never explained to his son. Everyone had been so welcoming and generous and there was no doubt in Mikey's mind that his father was well-respected. Mikey was having a great time—why leave now?

However, things were moving fast, and before they left, Mikey's cousin Peppina and her husband, Giuseppe, wanted Mikey to help pick olives off his mother's land. Jennie had left the land in trust to Peppina, since it was unlikely Jennie would ever return and her niece's family needed the produce to sell to survive. At six o'clock in the morning, Mikey and his cousin went to pick olives. Bending for more than six hours picking olives off the ground, Mikey learned the meaning of farming without tools.

After lunch, Giuseppe, who had picked them up two months before, transported them to the train station to board the *rapido* to Rome.

Once in Rome, Mike and his son got something to eat and talked a bit. Mikey said, "I had a great time here, Papa, but like you, I'm ready to get home."

With a nostalgic look on his face, Mike said, "I never wanted to come back here again, but I'm glad I got to show you where I was from."

4

DREAMS OF FLORIDA

Norwalk, July 1974

"Mike, you've got arthritis. The constant pain you're feeling is due to the trauma your body suffered all those years ago when you lost your right arm, to wear and tear on your joints from the work you've done, and a bit of heredity," Doctor Andrews said. "Warm compresses, showers, or baths can help ease it as well."

Joe Andrews had been Mike's doctor since he started his practice in 1970. "What can I take, Doctor, to make this pain better? It's so bad."

"It's safe for you to take Anacin. It's an anti-inflammatory, dulling the inflammation and the pain; it will not cure the arthritis. Nothing can. Keep moving as long as you can, although it hurts. It is important."

Mike thanked him, left the office after chatting with the receptionist, and walked down the stairs to the first floor instead of taking the elevator. Despite the excruciating pain, he had noticed that movement helped. He stepped out onto East Avenue and began his walk back to Godfrey Street. Every joint in his body hurt, from all the stress his painting work had put on his body. Some days he had painted for hours on stepladders and in odd positions, his left arm taking the brunt of the load. Now, he could hardly move his arm. His hand had become gnarled, clubbed, swollen.

He always felt better in the warm weather. He started dwelling on the possibility of moving to Florida. In fact, he had mentioned it to Jennie just yesterday. Her response was vehement. She wanted no part of it. She had gone on and on about how she would not leave the children and grandchildren.

"Who do I have in Florida?" she asked without expecting an answer.

"We'll just go for the winter months," he replied.

She went silent after that. Unusual for her, that meant she would not even give it any consideration.

On this damp, gray day, the sun looked as if it was trying to escape the grasp of its gossamer shroud, making short, faint appearances. He longed for warmth and sunshine. As he approached Norwalk's small retail business area, it seemed he was seeing the aging process of the community for the first time, and it was not for the better. He realized that he too had aged and not too well. At one point, he could not take two steps without being stopped by shopkeepers, friends, and acquaintances asking after his family. They were all gone now.

He made the trek up the small Godfrey Street hill that today seemed like a mountain. Arriving home, he was delighted to find Cliff, the mail carrier, sitting at the kitchen table. For several years now, Cliff had been coming for lunch at around three-forty-five in the afternoon.

"Hello, Mr. Ritzzo!"

"Good to see you, Cliff. I'm glad you're here today."

"Sorry, I had to handle a different route for a bit, but I told the boss I need this route back because my friend Mr. Ritzzo will miss me."

Jennie chimed in, "You no change route; you come here and eat with us."

"Mrs. Ritzzo, I ain't ever tasted good cooking like yours. And, Mr. Ritzzo, your wine is outstanding. I like our political and social discussions, too. I feel like you've adopted me, and I'm a grown man with kids myself."

"You could be my son, too," said Mike, his words carrying the warmth of a father's love. "I'm just gonna wash up, and I come an' eat with you."

As Mike headed to the bathroom, he thought about when Cliff had first started delivering the mail to their house. It had been sporadic when he would see the large, handsome black man, laden with his mailbag. He had always greeted Mike with a beaming smile. Mike recalled that he had asked Cliff to tell him what was in the packet in the mail bundle he had delivered. It was then that Cliff realized that the man, with whom he had exchanged occasional comments on the news of the day, could not read.

"Telephone bill. Electric and water bills. This looks like a letter from attorney Santaniello's office. These other two things, I'm sure are junk mail."

Mike recalled that he had asked Cliff to open the letter with the return address from his attorney and read it to him, please. As nice as Cliff had been in all their exchanges, his request led to a disappointing answer.

"Sorry, sir. If I open your mail, I could go to jail. I have a wife and kids. You wouldn't want that to happen to me."

Gasping, Mike apologized right away for asking him. The next day, when Cliff delivered the mail, Mike was eating a late lunch. He beckoned Cliff inside through the screen door.

"You come an' eat with me, Cliff."

The mail carrier's smile turned into shock. He had not yet had lunch, and he had taken a liking to this old man who was full of surprises. Still, the invitation presented a dilemma for the civil servant.

"Thank you, sir. I can't eat, but I'll just sit for a minute or two and keep you company if that's all right. My bag sure is heavy today; we have a lot of flyers to deliver on Wednesdays."

Despite his having said he couldn't eat, Mrs. Ritzzo had at once placed a dish of spaghetti in front of him with a thin-looking tomato sauce.

"You eat. It's just plain pasta. I have a veal cutlet for you after you finish that," she urged.

"Mrs. Ritzzo, what are these green odd-looking leaves? They smell really good."

"*Basilico*. I think you say basil in 'merican. I putta olive oil, garlic, and fresh tomatoes to make the sauce, and I putta the fresh basil. It's what makes it tasta good."

Despite his protests and concerns, Cliff was lured by the fresh, fragrant dish. He ate it.

"You like it?" Mrs. Ritzzo asked him.

With his mouth full and a look of delight on his face, Cliff nodded.

Then, Mike offered him a glass of wine.

"Oh. I'd love to try it, sir. But I'm still on the job until three-thirty."

"You eat now," Mike said, "then come back at three-thirty after your shift and have a glass of wine with me. I make it myself. It's good."

Cliff had done just that for several months, coming in the late afternoon for an after-work glass of homemade red wine. Then Jennie had suggested that Cliff come to eat after his shift so he could enjoy the wine with his food. For several years, at least once or twice a week, Mike would wait until around three-forty-five to eat so he could share it with Cliff. Sometimes Cliff came for lunch several days in a row, and sometimes they didn't see him for a week or two.

Mike respected the man. He admired his integrity and his commitment to his job. There was no temptation to do what he wasn't supposed to. Over time, Mike had learned a lot from this pleasant, hardworking, dedicated family man. Cliff had served his country. But also, Mike had come to understand that though the plight of a black man was different, it was similar to what he had lived through as an illiterate immigrant sixty years ago.

In recent months, they had discussed their disappointment with the Democrats. They commiserated that their party had forgotten about the working man. The two men were nearly two generations apart, different races and religions, yet they had so much in common.

Cliff's uplifting presence was a godsend. Mike had come to love this man and looked forward to his visits. The discussions they had helped Mike focus on something other than his pain, and Jennie enjoyed the time, too. She loved to talk and to serve food. She was a very charming woman, and engaging in conversation helped her take her mind off her own physical ailments. He would see glimpses of the younger Jennie he had fallen in love with. She was still there behind all her suffering.

Often, after they finished eating, she would get on the phone to check on the well-being of the children and grandchildren, leaving Mike and Cliff to discuss world events in quiet. Jennie hated discussions about politics.

It seemed that lately, she had nagged Mike about everything. She nagged about his napping. She nagged when he was doing a chore for her. He thought it ironic because she expressed her love for him through her cooking. She never failed to prepare him a fine meal, laying everything before him. She always served him first, whether they had eaten as a family with the kids at home, or when they visited with their own children, or when company was at the table. She respected him in a way that made him feel important.

He prized these seemingly small, but supremely meaningful and significant acts on her part. Jennie was a generous woman who loved everyone. But since that bad fall and the concussion ten years ago, she had trouble with her balance; she often felt dizzy and uncertain. She had been energetic and lively and then became fearful and tentative. The doctor diagnosed her as suffering from something called agoraphobia. She would often avoid large groups of people so she wouldn't have a panic attack, which caused her heart to race, and she'd break out into a cold sweat.

Mike understood that her past life's challenges and present health ailments had changed her. He knew it was not her fault. She didn't like being a complainer, she had said to him often. He thought she might have been a bit disillusioned with him as well. He'd aged. He had gotten a bit fat. He, too, was a bundle of aches and pains.

Yet, despite her own ailments, each night she would arrange the heating pad for him in the bed, then, after rubbing Bengay ointment on his back and shoulders, she would go to sleep on the sofa because the pungent smell would make her cough and her eyes water. He always loved her kindness and compassion as she helped him in the evenings.

Tenderness flowed between them during those times in the dimness of their bedroom, in which she rarely slept anymore. In fact, she barely slept at all. She'd stretch out on the sofa propped up on one of her arms. If he moaned, she'd come right in to check on him. He often accused her of sleeping with one eye open.

However, in the daytime, everything changed. When the sun was up, it seemed no matter what he did, she was unhappy with it. Her mind worked nonstop. She worried about everyone and everything. Sometimes, she would make him laugh with her salty mouth. He loved her. But he could not express it appropriately either.

Stepping back into the kitchen this afternoon, Mike said to her, "Jennie, you give Cliff some of that good eggplant parmigiana you make, and I getta the wine."

Then, to Cliff, he said, "I want you to tell me about your trip to Florida. I'm thinking of going there someday."

5

A CELEBRITY COMES TO VISIT

Godfrey Street, summer 1976

"Jennie, come hold the ladder for me," Mike said from the garden as she stood at the kitchen window washing some lettuce. From his short time in the garden, he had observed that the window trim paint was peeling. "I gonna scrape this off and then I paint it tomorrow."

"With your arthritis, you shouldn't be doing this. Mikey can do it when he comes over on the weekend," she responded.

But he insisted, and she came out and held the ladder steady. He scraped most of the peeling paint, and then Jennie announced that she had to get lunch going.

Jennie never missed anything. She often remarked that not even a fly could pass by without her noticing its color or its size. As she stepped to their screened kitchen door, she observed a car she didn't recognize parked in front of their neighbor's house across the street. The man and woman got out and walked right to her.

"Hello. I'm Haskell O'Brien," the man said. "I used to live in this house when I was a little boy. I remember a wonderful man who owned the house, Mr. Ritzzo, and his four lovely daughters. I was just telling my wife about my fond memories of the time we lived here."

"I'm Jennie Ritzzo; you must mean my husband, Mike."

The man's jaw dropped.

"You mean he is still alive? I guess when I was little, I thought he was old. I just assumed he would have passed away."

"Miche!" Jennie yelled. "Somebody's here who knows you."

Mike had been intent on his chores and hadn't heard the conversation, but as he walked around from the back of the house, he saw the visitors.

Haskell looked shocked. Then, regaining his composure, he strode toward Mike and hugged him.

"Mr. Ritzzo! I can't believe it! It's me, Haskell O'Brien!"

"Haskell, you are not only grown, but you are an old man now," Mike joked.

Right away, Jennie invited them in. Mike excused himself. "I go clean up, an' I comma sit down. You sit. Jennie will get you something to drink."

Jennie began peppering the visitor with questions.

"When did you live here? What do you do? Where do you live now? How many children do you have?" In a few short minutes, she had ferreted out all the pertinent details.

Haskell, the son of a musician, had also made a name for himself in the music world. The former bandleader and drummer had been living in California for many years. When Mike stepped into the living room, Haskell began his gushing again.

"I just can't believe it!"

Then, he shared a captivating story. Haskell's son was Cubby O'Brien, a Mouseketeer on the Mickey Mouse Club, Disney's first TV foray. Haskell spoke of Hollywood and TV; he talked about Las Vegas and the many places he had been. He explained that this trip was to reconnect with his roots. He wanted to show his wife where he came from.

"Mr. Ritzzo, I have been a lot of places and met a lot of famous people, but you know, I have never forgotten Godfrey Street and most especially you. You know, we didn't have anything." With a catch in his voice, the man continued, "My dad barely eked out a living or paid the rent, but you always gave us vegetables from your garden, you checked on us and treated us with respect, and your daughters were my friends."

Jennie broke in. "You stay for lunch." She went right to work to enlarge the meal she was preparing.

While Mike and Haskell talked, she dialed Mike's daughters and their children as well. Everyone was working. At last, she located their son Mikey. He came right over.

Mikey walked into the kitchen and watched as the visitor spoke with his father. Mikey thought to himself, *You'd think he had seen God, and it's just Papa.* What was with this guy? However, the unexpected visit was fortuitous. Mikey wanted to know all about Walt Disney and what it was like to be part of the Hollywood scene. While Haskell politely answered young Mikey's questions, it was obvious that he did so only out of respect and affection for Mikey's father. He quickly returned his attention to talking with Mike.

Mike pulled out the wine and Jennie started serving food. Looking Mikey right in the eyes, Haskell said, "Your father was verrry good to our family."

Summer passed and brought a peaceful autumn to Norwalk.

"You getta me a sock outta the top drawer, Gianni," Mike said to his grandson one October afternoon.

They had just finished talking about politics and the strides in aerospace; the seven-year-old was like an adult in his interest, knowledge, and attention. Mike was enthralled when his grandson described to him in vivid detail the Viking Lander on Mars and what the scientific outcomes would be from the mission.

His daughter Raffaela had been helping Jennie with canning the tomatoes, a huge job. He had been playing *scopa* with Gianni and his five-year-old brother, George, to keep them occupied while their mother and grandmother worked. The boys seemed to enjoy learning the Italian card game and were quite good at it.

Mike's stub throbbed non-stop from the chill in the late October air. Over the past ten years, he had taken to wearing a woolen sock over the stub in the cooler months; it seemed to help the pain.

When he returned to the kitchen, Gianni unpinned his grandfather's hanging right sleeve and rolled it up to his shoulder. Then, he slid the sock under the short sleeve of Mike' undershirt and over the arm's short stub. Gianni then rolled the sleeve back down and repinned it in place, as he had done countless times before. Mike was pleased with all the help and attention he often got from the twenty-two grandchildren that he and Jennie had between them. All seemed intelligent and did well in school. None seemed at all bothered by his amputation; he didn't mind their occasional curiosity about it.

"Does it hurt, Grandpa?" asked Gianni's five-year-old brother, George. A lively, blue-eyed blond with a charming smile, he and his sibling were as different as night and day.

"Not too bad," he answered.

"Okay if we go outside?" asked Gianni.

"You go, but you no go in the street," he admonished as they glided out the door.

Mike sat thinking about the cold winter ahead as he watched his grandsons play. He wanted so much to take a trip to Florida. He had asked just about everyone he knew who had ever been there to tell him about it; over time he had become convinced that his arthritic pain would ease there during the winter months.

As his wife and daughter appeared from their labors in the cellar, he asked his daughter a question. "You think you take a trip with me to Florida?"

Before he even finished, she said, "Sure, Papa! I can get some time off from work in January if you want to go then. I'll check on airfare. Gotta go now."

With a hug and kiss to him and her mother, she went out the door calling her children to pile into her little white car sitting in the driveway.

Jennie looked at him with a worried look but said nothing; she went ahead to start the dinner preparations.

He turned on the radio, and at once a song called "Don't Go Breaking My Heart" started playing. While he didn't like all the crazy songs of the younger generation, he did like a lot of it, as long as it wasn't too loud. The lyrics and tempo were good, he thought. He went to put the cards away and then cleaned off the table to help Jennie in his small way.

They sat down to an early dinner, as was their custom on Saturdays, when Jennie decided to break her silence. "I can't fly, you know that, and I know if you go to Florida, you will want to spend every winter there. I don't want you to leave me alone," she said, a catch in her voice.

6

WHERE TO REST IN PEACE

Godfrey Street, spring 1977

"When you die, I want to bury you at St. John's cemetery," Jennie said, as if talking about the weather.

Without looking up, he said in an even voice, "That cemetery is built on a swamp; it's all water. No good."

"It's much better than right next to the railroad tracks where you have those plots at St. Mary's. There's trash everywhere along the tracks. I want you buried right next to me. I don't want to go there with your first wife," she said with emphasis, in case he was not paying attention.

A loud ring emanating from the black rotary phone on the wall interrupted her tirade. Jenny moved from the kitchen counter where she was preparing her husband's lunch into the tiny alcove that separated the kitchen from the living room.

"'Allo," she announced in her Italo-American accent. "Marie," she said in recognition of her daughter's voice.

During the short probing discussion with her daughter, she managed to ferret out all the information she was looking for. She had left a message earlier at Marie's office to make a stop by her parents' house before she went home from work. Secure that her daughter had eaten, that the boys were well, and that Marie would stop by to write a check for them for the electric bill, she moved on to other matters.

During the phone call, she had stretched taut the phone's cord so she could finish the luncheon salad. The conversation, though for the most part spoken in her native Calabrian dialect, was also well peppered with broken English.

Admonishing her daughter to "no work too hard and to leave work on time," she hung up. Turning to her husband of thirty years, she sliced in again as if the interruption had not occurred.

"It's not wet. It's *spazioso* (spacious) and sunny, and I don't care what you want. If you die first, I'm burying you there." She sounded petulant. "Besides, my name is Giovanna, and I want to be buried in the cemetery named after my saint—St. John's Cemetery." She continued with her well-thought-out arguments. "St. Mary's Cemetery is old. Teenagers are always going there to break the stones. If I die first, promise me that I'll go to St. John's."

She paused. Her harangue ceased while she strained the pasta. He found his moment and said calmly, "We have a very good place at St. Mary's. It's dry and on a little hill with a shade tree over it. That's my place and there's room for you, too, right next to me. The stone is already in place."

"Why do I have to be buried near your first wife? I'm your wife now; you shouldn't want to go there," she declared. To Mike, she sounded like a well-trained attorney trying a civil case as she dressed the pasta with her home-made sauce. He ignored her and sat looking out the screen door, reveling in the aromas that emanated from her culinary handiwork. She placed the bowl of pasta and her other delicious creations on the table

"Eat your lunch before it gets cold," she ordered.

"Oh, okay, but be quiet about the cemetery," he said firmly.

He turned his attention to the magnificent bowl of *buccatini* just off the stove, swimming in a light fresh tomato sauce embellished with an aromatic abundance of basil from their garden. Another serving dish held two fragrant cubed steaks fully dressed in fresh parsley, garlic, and herbs from his garden, and an oblong platter held his garden-grown green beans. The tender lettuce-leaf and cucumber salad was drizzled with olive oil and garnished with fresh radishes with the tails on them. He helped himself, as she did also. They ate in a companionable silence.

The conversation had neither worried nor upset him. She had brought up the topic before, and he wasn't concerned. He knew their daughter would respect his wishes and that Jennie would come around. He also knew that, were Jennie to die first, he would honor her request as well.

PART FIVE

Ogni cosa avi u su stagione suttu lu cialu.
~ old Platanese proverb

Everything has its season under the heaven.

1

A TIME TO LOVE— A DAUGHTER'S PERSPECTIVE

Norwalk, August 1977

"You comin' down?" he asked.

I knew from the catch in his voice that it was important.

The early morning phone call had been from my mother. The topic, her usual. How were the kids? Had my husband gone to work? What did I have planned for the day? She wanted to know what I was going to make for dinner, even though we hadn't yet had breakfast.

The kids were still out of school for summer vacation. I, Raffaela Marie, worked for the *New York Times* Magazine Group at their Connecticut offices for Golf Digest, Tennis, and *Hockey* magazines. Previously, I had worked at the Board of Education in the Education Office, and my office had been literally in my parents' backyard. That's when holidays coincide with the school system. Now, I planned vacation days around my children's and parents' needs. The day I got the call, I had taken off from work to get my sons' annual physical examinations and immunizations.

My career no longer allowed summers off to be with my children and my parents. When after a few minutes, Mama said in Calabrese, *"Aspettta, Papa ti vo parare*—wait, your father wants to talk with you," I wondered what could be on his mind.

It was most unusual for my father to want to talk on the phone. To him, the phone was not for idle chitchat, but for emergencies. A non-emergency call was made solely for a specific purpose: to convey valuable information. Papa's telephone conversations were always brief and to the point.

My mother had different ideas. She used the telephone to stay connected with her children, grandchildren, and the world. It served as her social media outlet. She had never driven a car. Suffering from agoraphobia, she didn't get out much, even when we invited her to go out with us. Yet, through the convenience of the telephone, she kept up with all the activities and happenings of her children, stepdaughters, grandchildren, friends, *paisani,* and other distant relatives. She cared about people, and it mattered to her what was happening in their lives. Perhaps because of the tragedies she had suffered in her earlier life, she wanted to be sure that all her children, no matter how old, were safe and well. Perhaps she needed constant reassurance because life had taught her that tragedy could strike in an instant.

Mama stayed on the phone more than a secretary in a busy office. The long spiral cord on the black wall phone allowed her to make coffee, cook, and reach the sink while talking. Once connected, she talked for a long while, doing all sorts of things and never missing her meal-preparation deadlines.

Since there were no cellphones or message answering machines, when her ringing went unanswered, Mama would redial as many times as necessary until someone answered. She called all of the children at least once, more often, twice a day. Her second call was to check that everyone was home from work and to ensure the children were well and fed. More often than not, she called her daughters-in-law, asking them to stop by the house before going home from work. She would remark often that she recalled the burden of putting in eight hours working at the factory and returning to start the meal for her family.

To help alleviate their workload when they arrived home, she would often prepare extra pasta sauce, eggplant parmesan, meatballs, or fresh garden string beans fixed with olive oil and mixed with garlicky potatoes, or whatever the vegetable was in season. All fragrantly enticing, no one ever refused her care packages. If the truth were known, it may have been just a ploy to see her adult offspring and make sure they were fed properly. But the work and thoughtfulness she put into the preparations were her essence. Generous to a fault, she would do anything to help her family.

In many families, the words "I love you" are dropped often and expressed in a casual manner. In our family, that was not the case. It was rare for Mama or Papa to speak those words to us children. Mama said them to me about a dozen times in my life. And the two occasions my father told them to me are etched in my heart.

Nevertheless, I remember the numerous "I love yous" expressed without words.

During the summers, my mother called me at least six times a day. I concluded she believed that if she didn't remind all her children about what we were supposed to do for our family, we would let our kids go hungry or leave them alone to play with matches.

That's why I figured if Papa asked me to be sure and come by that afternoon, even though I did so on most days after work, it was probably something important. I assured him that I'd come after taking the children to the doctor for their annual physicals.

"I'll be there around three," I said.

The morning whizzed by as I prepared breakfast for my very active kids and got them dressed. Made beds, cleaned breakfast dishes, took a shower, and pulled on shorts and a sleeveless blouse. Then I ran a load of laundry, picked up toys, and made peanut butter and jelly sandwiches on whole wheat bread. After I packed them up, I announced, "Since it's special for Mom to be home during a weekday, we'll take our sandwiches and eat them at the Westport Nature Center. They have someone talking about animal habitats today. And you'll get to see the new snake they have."

"Yeah!" they yelled in unison.

"Now, we'll listen to the talk, pet if they allow it, but no trails today. You have to remain clean because we are going to Dr. Weinberger's office after that."

"What, no trails?" moaned George.

"You heard me then."

After a scintillating visit where we learned that snakes are not slimy, and we were all allowed to touch the head of a snake that the keeper held still, we jumped on the expressway to the pediatrician's office.

In the packed office, the boys busied themselves with blocks in the play area while we waited for their appointments. Then we were called in. After the boys had been measured, weighed, poked, prodded, and questioned, I met with Dr. Weinberger to get the exam results and to cover my list of questions and concerns.

By the time we arrived at Mama and Papa's house, it was nearly four o'clock. Papa smiled like a sunbeam when we arrived. He always delighted in the hugs and kisses from his children and grandchildren. Mama swooped up the kids and asked them if they were hungry. Always ready to eat and the early lunch already dissipated, they devoured two meatballs apiece and then ran outside to play.

Papa observed all the activity in silence, amid the flurry of food and little-boy excitement that filled the small but warm kitchen. Once the kids found other interests, I sat at the opposite end of the table waiting for what I thought would be a request to write something for him, a check or a letter, perhaps.

Instead, Papa got up and went without speaking to the kitchen cupboard and brought out something wrapped in a clean, freshly ironed white handkerchief. He set the bundle on the table in front of me and gently pulled back each corner of the handkerchief with his one hand as if he were unveiling a very delicate gift.

In the center of the handkerchief sat three perfectly shaped and freshly picked figs. They were the Italian white variety, a tender green, the size of an egg.

"You eat'em," he said.

I marveled at their perfection. I loved figs. There was almost no commercial fig production at that time. I had spent much of my childhood hearing about all the fig trees *ala Chianta* back in Italy. Growing up, my brother Joe and my sister Angie always spoke about the abundance of figs they had there. They talked about how much they loved them and of all the different types and sizes, the purple ones that resembled eggplants and the dainty "white" ones, really a pale green.

When people came from the old country to visit Papa and Mama, they always brought back some dried figs laid out in cruciform, called *croci,* that a cousin or other relative had sent. The *croci di fichi* always had a walnut half planted in the center of the cross. I loved those dried figs, too. But the fresh fruit was something I prized.

When I was eighteen years old, on my first trip back to my birthland, I reveled in the abundance of figs and the different varieties. Unfortunately, I couldn't bring them home.

Papa's fig tree in the backyard of our home in Connecticut was an anomaly. The tree had been a passion of Papa's. Fig trees don't flourish in cold environments and long winters. Initially, his tree had been nothing more than rootstock, about six inches long. Then, Papa planted it in the corner of the garden with the most sun and where, once it grew, it would not shade the vegetables.

When it grew taller, the small tree had to be buried or completely covered in carpets and other weather-resistant materials to survive the frigid Connecticut winters. With his one arm, once the tree grew to more than five feet tall, he could no longer bend it to bury it. He needed help. Each year, as winter approached, he would enlist the help of a son or son-in-law to cover the fig tree for hibernation.

The tree bore abundant fruit only every other year. In the off year, it could be coaxed to produce just a handful of figs. And it took great diligence to fend off the birds. One might think the small handful of fruit not worth the effort, but Papa never complained about the work, or how little fruit it bore. It was a labor of love and a connection to perhaps his few good childhood memories. I don't know. But he knew how much I loved figs.

He put the three oval-shaped figs in front of me, urging me to eat them while he watched. I took a bite. And savored the exquisite sensation. The lusciously sweet, reddish-brown flesh, combined with the smooth skin and crunchy seeds, was pure heaven. I looked up to see my Papa looking at me, his face serene. I saw a love so pure it brought tears to my eyes.

I was so lost in the moment that I almost forgot to offer him one. Thanks to God, my senses came to me, and I insisted he take the third one. He did so with reluctance, but then he bit in. I sat back and watched him eat it. I smiled as I recognized he loved them as much as I did. Our love went full circle. No words were necessary.

2

A TIME TO DIE

Godfrey Street, January-February 1978

The cancer had spread throughout his abdominal area. He was weak, too weak to stand even with help. He could no longer turn himself in bed, both from the cancer and from the lack of sustenance. Despite his physical weakness, his mind remained alert, his memory perfect; though he spoke slow, his voice was firm as it had been for several months now.

My brothers, Tony, Frank, Joe and Mikey, had dropped in almost every day, as had my sisters Rosie, Angelina, and Connie. They all lived within a three-mile radius. Antonietta, who lived the farthest away in the town of Meriden near Hartford, had made several trips recently with her husband, Lester. On her most recent visit, Papa's deteriorated state had caused her tremendous pain; recognizing she might not see him alive again, she had left in tears with her husband guiding her to their car.

Mike Jr., or Mikey, the baby of the family and my father's only son, felt more and more that he needed to be near Papa as much as possible. He knew, as we all did, that it was only a matter of time before God called him.

Despite the tremendous suffering, Papa displayed an incredible desire to live.

The evening of February 14, 1978, Papa had not been able to down more than a quarter-teaspoon of baby food. The Ensure product that Mikey tried to make him drink turned out to be just an ever-so-tiny sip. Then, just before we would go through the ritual of preparing Papa for the night, Mikey received a series of pleading phone calls from his wife, urging him to come home. It was snowing heavily, and she did not want to be alone if the power went out; she sobbed into the phone.

Mikey felt torn. He knew Papa was bad. Yet his wife's calls wouldn't let up. At around 11:20 p.m., he said, "I'm going to go home; my wife is scared of all this snow."

As he was leaving, he said, "Call me right away if anything changes."

I wanted to say to him, "Don't leave, Michael. She's just being selfish because she has never felt for anyone as much as you feel for our Papa."

However, I kept silent. I didn't want to make it any tougher for him than it already was.

"Be careful on the roads," stressed Mama.

I heard the door close and moments later his car started. I remember thinking, *You shouldn't be going.*

I sat by Papa's hospital bed, ensconced in the middle of the bedroom. He seemed to be resting comfortably. At the kitchen table, my husband's brother, Nick, sat with my mother as she lamented about Mikey's plight with his erratic wife.

Then, as Papa stirred, I called my brother-in-law and Mama to come help me get Papa ready for sleeping.

I gently washed his face with a soft washcloth soaked in warm water. Then, with Nick's help, we turned him onto his side to change the wet pads beneath him and help him move his chest fluids. My mother left the room with the wet pads, and Nick went with her.

With a glycerin stick, I swabbed the inside of my father's mouth, around his teeth, and across his parched tongue.

I said, "Papa, now you'll rest well tonight, you are nice and clean just the way you like it."

Suddenly, he grabbed my hand and almost lifted his entire upper body from the bed. There was a look of fear in his eyes as he said, "I die."

I called out for my mother, and she and my brother-in-law gathered at the foot of the bed. Papa still held my hand tightly and I squeezed back just as ferociously. He repeated his words, and from somewhere I do not know, a calm came over me.

I said, "Papa, do not be afraid. I love you. Do not be afraid."

My mother began wailing, but he was undistracted. She at once called Mikey and said, "Come right away, your father is dying."

Papa seemed oblivious to what Mama said and did. His eyes remained fixed on me. Then his eyes calmed. I suddenly heard a gurgling in his chest. He grasped my hand even tighter than I thought possible, and I found myself a broken record saying, "Papa, don't be afraid; I love you."

He continued to look straight at me. Then his eyes went from me to somewhere above and beyond me. Moments later, he spoke no more. His eyes remained fixed on the spot above and beyond me as if he had seen a great light. He looked calm and radiant.

My brother-in-law said, "That's it. There is nothing more."

At that moment, I hated him for saying those words; at the same time, I was grateful for his presence because he took my mother, who was inconsolable, into the kitchen. It had all happened so quickly that I realized my father had actually now passed to the world of life everlasting. I refused to leave the room because I felt his spirit was still there. I sat in the chair and kept holding his hand. I became ultra-calm. I felt I was becoming him. How would I handle this?

Mama called Dr. Andrews. Then, Mikey arrived, distraught. I will never forget the pain in his voice and eyes.

"I missed him. I knew he was bad. The snow is so terrible; I couldn't drive too fast," he said, covering his face.

I couldn't bear to watch him; his pain was so raw.

"Papa's spirit, his soul, is still here," I said, reaching out to hug him.

Then, I left the room, leaving Papa with his son.

In time, Dr. Andrews arrived. He had cared for Papa for so long, and he had grown to love the man. He asked me, "Did you notice the time?" I remembered looking at the clock on the dresser, and it had said 12:02 a.m.

He asked us who we wanted to handle the arrangements. Without question, I said, "Magner." Papa's old friend's son would be doing the honors.

Dr. Andrews seemed intent on knowing every detail.

"Exactly what did he say as he passed away?" he asked gently.

I recounted the events. He listened and seemed to be making notes in his head.

All of it became extremely vivid, as if a neon light had begun to shine. The room. The house I grew up in. The hospital bed where Papa had lain in these last two months.

I walked over to the door, and I gazed through the large glass pane. Outside, I saw the beautiful fluffy white blanket that covered the road and hooded the streetlights. The reflection upon the snow made it glisten like a million tiny diamonds.

It was peaceful. It was calm and beautiful, like Papa was now. I prayed that his soul went straight to heaven. That all the suffering he had had throughout his life was enough.

"Please, dear God, no purgatory for Papa," I begged.

Tranquility overcame me, spurred by an inner knowledge that I didn't understand, but it told me all was well with Papa.

I called my husband. We continued to wait for the undertakers. When they arrived with a stretcher, they asked us to leave the room. In short order, they came out with what looked like a black vinyl zippered bag, strapped to the stretcher.

It struck me then. He was truly gone from this earth. Quiet tears welled, then flooded and dropped. Then, after they took Papa's body away, we packed up things my mother would need, and my brother-in-law and I headed for my house with her. Michael went home to his wife. From the house to the car, from the car all the way to my home, Mama was still wailing. Once at my home, she didn't want the extra bed in my kids' room but instead stretched out on the living room sofa.

When I got into bed, the water gate broke and a torrent of tears poured forth like a monsoon down my face, soaking my nightclothes.

Why? I thought. I'd been prepared. I knew he was terminally ill. I didn't want him to suffer any longer. The conversation raged in my head.

Had I been kidding myself that I understood that?

A physical pain that started in my stomach progressed through my heart. It cut a hole into my entire being as if someone had dug a tunnel through my middle and driven a truck through it. My arms and legs felt limp. I remember thinking, *I didn't know anything could hurt so much.*

3

A TIME TO CRY

Norwalk, February 15, 1978

A solemn-looking man came out to greet us.

"We are the Ritzzo family," I said. "We have an appointment."

"Yes. Thank you for choosing Magner. We collected your father's body about twelve hours ago. We will be glad to handle all the arrangements for you."

With that, he pulled out a multi-page form and proceeded with his questions. "Is there an insurance policy?"

"No," we said in unison.

"Oh," was his stunned reply.

"I assure you our father set aside sufficient funds for a dignified funeral," I said. With that verbal assurance, he laid out all the decisions we needed to make. Calling hours, church, cars and caskets. Once satisfied that he had all the information he needed, he asked that we follow him downstairs.

The puzzled look I must have worn was mirrored on the faces of Mikey and our eldest sister, Rosie. At the bottom of the stairs, the funeral director pulled out an enormous key ring from where I do not know; then he unlocked the door and opened it just a crack. He slid his hand in to hit a light switch. Then, he swung open the door and invited us in.

What I saw startled me. It looked exactly like a new car showroom, brightly illuminated in some areas, and soft spotlights focused in others. There were coffins of every type and model. Wooden caskets, bronze models, and shiny chrome metal ones. Some were open, to show the satin and velveteen linings. The metal caskets came in pink and charcoal, and the wood, light and dark mahogany, and there was even a very plain pine casket. The funeral director commented on each model he deemed appropriate for a man. Most had the prices right on the model. One sign even said, "Price reduced."

We reached a consensus quickly. We zeroed in on a smart, quality, and sturdy choice. Once we settled on that, he asked us to think about the lining and draping, again making suggestions about what he thought would look best. He indicated pricing for each item as everything was an a la carte cost. Lastly, he announced that the coffin should be encased in a cement liner to protect it from moisture. Moreover, he had a miniature model of the types and styles, as well as the differences in pricing.

"Upstairs, we will finalize all the arrangements," he announced.

We ascended to the upper floor, and we sat awaiting his return. I felt tired and mentally exhausted.

Returning, the funeral director offered us coffee, which we gratefully accepted. As we sipped our hot beverage, he reviewed the charges on an intricately detailed invoice. As executor, I signed the papers showing the total cost, a scary sum.

Then he added, "You will need to bring a full set of clothing, as you have chosen to have an open half-casket." As an afterthought, he added, "But you don't need shoes since they won't show."

Mikey and I looked at each other and said in unison, "Papa must be buried with his shoes on."

4

A TIME TO MOURN

Norwalk, February 15, 1978

The outpouring of love and the hundreds of people who filed through Magner's funeral home were mind-boggling. We all remained attentive to my grief-stricken mother. I recognized that we all had our own pain as I watched my sisters and brothers' faces. Many of the visitors were people I did not know, but they had known Papa throughout the years. Some came, though they hadn't had contact with him in a long while; however, they came because, as they said, "I wanted to pay my respects," and then would proceed to tell us what Papa had meant to them.

Many were our friends and coworkers who hadn't known that the one-armed man in town was our father. Among the ten of us, we were all outgoing people with friendships extending throughout the community and beyond. Many who came to call shared words of praise with each of us for the man who looked so stately and handsome in the mahogany box.

At some point during the three-hour visitation period, my son pulled at my hand as I was hugged by a procession of people that seemed never to end.

He said, "Ma, look, Mr. Cliff is here."

There, at the coffin, knelt the kind mail carrier. With his large frame bowed, his handsome, dark face covered with tears while he spoke to the soul who was gone.

After a few minutes, he rose and hugged my mother, seeming never to let go. Then, he spoke briefly to me and said, "He loved me."

Then, he left.

5

A TIME TO CELEBRATE A LIFE WELL-LIVED

February 16, 1978

The last prayers said, the funeral director wanted us to load up into the limousine that would take us to St. Mary's Church and later to the cemetery. We learned that the ground was so laden with ice that the procession could not reach Papa's burial site on Broad Street. Instead, after mass, we would all go to St. John's Cemetery for a graveside service to be held indoors at an outbuilding. St. Mary's ancient and historic cemetery had no such accommodation.

"We will then transport the coffin later and bury him where he belongs," assured Mr. Magner.

My brothers, sisters, and mother proceeded to say our final goodbyes before they closed the coffin for transportation to the church.

My thoughts were a jumble. I thought back to my growing-up years with my mother and my father. I remembered so vividly when I pressed him for the forty-four-thousandth time to tell me why, after all those years of being alone, he had married my mother, a widow with four children. His answer was short but spoke volumes. I could still see his face and hear the catch in his voice.

"I saw those children without a father, and my heart went out to them. They had no father, nothing to eat, no one to guide them." Then he added, "And your mother was very beautiful."

Now, approaching the funeral bier, I was once more taken aback by the enormous collection of flower arrangements. The fragrance was overpowering. I walked to the bier holding Papa's coffin and stood for a few minutes before kneeling to say prayers for his soul.

He looked good.

His suit looked smart. His unlined face, despite its eighty-one years, was as handsome as always. His one hand lay on his chest when he rested. I thought about its significance in this man's life and our lives.

That one hand was large, strong, and had prominent veins that stood out like blue dunes on a brown desert. Solid and dependable, that lone hand had never apologized for its lack of a right-side mate. In the later years, it became thick, gnarled, and clubbed by arthritis. However, even in this afflicted state, it never wavered. This one hand had raised two families—three, by some people's count. It wore its disappointments no more prominently than its triumphs. I stood in awe of all that it had accomplished.

It had ignited the town's gas lanterns and bagged many groceries. It had dug ditches on railroad beds and swung a pickax, building roads. It mixed the oils and tints in drums full of paint. It had hoisted its owner up heavy, wooden extension ladders and wielded the brush that restored brightness and color to countless three-story, Victorian-style homes. It had set clocks at sequenced intervals during the wee hours in factories and counted change to the numerous customers who clamored for ice cream, candy, and cigarettes from his pushcart at the local ball games.

That lone hand had carried a briefcase, ferrying important documents into New York City for a printing company, and annually planted a huge vegetable garden that grew tomatoes, peppers, eggplant, basil, parsley, squash, green beans, and even a fig tree. On occasion, it had held a cigar to its owner's lips. It had hauled crates full of grapes and turned them into delicious wine every year until his last.

That hand had faithfully sent money to his adopted sister to try to repay her for his first shoes. The hand played a sharp game of *briscola*. He had often used it to cross himself as he prayed every night before sleeping. It held my hand through sickness and hospital stays, and as I came out of surgery.

This same hand had gently bathed his four motherless daughters. It had cut his first four daughters' hair in a neat Buster Brown look that kept them lice-free. It patted us on the head and stroked our faces when we cried. This hand's owner had stood vigil with dying friends and had mourned with their families. It had helped its owner work for a living, yet it never lived just for today. It carefully and systematically put small amounts of money into a passbook savings account each week at the Norwalk Savings Society Bank on River Street.

This hand had shaken warmly and strongly with politicians, judges, bank officials, and company leaders as proudly as with the last-coming Italian *paisano* who needed guidance and help finding a job. It had lovingly caressed the only two women he had ever loved. It had learned to pen a name, although the owner was illiterate, and it had faithfully pulled the lever in the voting booth in every election since he had become a naturalized U.S. citizen in 1936.

It had bought lacy lingerie for his second, much younger wife. For twenty-five years, it sported an elegant gold ring with a flat, jade stone centered with a small diamond on the third finger.

Despite all of its talents, there were many things this hand had never done. It had never driven a car. It had never taken or paid a bribe. It never intentionally hurt or cheated anyone. It never destroyed anything, and it never went to war.

What had kept it going? Its spark flinted by a passion for living, its engine fueled by respect, love, and compassion, it served Michelangelo, Michele, Miche, or Mike Rizzo, or Ritzo, or Ritzzo, as well, if not better, than any pair of hands, or any hand you and I have shaken any day of the week.

No, I thought, Papa was not famous or accomplished in the modern sense. He did not write books or invent the internet. He was not a politician and never had a 401(k), or even a life insurance policy. He was not particularly athletic; he was neither tall nor short at five feet nine inches. He was not outstandingly handsome, nor would anyone ever describe him as homely. He was distinguished-looking and a clean person. He admired quality and good taste in contrast to flash and gaudiness.

He was an enormously complicated yet simple man who never followed convention but created his own. He had numerous acquaintances, inquired about everything, yet kept his lone counsel. He was the living embodiment of incongruity—caring and tough, compassionate and cold, intelligent and stubborn, humble and proud, doggedly determined and yet reverently afraid.

No wonder he had such a profound effect on me. How could you ever say "I can't" to a one-armed man?

AFTERWORD

Fernandina Beach, Florida, September 1999

It was one of those spectacular September days with a nip in the air, portending the coming fall, yet the cloudless sky and blazing sun intimated that summer was still kicking.

The much-anticipated reopening of St. Michael's Academy, a Catholic school with a rich history, marked the beginning of a new and special school year in the quaint town of Fernandina Beach on Amelia Island, Florida. The restoration of this 117-year-old institution, a symbol of resilience and continuity, had started two years prior.

Once again, the landmark three-story school with the mansard roof and cupola graced the historic block, looking precisely as it did in photographs dating back to the early 1900s. The sixty or so children, looking learning-ready in their uniforms and excited to be with old and new friends, appeared oblivious to all that had happened over more than a century to bring them the education they were about to receive. It was an education shaped by selflessness, humility, and love, committed to and fashioned in a Christ-centered environment that challenged them to grow academically, physically, and spiritually.

Those who know me best are privy to my lifelong quest to understand where goodness comes from. In psychology classes, this nature-versus-nurture question is often debated but never answered. Experts tell us that role models and a father figure are essential in a child's development. All know that family and staying connected to each other mean everything to me.

I pondered the possibility that these children might one day learn about the profound goodness exemplified by the historic sacrifices of the Sisters of St. Joseph from Le Puy, France. These courageous women, who left their homeland, language, and culture to answer the call of their bishop to educate the newly freed slave children in the 1860s, left an indelible mark. Their mission, guided by the Holy Spirit, was to serve those in need, with education as their focus and the quote *"that all may be one"* from John 17:21 as their mantra.

They set up free schools for black children, whites, boys, and girls, took in orphans, and set up a boarding school for girls from families who could pay. They taught French, English, and the three "R's," as well as art, music, and piano. They worked selflessly under conditions almost at the stable level of Christ's birth. They regarded everyone as children of God, rich and poor alike, regardless of race or ethnicity.

My thoughts wandered. I moved to Florida in 1990 because of a corporate relocation. I quickly became immersed in community organizations and the historic St. Michael's faith community. "Papa, you always wanted to come to Florida. Here I am, living the Florida life for you," I whispered. "Guess what, Papa, back in Connecticut, you have three handsome grandsons with your last name, courtesy of Mikey and his lovely second wife—grandsons whom you never met. Our Ritzzo legacy lives on."

I gazed up at the stained-glass window with its beautiful colors depicting St. Joseph, and I wondered about this spiritual, faithful, selfless man who cared for Mary and Jesus—once again, a life that demonstrated goodness. And again, my thoughts returned to those women known as the Sisters of St. Joseph, teaching, guiding, loving, protecting, and emptying themselves for the glory of God.

No grand monuments mark the heroic nuns who nursed the town during the mysterious fever that became known as the Yellow Fever Epidemic of 1877 and again in 1888. When the fever struck, the Sisters had been on retreat in St. Augustine. Filled with the Holy Spirit to move quickly to the side of those who desperately needed them back home in Fernandina, they went, knowing full well they might be going to their deaths; they did not hesitate to race to the aid of others. As quarantine cut the island off, they nursed the sick, bathed fever-wracked bodies, fed the hungry and abandoned, sewed lifeless bodies into shrouds, and even buried the dead with quick prayers of faith and consolation.

Again, my wandering thoughts returned to my family, particularly my father. I thought of the unselfish love he, a man of few words, had lavished upon me after raising his first four daughters without a mother. He had worked against all odds to keep those girls together, always treating them with kindness and care, and they had grown into loving and wonderful women.

"I'm proud to have them as my sisters. My younger brother, my half-siblings, we all learned so many important lessons through your quiet example, Papa," I whispered. "I continue to marvel at how you took on Mama's four children. Not your own, but you provided for them as well. I think of your loving relationship among all of us—whole, half, step, all irrelevant labels."

Could I be as courageous as the Sisters of St. Joseph or as Papa if called by the Holy Spirit to live such a selfless love? I wondered.

I moved to the wall, where a small plaque indicated that the stained-glass window depicting St. Joseph had been restored in memory of Michael and Jennie Rizzo. Paying for that window restoration had been a small sacrifice, but I felt compelled to do it. Papa, a humble father, honest citizen, and loyal friend, was a faithful believer. He was a man of goodness. Mama was a hardworking, generous, and loving woman who never lost her faith despite the immense losses she endured throughout her life.

For decades, I have searched to understand where goodness comes from. Is it taught? Does an example teach it? Without any of that, where, Papa, did you get your goodness?

At that moment, the wellspring of goodness came to me in that chapel.

Clear as a school bell, I heard it. "Goodness comes from God. We are all heirs if we choose it." I recognized then that it doesn't have to come from grand declarations, or epic events, or significant acts of heroism. It is, instead, built from all the small things that prove love for our fellow human beings in the glory of God Almighty.

As I left the chapel, I murmured to no one in particular, "Thank you, Sisters of St. Joseph, for your selfless examples of courage, love, and humility, all adding up to the greatest sacrifice, that of your life for your fellow man.

Thank you, St. Joseph, for taking Mary and Jesus into your care, love, and protection. And I'm eternally grateful to Papa and Mama for teaching me that where you come from and what you materially have or don't have are all irrelevant. It's your character, integrity, the love and compassion in your heart, and most of all, your goodness that is important."

ACKNOWLEDGMENTS

This book could never have become a reality without the generous gifts of time, talent, encouragement, and love from numerous people—a million thanks to each of you.

I appreciate the dedicated curators and volunteers at historical libraries, societies and museums everywhere, especially, Paul Keroack, at the Norwalk (CT) History Room; Richard Stanislaus, Anthracite Heritage Museum, Scranton, PA; Bode Morin at the Eckley Miners' Village in Weatherly, PA; Elizabeth Van Tuyl at the Bridgeport History Center; and Paolo Nicolazzo, Pro Loco Platania-Italy.

I'm forever grateful to my extended family and friends in Italy who showed me all the places, helped me find the records, and told me their stories, especially my cousin Franco Cuiuli, Signora Furci, and the late Zio Michele Bonaddio, and my late cousin Anna Cuiuli Ferraro, and my dear friends the late Gino and Rosetta Giampa; and to my cousin Anna Cuiuli Parinettto in Sydney, Australia, who remembered her birth land and the events.

A heartfelt special thanks to my dear friend and mentor, the late Don Shaw, who believed in me and made me finish writing this story. And to all those friends and champions who fanned my frequently stalled flame of writing over the years, Martin Arnold, Suzy Sabadie, and especially those friends who have passed on, Shiela Fountain, Patrick Sabadie, and Marsha Arnold.

My sincere gratitude goes to Emily Carmain and Kenneth Overman, who made this book better in every way. And special thanks to Roseanne White for the new cover and interior design, who, despite her health challenges, persevered to help finish this.

A million thanks to my late mother, Giovanna, who painted pictures with words and provided me the insight into her soul, the ethos of Calabria, and who shared what my father found too painful; and to my late father, who told me the important stuff, each word as precious as a diamond.. To my wonderful brothers Joe Bonaddio and Michael Ritzzo, Jr., and my sisters and brothers in Heaven, Rose Mola, Connie Marotto, Lena Casavecchi, Ann Redican, and Angie Ciliberto, and Antonio and Frank Bonaddio. Over the years, in addition to looking out for me, each of my siblings shared innumerable stories about the old days in Norwalk and *La Chianta* in Italy, and about the times they shared with Papa and Mama. I love you all.

For sharing their memories, thank you to my children, George and Holly, and all my cherished nieces and nephews.

And to my granddaughter Selena and grandson Jackson Girardo. You are the joy and spirit that make everything I write and all that I do worthwhile.

Saving the most important for last, to my best friend, my love, my husband, Mark. Thank you for your exceptional patience, understanding, love, support, encouragement, technical skills, and for delicious dinners, and for ensuring I could travel to all the treasured places. You have shared freely and unconditionally, and for all these things and much more, you have my eternal gratitude and love.

With heartfelt thanks to you, my readers, and may love be your most profound emotion.

RMR, Amelia Island, Florida, November 2025

ABOUT THE AUTHOR

Raffaela Marie Rizzo is a former senior executive with numerous business and marketing communications awards. She earned an MBA from Jacksonville University and a BA degree in media studies from Sacred Heart University in Fairfield, Connecticut, where she graduated magna cum laude. She has been a lifelong volunteer with community and faith-based organizations. In addition to her strong Catholic Christian faith, her passions are people, family stories, community, genealogy, history, and travel.

She founded the Ritzzo Family Education Foundation, whose purpose is to fan the flame of education for Italian-American children, a cause for which Michelangelo (Mike) Ritzzo (Rizzo) was a strong proponent. The foundation also offers college or trade school scholarships to Italian American children, especially those with Calabrian heritage. Calabria remains one of Italy's and Western Europe's poorest regions.

To learn more, visit https://www.ritzzofoundation.org/ The Ritzzo Family Education Foundation Inc. is a 501(C)3 organization. If you enjoyed this book, please consider donating.

Born in Italy, raised in Connecticut, Rizzo and her husband now make Amelia Island, Florida, home. To learn more about her, visit https://www.rmrizzo.org.

From humble beginnings in the Mercuri-Tedesci area of Platania, Italy.

October, 12, 1912—Michelangelo (Mike) Rizzo arrives in Norwalk, CT, after a circuitous route from Calabria in time to share in his first family milestone in the new world, the wedding of his cousin Innocenza (Jennie) Nicolazzo (front row, second from right) to Antonio Lo Schiavo, the groom. Second from left (front row) is Mike; standing beside him is his cousin, Mickey Nicolazzo, the bride's brother. Second row, standing behind the bride is her uncle, Zio Michelangelo Gallo, and next to him is his wife, Zia Giuanna, Mike's mother's sister.

Michelangelo Rizzo married Maria Raffaela Russo at St. Mary's RC Church in Norwalk, CT Jan. 7, 1918. It took a year to pay for the portrait and have it released to them by the photographer.

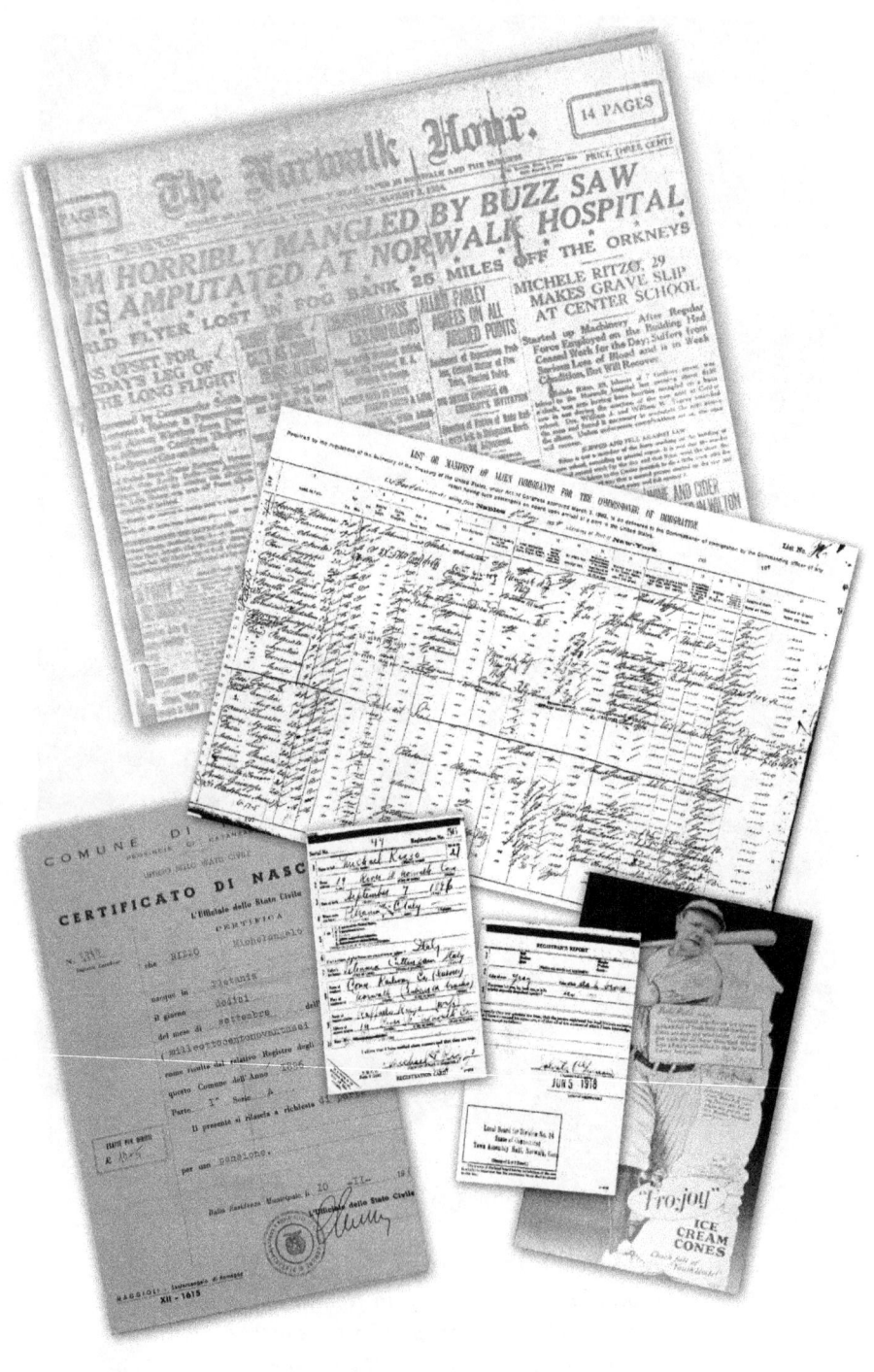

LIST OR MANIFEST OF ALIEN PASSENGERS FOR THE UNITED
COMUNE DI SAMBIASE
UFFICIO DELLO STATO CIVILE
CERTIFICATO DI MATRIMONIO
Il sottoscritto Ufficiale di Stato Civile del Comune di Sambiase
CERTIFICA
REPUBBLICA ITALIANA
REGNO D'ITALIA
COMUNE DI
IN NOME DELLA LEGGE

January 1929—Mike gets his four motherless daughters home again and takes them for a portrait sitting to memorialize the reunited family.

Spring 1956—Confirmation day for Joey Bonaddio, age thirteen, with little sister Marie, eight, and little brother Mikey, Jr., six, on Godfrey Street.

Mike at work at O'Brien Press, circa 1957

April 1958—Mike, with wife Jennie, at the wedding of her son Antonio Bonaddio to Maria Parisi. Also in the photo are Jennie's other children, Angie, Frank and Joey, as well as their children together, Marie and Mikey Jr., and Mike's Nicolazzo cousins, Mickey and Innocenza (Jennie) and her second husband, Nicola Fiumara.

Circa 1964—Mike and his second wife Giovanna "Jennie"

www.ingramcontent.com/pod-product-compliance
Lightning Source LLC
Chambersburg PA
CBHW050954050426
42337CB00051B/839